Simón Bolívar

I0792539

UNIVERSITY PRESS OF FLORIDA

Florida A&M University, Tallahassee
Florida Atlantic University, Boca Raton
Florida Gulf Coast University, Ft. Myers
Florida International University, Miami
Florida State University, Tallahassee
New College of Florida, Sarasota
University of Central Florida, Orlando
University of Florida, Gainesville
University of North Florida, Jacksonville
University of South Florida, Tampa
University of West Florida, Pensacola

Simón Bolívar

Travels and Transformations of a Cultural Icon

Edited by Maureen G. Shanahan
and Ana María Reyes

University Press of Florida
Gainesville · Tallahassee · Tampa · Boca Raton
Pensacola · Orlando · Miami · Jacksonville · Ft. Myers · Sarasota

Printed in the United States of America on acid-free paper

This book may be available in an electronic edition.

21 20 19 18 17 16 6 5 4 3 2 1

Library of Congress Cataloging-in-Publication Data
Names: Shanahan, Maureen G., author. | Reyes, Ana María (College teacher), author.
Title: Simón Bolívar : travels and transformations of a cultural icon / Maureen G. Shanahan and Ana María Reyes.
Description: Gainesville : University Press of Florida, [2016] | Includes bibliographical references and index.
Identifiers: LCCN 2015048926 | ISBN 9780813062624 (alk. paper)
Subjects: LCSH: Bolívar, Simón, 1783-1830—Travel. | Heads of state—South America—Biography. | Generals—South America—Biography. | South America—History.
Classification: LCC F2235.3 .S53 2016 | DDC 980/.02092—dc23
LC record available at http://lccn.loc.gov/2015048926

The University Press of Florida is the scholarly publishing agency for the State University System of Florida, comprising Florida A&M University, Florida Atlantic University, Florida Gulf Coast University, Florida International University, Florida State University, New College of Florida, University of Central Florida, University of Florida, University of North Florida, University of South Florida, and University of West Florida.

University Press of Florida
15 Northwest 15th Street
Gainesville, FL 32611-2079
http://www.upf.com

Contents

Figures

Plates

Following page 114

Prologue

An appropriate way to preamble this multidisciplinary study concerning the sociopolitical phenomenon of the Bolivarian cult would be to provide certain clarifications about the origins of my work entitled *El culto a Bolívar: Esbozo para un estudio de la historia de las ideas en Venezuela,* published in Caracas by the Institute of Anthropology and History, Faculty of Humanities and Education of the Central University of Venezuela, in 1970 after being presented as my doctoral thesis in history. This book is the result of two main motivations and one circumstance, as I explain in what follows.

As a consequence of the growth and refinement of my own critical thinking, one tacit but dominant motivation was to contribute to and strengthen our historical understanding of the discourse concerning the role of the individual in history. This occurred starting in 1948 when I was impacted by the intellectually stimulating ideological and political reconfigurations in the post–World War II era.

The second (and explicit) motivation emerged after I returned to Venezuela in 1958 when the fall of the military dictatorship ended my decade-long period of political exile. With great trepidation I witnessed how the Bolivarianism that characterized both the Liberal Autocratic Republic (1830–1945), especially in its most degenerate phase during the Liberal Regionalist dictatorship (1900–1945), and the recently overthrown regime was casting a shadow over the newly restored Liberal Democratic Republic (initially established in 1946–48).

The seeds of the project were planted with an academic task. Charged with inaugurating the *cátedra* in Venezuelan historiography in 1961–62, I set out to compose a manual that would provide a general characterization of such historiography along with a compilation of the case studies from which I derived my assessment to date. This procedure, based upon critical analysis and not adopted from other historiographic discourses, allowed me to identify twelve historical conditions or characteristics. From this grouping, compiled in October and November 1961, there were two characteristics that fundamentally influenced the conception and design of my aforementioned work and motivated me to write my doctoral thesis. The first one is what I called "exorbitant hero cult," and the second consists of its "close relation to public power."

May this narrative serve as evidence for the scientific, academic, and political motivations that converged in the conception and elaboration of my work, without any one of these taking precedence, and which corresponded with my views on the social responsibilities of the historian. I aimed to serve two criteria: first of all, to be careful not to confuse the historical character of Simón Bolívar, the cult formed around his signification—real and attributed—and the hold of this cult, once it was converted from the initial cult of the people to a cult for the people in both political and ideological terms. The second criterion consisted of discerning critically what Simón Bolívar witnessed and, from our contemporary perspective, what we think he could have witnessed.

After completing this work, I became occupied with several aspects of Simón Bolívar's historical work, particularly in the area of constitutional law, which resulted in more recent works such as *Colombia, 1821–1827: Aprender a edificar una república moderna liberal: Demolición selectiva de la Monarquía, instauración de la República y reanudación política de la disputa de la Independencia,* published in Caracas in 2010. In this work, a more systematic study of Simón Bolívar's most elevated political and strategic genius, I sought to counterweight the ongoing degradation of his historical significance, a process of perversion of historical conscience that engendered a response captured in my work titled *El bolivarianismo-militarismo: Una ideología de reemplazo,* first published in Caracas in 2005. This book arose from a graduate seminar, "Alternativas ideológicas en América Latina contemporánea (El caso de Venezuela: el bolivarianismo-militarismo)," held at the University of Florida, where I had been invited to be a distinguished visiting scholar funded by the Bacardi Family Eminent Scholar Chair in Latin American Studies.

The assessment of *El culto a Bolívar* by the eminent Venezuelan scholar Luis Castro Leiva critically endorses this argument. In his essay "El historicismo político bolivariano," published in 1984, Luis Castro Leiva writes,

> Perhaps this may partially explain the [official] Bolivarian reaction to Carrera's thesis. If we consider the epochal context and the general opposition to Marxism, *El culto a Bolívar* should be seen as a "political action" aimed to critically subvert the order and form of legitimation during the era. . . . In both readings (that of *El culto a Bolívar* and that of its detractors), the confrontation focuses on Bolívar's own thought and its event-driven interpretations. It did not occur—nor could it have occurred—to anyone at that time to question whether the battle for Bolívar, as synonymous with the struggle for history, depended less on the sociopolitical "adequacy" and "efficiency" of his presumed ideas than on that other previous problem of knowing if these ideas were really—and in which way—his "ideas" and his "actions." In other words, if Bolívar's "texts" were Bolívar's ideas and not a hypostasis. On both sides of the dispute, whether in the Cult of Bolívar or in the "Bolivarian criticism," there is a common hermeneutic strategy: that texts speak for themselves from their literal sense and as such affect the surrounding reality. Therefore, the "error or heresy" committed by the author of *El culto a Bolívar* consisted of frank irreverence, or in not having consulted other texts or other readings of Bolívar. (81–82)

All of the above has the objective of explaining my interest in this collection, which I am pleased to prologue and to which I have been introduced by the intriguing text that the co-editors sent me. Suffice it to say that it sparked my interest in studying a work that promises to deliver wide-ranging interpretations of the cult of Bolívar. Moreover, I confess that I have been eagerly awaiting something like the scholarship offered here by this dedicated group of scholars. Thank you.

Germán Carrera Damas
Caracas, March 10, 2015

References

Carrera Damas, Germán. 1970. *El culto a Bolívar: Esbozo para un estudio de la historia de las ideas en Venezuela.* Caracas: Universidad Central de Venezuela.

———. 2005. *El bolivarianismo-militarismo: Una ideología de reemplazo.* Caracas: Ala de Cuervo.

———. 2010. *Colombia, 1821–1827: Aprender a edificar una república moderna liberal:*

Demolición selectiva de la Monarquía, instauración de la República y reanudación política de la disputa de la Independencia. Caracas: Universidad Central de Venezuela.

Castro Leiva, Luis. 1984. "El historicismo político bolivariano." *Revista de Estudios Políticos* 42 (November–December): 71–100.

Bolívar Unhinged

An Introduction

MAUREEN G. SHANAHAN AND ANA MARÍA REYES

Simón Bolívar (1783–1830) is arguably Latin America's most famous historical figure and certainly the most studied. He is honored as El Libertador for his role in achieving independence from Spanish rule for Venezuela, Colombia, Ecuador, Panama, Peru, and Bolivia. But while his military successes provide a heroic narrative for myths of liberation and national foundation, Bolívar's political ideas were controversial during his lifetime and have continued to fuel disparate, if not antagonistic, political imaginaries. His truncated dream—of a unified federation of Spanish American nations—constitutes a recurrent topos that helps us to understand why Simón Bolívar remains such a powerful icon and symbol. Bolívar's frustrated vision and tragic end as a politically disgraced figure, reviled in both Colombia and Venezuela, have morphed into an unsettled debt to be paid, a legacy left open for future generations to fulfill. Simultaneously, however, the mythologized Simón Bolívar filled a vacuum left after the bitter political rivalries of nation formation and provided a foundational icon used to pacify the conflictive environment that characterized nineteenth-century Latin America. Bolívar has thus become the quintessential myth mined for authority and legitimacy. For more than two hundred years, "Bolívar" has served as a privileged signifier in public debates. Governments have deified Bolívar as the guiding father of the nation, while individuals and communities have refashioned his image and ideals in positioning themselves vis à vis the nation or state in what we call cultural Bolivarianisms. Bolivarian symbolism has been both anchored and destabilized—hinged and unhinged—to stand for competing notions of liberation, nation, history, the state, revolution, and the people, among others.

The essays in this volume further unhinge Bolívar from any one meaning and, taken together, show the multiplicity of cultural forms that constitute the public sphere: the interstice of culture and politics. The many faces and functions of Simón Bolívar elaborated in this collection illuminate the complex dynamics of cultural grammar and complicate cohesive national mythologies. Furthermore, this volume demonstrates that Bolívar's relevance as a political and cultural sign extends outside of Latin America, where he has functioned as a vehicle for Enlightenment ideals, including citizenship, the republic, and liberty, and where he has been redeployed both to critique oppressive regimes and to legitimize them.

Historian Jorge Orlando Melo (2010) considers the perennial political retrieval of Bolívar a sign of impatience with the arduous, slow road of democratic debate. The conception of nation according to a Bolivarian tradition is not a project of "daily debate among citizens, but rather an inherited project, a messianic goal, whose search we must all embark upon, a forever imposed obligation" (134).[1] If political Bolivarianisms are the antithesis of messy, contingent, unpredictable, and agonistic democratic practices, then cultural Bolivarianisms may provide a way out of the conundrum of heroic appeal. Making Bolívar an artistic medium—*material de trabajo* to be transformed or repurposed—signals a path out of a hierarchical conception of society or the messianic role invested in political leaders and toward a dialogical relation between the individual, group, and community and the state, nation, and public sphere.

Bolívar may seem like a questionable starting point for any discussion on democracy since his political thinking and especially his Bolivian constitution sided with centralist authoritarianism, patriarchal militarism, and a distrust of the masses. For this very reason we wanted to investigate cultural appropriations and reworkings of Bolívar the icon and myth, including examples from inside and outside the state, to illustrate the roles played by arts and humanities in both constituting the public sphere and decentering authority. The idea of this collection was to take a, if not the, symbol of authority (Bolívar) and see what happens when it runs through the cultural grinder. That is, the studies presented here analyze those sites of creative cultural agonism where Bolívar serves as the vehicle for reaffirmation or dissent of the established order. A book on cultural Bolivarianisms illuminates the battlefield that constitutes a public sphere. As such, this volume is a contingent experiment, necessarily incomplete, inconclusive, and anti-authoritative. It is also an open invitation for further interventions.

Bolívar's dramatic ascent and descent during his life offered a properly malleable narrative not only for statesmen and for the leaders of the early republics but also for those making claims against the state's shortcomings, a trend that has continued today. While historians, journalists, and politicians claim proximity to Bolívar's ideas in order to endorse their own positions, cultural producers are not necessarily held responsible for retrieving an authorial voice from the past, nor do they carry the burden of providing historical veracity. Rather, they have the creative license to refashion the Bolivarian icon into something new. Yet the Bolivarian case poses a challenge to cultural producers: a history of strong reactions to his symbolic presence signals treacherous ground.

Following Antonio Gramsci, culture is understood as a process or set of practices that constructs meaning and thus constitutes social and political realities. Images, music, theater, dance, material culture, and other cultural media are produced within signifying practices that organize and structure social actions. In this sense, cultural practice is a field of debate, dissent, and contested meaning. Indeed, political theorists Ernesto Laclau and Chantal Mouffe (2001) argue for dissensus or creative conflict, and they call for "agonistic public spheres," which, they assert, operate in a dialectical relationship to democracy. If we are to conceive of democracy as a terrain of perpetual agonism and understand hegemony as processes of complex dialogical relations between unstable and unequal "relations of force" within the cultural sphere, then we must also look at cultural production for heretical reformulations. Bolívar becomes a symbolic battleground on which the struggle for hegemony can be fought. As the cultural analyst Doris Sommer reminds us (2014), the arts are endowed with the creativity, criticality, and even freedom to take risks that are necessary for civic agency.

At once a focused iconographic study and a broad investigation of representation itself, our project engages history, literary criticism, art history, film studies, and musicology to examine cultural employments of Bolívar as myth and sign, and it forms a substantial contribution to the growing field of cultural studies. By studying the various permutations of the Bolivarian myth in the cultural arena, one can trace the ways in which myths and regimes of representation are transformed by different media and repurposed for diverse objectives. One must not forget the importance of ritual performativity in maintaining certain historical figures' value in the public sphere. Bolívar's power over the imaginary rests on the resurfacing of his image in the multimedia spectacle of civic ritual inherited from the American Baroque. Baroque religious pageantry, that is, the Catholic Church's efforts from the time of the sixteenth-century Counter-Reformation to propagate the faith by overwhelming the senses, has metamorphosed in the modern era but retained its power through civic forms. Just as Baroque ritual incorporated huge stage designs for *retablos,* artful oration, musical compositions, the smells of candles and incense, and the processional animation of paraded sculptures, paintings, and *tableaux vivants,* so too contemporary patriotic celebrations, operatic performances, and televised rituals manifest civic versions of these multimedia spectacles. An approximation of the many Bolivarianisms necessarily must embrace the multisensorial, multiperspectival, multigeographic, and multitemporal dimensions of the spectacle.

Ever since Pedro José Figueroa (ca. 1770–1836) painted his now iconic image *Simón Bolívar, Libertador y Padre de la Patria* in 1819 (plate 1), the issues of race and gender have been central to cultural representations of Bolívar (González Aranda 2013). As Emily A. Engel argues in the first chapter of this collection, pictorial production during the revolutionary era appropriated existing practices to forge an icon and a national imaginary. The Bogotá Assembly of Notable Citizens commissioned Figueroa's painting to celebrate Bolívar's victory at the Battle of Boyacá that secured New Granadian independence from Spain and to accompany the inaugural ceremony of the Cruz de Boyacá, the highest medal awarded for services rendered to the nation. Full of fear at the changing tide, the royalist New Granadian artist hastily repainted over his portrait-in-progress, which was either of King Ferdinand VII or Spanish General Pablo Morillo, in time for the September ceremony.

The Bogotá *cabildo* (council) had petitioned the artist to paint "Liberty supported by General Simón Bolívar's arm." Instead, Figueroa painted in the inscription *Post Nublia Faebus, Simón Bolívar, Libertador y Padre de la Patria,* effectively replacing "Liberty" with "Nation." In this reluctant and unflattering portrait (more fully discussed in Paul Niell's essay), the Liberator awkwardly places his arm around the young *patria.* Figueroa not only transformed liberty into nation but also the allegorical "America"—traditionally depicted as a seminude Indian woman with a plumed crown—into an elegant *criolla* wearing a neoclassical dress along with pearl earrings and necklace. Unlike America, however, the nation would not be represented by an image of a strong, idealized, indigenous female but a fragile, dainty lady who needed to be defended. Like America she wears a plumed crown and holds a bow in her hand, in this case gesturing toward the other, celestial Father. Here *patria* is a conflation of both allegorical America and the Virgin and saint statues lavishly dressed and processed ritualistically throughout Spanish America. Figueroa's Bolívar is father to the young *criollo* and Catholic nation and thus guardian of the protective Church.

In one ephemeral image circulating on the Internet but now lost, the Catholic hierarchical conception of social order remains intact: Bolívar as Father of the Nation serves as terrestrial equivalent to the celestial God the Father. The anonymous artist overlaid an image of Bolívar in military uniform on the Mano Omnipoderosa (All-Powerful Hand), which conventionally depicts the all-powerful hand of God upright with the palm toward the viewer and surrounded by angels, saints, and the Holy Family. In this version, an apotheosized Bolívar, standing erect in gilded military regalia, stands before God's hand among the heavenly figures and turns toward the Christ Child, who holds a terrestrial globe as though recalling Bolívar's military triumphs and earthly ambitions for a Gran Colombia. At the same time, the saints and angels who hold the symbols of Christ's crucifixion invite the viewer to read Bolívar's final days—his expulsion from his role as president of Gran Colombia and his lonely death of tuberculosis—in terms of Christ's suffering. By transforming Bolívar into a resurrected martyr and spiritual-political leader, the image organizes spiritual desire for a church-military consolidation that would yield the fulfillment of Bolívar's utopian vision. Bolívar's spiritual aura backed by the Mano Omnipoderosa in this popular image, most likely associated with Santería practices, evinces how deeply entangled the figure of Bolívar is with notions of political messianism and legitimacy, whether mythified and idealized or debased and satirized.

One of the most iconoclastic versions of Bolívar, which generated enormous controversy and created a diplomatic incident, has been the satirical painting *El Libertador Simón Bolívar* (1994) created by Juan Domingo Dávila, a Chilean-born, Australian-based artist. Dávila's Bolívar is a bald, dark-skinned equestrienne, a transsexual who wears only a blue cape, a military jacket, and boots, exposing female breasts and perhaps a male phallus strategically obscured by pubic hair. The Liberator holds up his/her left hand to the viewer in a "F— you" gesture. The painting, which was originally exhibited in 1994 in the Hayward Gallery in London and then circulated through Latin America as a postcard, created an uproar requiring a formal apology issued by the Chilean government to the people of Venezuela, Colombia, and Ecuador (Mejías-López 2005, 148).

The success of Dávila's attack upon hegemonic orders of "nation" is contingent upon the commodified and debased female body and may only reinscribe hierarchies of race, gender, sexuality, and aesthetics. Yet Hugo Chávez ignored the deliberate gender-bending in order to interpret the work as a "true" representation of Bolívar's race, even embracing the term *zambo* (Guerrero 2008, 1–2). In Chávez's interpretation, Bolívar as *zambo*, a term used to reference a person of mixed African and Native American ancestry, embodied the new conception of a racially mixed body politic that excludes white-*criollo* ethnic identity.[2] An effeminate Bolívar, however, betrayed the pervasive patriarchic and militaristic conceptions of public authority. Writers have variously interpreted Dávila's work as mocking "the heteronormative protocols of national projects" (Allatson 2006, 20), a "monstrous refusal of the nation" (Guerrero 2008, 3), an attack upon the "monumental Bolívar" as history and patriarchy (Conway 2003, 3–4), and a challenge to "masculinity, the authority of fixed language and progress . . . at the core of the cult of Bolívar" (Mejías-López 2005, 149). The dilemma of how to critique hegemonic orders and the entrenched position of Bolívar as myth and icon for the nation explain in part the polarized responses to Dávila's painting.

Even today, vanguard adaptations of the Bolivarian myth equally rely upon the viewer's understanding of the icon's function as synecdoche for nation. One example is *La bandeja de Bolívar* (1999) (plate 2), a video installation by the Colombian photographer Juan Manuel Echavarría. For this work, which was included in the exhibition "Arte y Violencia en Colombia" at the Museum of Modern Art in Bogotá in 1999, Echavarría commissioned a replica of the porcelain tray gifted to El Libertador during the consecration of the newly founded republic of Gran Colombia. Among the painted flowers of an Edenic garden are inscribed the words "República de Colombia para siempre" (Republic of Colombia forever), capturing the sense of incorruptible achievement following the success of Bolívar's military campaign against Spain. The video begins with an image of this tray, and as the video progresses, the sound of shattering porcelain echoes as the tray breaks apart. The last image of the tray, now reduced to a pile of white powder, uncannily resembles a mound of cocaine.

Bolívar's utopian vision for a prosperous Spanish American nation at first seemed plausible in a continent so rich in diverse natural resources, yet a product of this very land—coca—destroys the Bolivarian dream. Echavarría produced this work at a historical juncture when Colombia seemed to disintegrate with ceaseless waves of violence, fueled by the lucrative and uncontrollable drug trade. *La bandeja de Bolívar* is at once beautiful and terrifying, evoking nostalgia for a united nation that never came to fruition (Reyes 1999). It is a reflection on the ideal of republican unity amid its unraveling, one that echoes the sentiment of bereft frustration Gabriel García Márquez wrote into his controversial representation of the Liberator navigating up the Magdalena River toward his death in *El general en su laberinto* (1989).

Dávila's painting and Echavarría's video installation respond to dominant narratives of Bolívar as a state-sponsored myth and symbolic system. Official forms of Bolivarianism have generated the Bolívar statues (often state gifts from Venezuela) that populate global civic centers, the portraits that adorn institutional buildings, and the *cátedra bolivariana* textbooks that teach his political ideas as part of national school curricula. The above-described visual examples, however, represent a vast array of unofficial cultural production—from popular forms to avant-garde art—that raises questions about the interpretation, manipulation, and reception of Bolívar beyond state-crafted stagings. The cultural study of Bolivarianism is thus an investigation into not only the static object of the icon but also the dynamic environment of its production and uses. The ritualistic uses or activation of "Bolívar" is necessarily performative and presupposes a variety of audiences.

The cultural studies approach of this collection is significantly indebted to the demythification and historicization of Bolívar initiated by historian Germán Carrera Damas. With *El culto a Bolívar* (1970), Carrera Damas launched an influential critique of the Venezuelan national mythology and an intellectual revolution as well as a larger postmodern criticism of the "great man" theory of history formulated by Thomas Carlyle in the nineteenth century. Carrera Damas traces the emergence of the Bolívar cult in nineteenth-century romantic literature, including its extension into sociopolitical life, popular expression, and manipulation by the state according to shifting political ideologies. He identifies key historical moments in the cult's formation, particularly the repatriation of Bolívar's remains in 1842 from Santa Marta, Colombia, to Caracas; the construction of the Venezuelan Panteón Nacional in 1876 as a secular temple for Bolívar's remains and those of other national heroes; and the centennial celebrations in 1883.

Those responsible for the cult's formation and perpetuation as a state institution—as Carrera Damas writes, "the priests of the Bolivarian cult"—have shaped Bolivarianism, that is, ideas about what constitutes a united nation and orderly government as well as the self-improvement and destiny of the nation. Bolívar's deeds, both documented and apocryphal, his extensive writings, and historical sites have been transformed by successive military and political leaders into the cultic tools of a "second religion," especially under the regime of Antonio Guzmán Blanco (1829–99), president of Venezuela for three discontinuous terms from 1870 to 1887. The Bolivarian cult has, Carrera Damas argues, functioned as both censor and promise, in that all social ills are understood to be failures in meeting Bolivarian ideals. Such exalted patriotism forges a monumental Bolívar that fictionalizes rather than historicizes the man and his times. Bolívar as a cult figure and Bolivarianism as a second religion are subject to myriad manipulations. Carrera Damas's project thus engages in methodologies of cultural studies that are important to our contributors as well: a discursive analysis of the texts that shape the Bolivarian myth; a structural critique of the institutions that perpetuate it; a sociological contextualization of its monuments, rituals, and gestures; an ideological investigation into multiple Bolivarianisms; and a kind of semiotic assessment of the malleability of the Bolívar cult according to shifting political regimes and popular practices.

Our collection joins other scholars' work extending Carrera Damas's social-historical research into Bolívar's self-mythification and the multiple cults of Bolívar, their state-generated forms, populist interpretations, and creative appropriations. Historians and anthropologists Manuel Caballero, Luis Castro Leiva, John Chasteen, Elias Pino Iturrieta, Yolanda Salas de Lecuna, Tomás Straka, Ana Teresa Torres, and Michael Zeuske provide important social-historical research into the multiple cults of Bolívar, state-generated and populist alike.

While demythologizing the Bolívar cult has created space for many critical approaches, one particularly important approach has been that of mapping the terrain of race, class, and gender formations in independence-era mythologies. In this collection, several scholars take up the entwined concepts of race and nation. The essays by Paul Niell, Alicia Ríos, and Maureen Shanahan rely upon new histories by José Antonio Aguilar Rivera, Aline Helg, Christopher Schmidt-Nowara, and others who have advanced contextualized notions of liberty and equality for Afro–Latin Americans and have explored Bolívar's fear of *pardocracia* (rule by mixed-race people) as well as his conception of the *patria* in terms of racial diversity and cultural inequality. All of these studies focus on the uses of Bolivarianism and race as social-historical and discursive formations rather than engaging in a search for a "true" Bolívar. In other words, the liberation narrative that has previously been condensed into the privileged sign of Bolívar is now an expanding field.

While much of Carrera Damas's famed historical project focuses on the state-produced cult—as do the essays in this collection by Luis Duno-Gottberg, Juan de Dios López Maya, and Tomás Straka—other contributors, notably Alicia Ríos, build upon the work of scholars who focus on popular, iconoclastic, and counterhegemonic interpretations of Bolívar. In this regard, Yolanda Salas de Lecuna's study on the reinvention of Bolívar in oral culture in southern Venezuela, *Bolívar y la historia en la conciencia popular* (1987), is particularly noteworthy. A major anthropological case study and oral history, Salas's work draws from 123 informants, ultimately showing the ways in which Bolívar figures into the pantheon of a constantly transforming, dynamic, Afro-indigenous-Venezuelan (Zambo) religion organized around María Lionza, the goddess of nature and love. Through her research, Salas foregrounds Bolívar as a part of a liberatory discourse for indigenous people and Afro-Venezuelans and, in so doing, orients her readers to issues of justice for the poor.

Although the Colombian context did not engender a cult to Bolívar to the degree found in Venezuela, Colombia's political landscape is the context for case studies analyzed in this collection by Armida de la Garza and Ana María Reyes. As Straka shows in his essay, the Venezuelan Liberal Party and the Colombian Conservative Party (both founded in the nineteenth century) claimed to be Bolívar's heirs. In Colombia the traditional, two-party system provided the backdrop for a foundational myth predicated on the double leadership of Simón Bolívar (as military hero of independence) and Francisco de Paula Santander (a talented administrator and legislator).

Beginning with the rift between the two that occurred during 1827 and 1828, a simplified but pervasive understanding of Colombian history has for the most part credited Bolívar with laying the ideological foundations for the Conservative Party and Santander for the Liberal Party (Safford and Palacios 2002, 118).

Prior to the 1950s, Colombian Bolivarian historiography was caught in this bipolar understanding of history. However, the Cold War brought about a profound rereading of the Bolivarian legacy. Following the Cuban independence hero José Martí, later Latin American intellectuals of the Left, along with Soviet scholars, reoriented Bolívar from an icon of national foundation to a revolutionary anti-imperialist reinterpreted through a Marxist ideological lens (Melo 2010; Pividal 1977; Schelchkov 2002). Tina Potočnik argues, based upon her archival findings, that in the 1960s "Bolívar" signified a new kind of revolution that informed plans for Revolution Square in Ljubljana, Slovenia. This kind of radical revision still operates today in the Bolivarian Republic of Venezuela, ALBA (Alianza Bolivariana para los Pueblos de Nuestra América), and the guerrilla movements in Colombia. In their contributions to this volume, Potočnik, Reyes, de la Garza, and Alejandro E. Gómez Pernia further develop the instability of the Bolívar signifier as it shifted from patrimonial to revolutionary icon.

Many of the critical histories generated by Carrera Damas, Salas, Straka, Melo, and others emerged as landmark texts on cultural studies; their work demonstrates that Latin American cultural studies has had its own locally and historically grounded practice whose canonical texts often preceded the field's consolidation during the "cultural turn" of the 1980s and 1990s (del Sarto, Ríos, and Trigo 2004). More recently, a number of literary and cultural studies (Conway 2003; Hart 2005; Ríos 2013; Shanahan 2005; Zeuske 2013) have outlined the rich array of Bolivarian significations in historical writing but also in contemporary visual and literary culture, thus pointing to a rich cultural field awaiting analysis. While an extensive body of scholarly writing exists on authors such as Pablo Neruda and Gabriel García Márquez, including their poetry and novels about Bolívar, many other literary examples have been neglected. Christopher Conway's 2003 literary study of the cult of Bolívar is a rare exception that extends the critiques of Bolivarianism as a field through which nation, gender, and modernity are debated. Alicia Ríos's recent study *Nacionalismos banales, el culto a Bolívar* (2013) provides an overview of the historical texts on the cult of Bolívar while focusing on examples in literature, film, and the visual arts. A translated chapter from that book appears in the present volume.

The aim of this book, however, is not to correct all imagined omissions in the analysis of Bolivarianism or Bolívar as a cult figure but to engage in an iconographic and cultural study of a more capacious notion of "Bolívar" as a symbolic system and cultural field. Furthermore, this project does not posit a battle between the state and the popular as fixed coherent positions—that is, between the hegemonic and counterhegemonic, however imagined (colonizer and colonized, *criollo* and *pardo*, male and female). Cultural studies examine objects from all arenas of production as signs engaged in a dynamic and contested field of power and meaning. "Hegemony," in the Gramscian sense, refers not only to state control but also to processes in a complex dialectical relation between unstable and unequal relations of power, making culture a dynamic and contested field contingent on institutions, audiences, media, and reception.

Our project extends beyond the cult of Bolívar and its multiple ideological formations, or Bolivarianism, to a wide range of representations of Bolívar. Music's important role in the Venezuelan patriotic celebrations and its ideological uses in promoting Bolivarianisms have received even less attention than literature or the visual arts. Our collection initiates an intervention in this arena. Juan Francisco Sans shows how Bolívar used dance and music as diplomatic tools to unify newly liberated terrain, while López Maya's research in the Venezuelan archives documents just how important state-commissioned music was for the centennial celebrations in 1883.

Although the cult of Bolívar had its consolidation in the Guzmán Blanco era in the late nineteenth century, essays in this book argue for looking back to Bolívar's era to study his role in his own iconicity as well as his uses within contemporary revolutionary iconographies. Moreover, they contend that one should look outside the Latin American context to understand how Bolívar functions beyond *el culto a Bolívar*. We also argue for the significance of the visual and performing arts, which have previously received little attention in Bolivarian studies, because they reveal its artifice and performativity. The new archival findings and previously unpublished material presented here show the role of the arts in codifying and institutionalizing the sign as well as in critiquing and contesting it. Such performative processes go to the heart of democracy's work as a contested field, the need for dissensus, and agonistic public spheres. Our series of case studies spanning from the nineteenth century to the contemporary era provides insight into the diachronic and synchronic mutability of the sign. The collection is organized chronologically—rather than by discipline, geography, or thematics—in order to trace a genealogy of the sign of "Bolívar" while also making the subject accessible to the specialist and the nonspecialist, the advanced scholar and the undergraduate.

Part I of the collection, "Emergence and Consolidation in the Nineteenth Century," pushes back the origins of Venezuela's cult of Bolívar to present original research examining how ideas associated with Bolívar circulated during the revolutionary era. We then show how the national cult was forged during the postrevolutionary era in the mid- to late nineteenth century, culminating with the presidency of Guzmán Blanco in Venezuela. Drawing upon an extensive body of images, Emily A. Engel charts the explosion in portrait production from 1799 to 1830, explains the iconographic development of Bolívar's portraits based upon earlier viceregal traditions along with new modes of representation, and argues for the strategic social and political uses of Bolívar's "body" to signify unity, independence, and political transformation during the military campaign and early years of the republic.

Arguing against the dominant image of Bolívar as either a heroic warrior in the battlefield or a frivolous and womanizing bon vivant, Juan Francisco Sans interprets neglected primary sources to make the case that Bolívar used dance as a powerful political weapon, embodying the dialectics of negotiation, diplomacy, and even intimidation. Paul Niell draws upon his archival findings of the Cuban branch of the international movement Soles y Rayos de Bolívar, demonstrating that the movement appropriated Amerindian figures to represent American identity and cultural authenticity within the Spanish colonial system. Niell brings to light the entangled notions of liberation and emancipation that complicated Bolivarian campaigns in Cuba, a slave-dependent economy in the early nineteenth century. In a close reading of archival documents on the centennial celebrations in 1883, Juan de Dios López Maya shows how state-commissioned music was a crucial part of Guzmán Blanco's transformation of the cult of Bolívar into a secular religion. An expert on the cult of Bolívar, Tomás Straka addresses the formation of the Venezuelan Liberal Party's historiography during Guzmán Blanco's era, when the party's founders attributed progressive values and modernity to Bolívar. Straka foregrounds the state process of secularizing a cult that had been in the control of the Church through the creation of national monuments and symbols dedicated to the Liberal narrative of Bolívar.

Part II, "Disruptions and Unhingings in the Twentieth Century," focuses on visual, literary, and architectural examples from the twentieth century to the contemporary period that represent both attacks upon an iconic Bolívar and the polyvalence of Bolívar as a cultural sign beyond the Latin American context. In analyzing the staging, performance, and reception of two operas about Bolívar—one in 1950 in France and the other in 1994 in the United States—Maureen Shanahan investigates the contingent meanings of empire and liberation associated with the Bolivarian narrative. Tina Potočnik presents new findings from the Slovenian archives that suggest that the initial plans for Revolution Square (now Republic Square) in Ljubljana, Slovenia, created in 1960 during the formation of the nonaligned nations, drew upon Centro Simón Bolívar in Caracas as an architectural model and as a representation of revolution, national autonomy, and anti-imperialism.

Looking at the Colombian context, Ana María Reyes argues that Beatriz González's installations *Apuntes para la historia extensa* (1967) and *Mutis por el foro* (1973) appropriated canonical images of Bolívar in order to make strategic interventions that have gone unrecognized by the fine arts establishment. In Reyes's reading, González capitalized on the destabilization of Bolívar in order to revitalize contemporary history painting. González's works functioned as a critique of the two dominant ideologies at the time: the two-party political system in Colombia during the National Front and the aesthetic of technological "advancement" fostered in international art circuits. By turning to literary forms of iconoclasm in novels such as Manuel Trujillo's *El Gran Dispensador* (1983) and Francisco Herrera Luque's *Manuel Piar, caudillo de dos colores* (1987), Alicia Ríos provides a rare analysis that decenters Bolívar in the revolutionary narrative and unpacks the gendered and racialized assumptions of the Bolívar myth. Finally, Armida de la Garza's theorization of the much-acclaimed film *Bolívar soy yo* (Jorge Alí Triana, 2002) shows just how the performativity of "Bolívar" is contingent upon the reception of the "spectator" as citizen to imagine an alternative ending to the Bolivarian narrative.

Part III, "Re-Anchorings in the Late Twentieth and Early Twenty-First Centuries," returns to the Venezuelan context to assess the new forms of cultic political spectacle generated by the Chávez-Maduro regime in their

Bolivarian Revolution. In a rare analysis of Bolivarian relics, Alejandro E. Gómez Pernia shows how the Liberator's three swords—in Lima, Bogotá, and Caracas—have served multiple political positions: at one time seized by dissident Colombian guerrillas and later manipulated by Hugo Chávez in sacralizing his own claim to power. Nicholas Roberts argues that "Bolívar," once a floating signifier in Eugenio Montejo's poetry, became anchored to Hugo Chávez, thus permitting Chávez/Bolívar to become an object of iconoclastic dissent in the routines of the celebrated comics Emilio Lovera and Er Conde del Guácharo. Finally, Luis Duno-Gottberg explores the televised spectacle of disinterring and reconstituting Bolívar's physical body as a metaphor for the politics and poetics of the contemporary Venezuelan national body.

* * *

As we began this introduction with several examples of cultural Bolivarianism, we conclude with the extraordinary case of Mulaló, a *corregimiento* (small town) of less than two thousand inhabitants in southwestern Colombia. Historians confirm that during his military campaign in 1822, Simón Bolívar stayed at the slave-owning hacienda El Mulaló, which belonged to his friend José María Cuero y Caicedo. Oral traditions claim that Bolívar's white horse Palomo was interred next to the former hacienda chapel on September 17, 1840, and that both their spirits can be heard every September 17 at midnight. More significant is the belief that Bolívar's amorous interlude at El Mulaló with the slave Ana Cleofe Cuero produced his only biological heir. On September 13, 1823, Ana Cleofe gave birth to an infant, Manuela Josefa Bolívar Cuero, who went on to become the matriarch of an Afro-Bolivarian family (Valencia and Correa 2005). As the descendants of slaves claiming to be the only biological successors of Simón Bolívar, the community of Mulaló has invested "Bolívar" with the double meaning of independence from Spain and emancipation from slavery (Calle 2012; Tobón 2007). The Museo de Bolívar, located adjacent to the San Antonio town chapel, makes this connection manifest by displaying evidence of Bolívar's sojourn, a document popularly believed Manuela Josefa's baptismal record, as well as other nineteenth-century artifacts including *cepos* (mantraps) used to capture and punish slaves (Valencia and Correa 2005). Mulaló residents, in a gesture of familial recognition, painted black the bust of Bolívar located in the town's central square and altered his nose to resemble those of his descendants (Nascimento/Lovera 2014).

It is no surprise that this small, sleepy town on the banks of the Cauca River became the site for the remarkable Memoria Viva bicentennial celebrations on July 20, 2010. One would surmise that the Mulaló organizers would give Bolívar's impersonator center stage. Instead, the Liberator followed a long and dynamic procession that reenacted the arduous battles over slave emancipation, battles that eventually triumphed with the final assistance of patriotic reinforcements. This *macro-escena,* directed by John Jairo Perdomo, honored Bolívar but also Manuela Sáenz, Francisco de Paula Santander, Colombian independence heroine Policarpa Salavarrieta, and above all, the insurrectionary slave community that had been fighting for freedom long before (Bicentenario Municipio Yumbo 2010). Just as the Museo Bolívar displays an image of a mutilated Christ with a text describing how he stood alongside slaves who battled with Bolívar (Valencia and Correa García 2005), the bicentennial procession also accentuates the long-term and crucial role played by slaves in the liberation of the Americas.

Two years earlier, the Venezuelan artist collective Nascimento/Lovera picked up on the ritual centrality of Bolívar and Palomo in Mulaló. Their performance, *Untitled Mulaló* (2008), punctured Mulaló's sleepy calm with a cacophonous dialogue between the town band and a procession of rearing motorcycles that circulated around the ceiba tree under which, it is claimed, Palomo's remains are buried, a performance that evoked the virile image of Bolívar heroically crossing the Andes on the rearing Palomo. Nascimento/Lovera staged a funerary rite around Palomo's marble tombstone that included a tributary floral arrangement of Bolívar's "War to the Death" banner made of local flowers and coca leaves (figure I.1). In this way, the artists critically commented on the uses of Bolivarianism—by Bolívar himself, by the Bolivarian state, and at the fringes of society—opening questions about the connections among militarism, virile masculinity, the cocaine trade, and funerary rites.

These interventions in the public sphere by the community of Mulaló and collaborative artists Nascimento/Lovera operate as forms of dissensus upon the national imaginary, raising questions about who narrates which story of the nation, liberty, and revolution and whose "body" in all its metaphoric and material manifestations becomes iconic. This final example thus

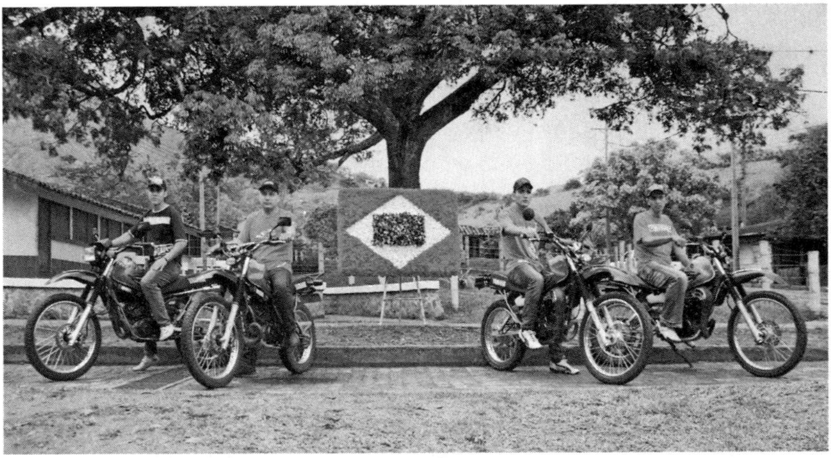

FIGURE I.1. Nascimento/Lovera. *Untitled Mulaló*. Performance, 2008. Tomb of Palomo, Simón Bolívar's horse, in Mulaló, Colombia. Motorcycle acrobats and floral arrangement with coca leaves and chrysanthemums. 41SN Cali URGENTE, curator Wilson Díaz. Photograph by Carlos Mario Camacho.

points to the larger dilemmas inherent in ritualization and cult practices of any privileged sign considered to embody abstract values; the sign's very performativity serves as evidence of its formative processes, its naturalization through repetition—and so too the apparatus for its undoing.

Many other cultural practices and producers intervening in the contested field of Bolívar as a cultural sign and as a cult figure also merit attention. How, for example, might we understand the activation (or neglect) of the many Bolívar statues around the world, the recent explosion of artistic and literary representations of Sáenz and Salavarrieta, or the rare envisioning of the lives and subjectivities of their slave women (a notable example being Jaime Manrique's 2007 novel, *Our Lives Are the Rivers*)? Similarly, many questions remain about how the body of the nation is materialized in culture and sacralized in ritual. We do not claim this collection to be an authoritative or comprehensive study but quite the inverse; our objective is to decenter iconicity and authorial texts as well as to contribute to the exploration of Bolívar as a cultural vehicle through which the public sphere is negotiated. It is our hope that we will foster new avenues of exploration for this inexhaustible and very rich subject.

Acknowledgments: Maureen G. Shanahan

As an idea that has migrated among many collaborators and several continents, this book owes its materialization to a wealth of supporters and colleagues. The project arose over a decade ago in the course of my research on the French avant-garde artist Fernand Léger, his experiences of war and historical trauma, and his uses of art as a form of resilience. In a forthcoming book on Léger, I argue that what constituted resilience for Léger and his contemporaries was an ongoing process highly contingent upon the shifting cultural, economic, and social dynamics of their time. During World War II, while France was under occupation, Léger was in exile in the United States and began collaborating with composer Darius Milhaud on plans for a Bolívar opera. For them "Bolívar" was a privileged sign of heroic masculinity, a site of investment that functioned as a vehicle for envisioning "liberation" and a reempowered future. As I studied more cultural iterations of the Bolívar story, including Thea Musgrave's Bolívar opera, I began to understand how "Bolívar" functioned as a complex discursive field of contested meanings for many interrelated ideas: oppression, colonialism, the rights of man, liberation, the Enlightenment, and the nation. I also began to see the Bolívar narrative with its iconic heroes and heroines as a lens through which to enact a postmodernist critique of history's metanarratives, its types as cultural condensations, and its reformulations as sites of agency and subjectivity.

Many individuals and institutions supported my research on the Milhaud and Musgrave operas, particularly Thea Musgrave, who generously shared her work with me; the Virginia Opera and the Bibliothèque nationale de France and their respective archivists and managers; and my home institution of James Madison University. I am very grateful to those who have commented on earlier iterations of the research presented here, particularly Defne Demir, Kristen McCleary, Sue Peabody, Daniel Silander, and Charlotte Wallin.

As a nonspecialist in Latin American studies and an agnostic outsider to the cult and culture of Bolívar, I sought many advisers and collaborators, which in turn led to the development of this edited collection as a dialogue about and genealogical study of an iconic figure and the many narratives in which he figures. My first co-editor to whom I owe thanks is Pedro Aponte, a musicology specialist in Venezuelan nationalism and, in 2010, a newly hired colleague at James Madison University. As soon as I broached the idea of a collaboration, we began planning a panel for a Latin American Studies Association conference. In the course of developing our panel proposal in 2011, I met Ana María Reyes at the College Art Association's conference, where she presented a paper on Beatriz González's Bolívar and Santander medallions as part of a panel organized by our mutual friend and colleague Roberto Tejada, who has generously advised and supported this and other projects. Pedro, Ana María, and I joined forces and launched a call for proposals along with a panel at the Latin American Studies Association conference in San Francisco in May 2012. As a result of the call, we received many exceptional proposals; my thanks thus also go to the contributors in this volume for their illumination of Bolívar's polyvalent significations. Although Pedro was not able to continue with this project due to other demands, we thank him for his many contributions, including his efforts in recruiting several contributors: Juan de Dios López Maya, Juan Francisco Sans, and Tómas Straka.

In 2012, my research on Milhaud's opera took an extraordinary turn when Pedro alerted me to a planned reconstruction scheduled for performance in Caracas in March of that year. Despite only about two weeks' notice, many people and offices at James Madison University supported my travel for the historic event: the College of Visual Arts and its dean George Sparks; the School of Art, Design, and Art History and then director William Wightman; and the Office of International Programs and its study-abroad director Felix Wang. In addition, Pedro provided me with many introductions, most importantly to Juan Francisco Sans, who graciously hosted me at the Universidad Central de Venezuela (UCV). There the university leadership and Juan Francisco's colleagues received me with great hospitality. I am especially grateful to Nila Sareet Lista, director of university conservation, for the tour of the university's exceptional modernist art and architecture.

While I was in Caracas, my visit was generously supported and hosted by numerous institutions and people, many of whom permitted interviews on the production and history of the opera. These include the Embassy of France, Ambassador Jean-Marc Laforêt, and cultural attaché Lionel Paradisi-Coulouma; the Alliance Française, then director Alain Villechalane, and cultural coordinator Clarisse Lavaure; the Institut Français and its cultural minister Jean-Louis Gavatorta; and the Teatro Teresa Carreño, whose archivist Asdrubal Urdaneta was most helpful and whose musical director Alfredo Rugeles and then cultural director Diana Arismendi were very welcoming. The producers, Atahualpa and Diana Lichy, who have conducted years of research on the music and history of the opera, were extremely generous in meeting with me and sharing their findings. In addition, Pierre-Yves Pruvot, who sang the role of Bolívar, documentary filmmaker Xavier d'Arthuys, and independent researcher Héctor Pérez Marchelli answered my many questions about the production. While my essay in this volume focuses on a particular aspect of representation in the libretto and Léger's designs, the history of Milhaud's opera, including its performances in Caracas in 1983 and 2012, deserves much more scholarly attention than is possible here.

Finally, this book would not have been possible without two important partners. One of the greatest pleasures in working on this book has been developing a wonderful friendship and professional partnership with my admirable co-editor, Ana María Reyes. Her energy and intellect and our many conversations about culture and democracy have shaped my thinking as well as the text itself. None of my work would be possible without my loving life partner, Diana Elizabeth Haddad, whose linguistic coaching helped make my talk at the UCV a success and whose support and encouragement have cheered me on throughout.

Acknowledgments: Ana María Reyes

This book would never have come to fruition if it were not for Maureen Shanahan's daring vision to fill a gap she identified in the massive sea of Bolivarian literature. While Bolívar has captivated the imaginations of many cultural producers, no scholarship to date compiles in one volume a synchronic, diachronic, international, even intercontinental dialogue concerning the polyvalent "Bolívar" as icon and myth. When Maureen asked me join her and Pedro Aponte as co-editors for a collection of essays on Simón Bolívar, I was apprehensive about entering unfamiliar territory, perhaps moving away from the anti-authoritarian ethos of my scholarship. Maureen approached me in 2011 after I delivered a paper at the College Art Association at which I interpreted Beatriz González's Bolívar and Santander medallions (1967) as assaults on authoritarian patrimonial institutions such as the National Academy of History in Colombia. However, Maureen's vision concurred with my own conviction about the important role that arts and humanities play in democratic practices. Her idea was a wonderful opportunity to combat the endemic political and cultural messianism that interferes with laborious yet worthwhile civic participation. This collection of essays thus serves as both an exercise in and metaphor for the polyvocal and agonistic public sphere. Therefore, I thank Maureen first and foremost for inviting me to join her in this rich journey through the complex interstices of art and politics. It was her path toward Bolívar via France and Virginia that illuminated my understanding of this iconic figure's plasticity.

The book is the outcome of many exchanges that began at the 2012 Latin American Studies conference in San Francisco and continued in written form and through engaging conversations. *Simón Bolívar: Travels and Transformations of a Cultural Icon* has benefited tremendously from the compelling scholarship presented here by each one of the contributing scholars whose essays complicate any facile reading of cultural history.

I owe a debt of gratitude to many people who, intentionally or not, have contributed to the development of this book. I especially would like to thank Andrea Giunta and Roberto Tejada for inviting me to join their panel, "Conspiracy Methods: Revisiting Latin American Art 1960s to the Present," at the College Art Association in 2011, which led to this collaboration with Maureen. I am greatly indebted to Beatriz González, who patiently and generously allowed me to interview her several times, digitize her archives, and reproduce her works.

Writing is a collective endeavor, and this process was greatly nourished by the intellectual community that surrounds me. I would like to thank those who have read the many iterations of my writing on Beatriz González, including Tom Cummins, Marty Ward, Agnes Lugo Ortiz, Darby English, Ingrid W. Elliott, and E. Carmen Ramos Alfred at the University of Chicago, Jill Bugajski from Northwestern University, and Gina McDaniel Tarver from the University of Texas at Austin. My research also greatly benefited from assistance in Colombia by María Antonia Uscátegui, Nicolás Duque, and Zoad Humar. I express my gratitude to Juan Manuel Echavarría, Juan Nascimento, and Daniela Lovera for their generosity with materials and fascinating discussions on contemporary interventions in Bolivarian territory. This book also benefited from the generosity of Jorge Alí Triana, Sandra

Padilla, and Carlos Duque at Dramax, Colombia, as well as Daniel Castro, director of both the Museo Quinta de Bolívar and the Museo de la Independencia Casa del Florero, Bogotá, and his assistants Norma Juliana Jiménez (Museo de la Independencia) and Angela María Eraso (Quinta de Bolivar).

Funding for research came from the University of Chicago Department of Art History Field Research Grant and the University of Chicago Center for Latin American Studies Field Research Grant. Funding for writing came from the American Association of University Women (AAUW) American Dissertation Fellowship. I am especially grateful to the AAUW members who work hard at raising funds so that scholars like myself can achieve our professional goals. I would like to express my gratitude to the Boston University Center for the Humanities for their generous publication production grant and for their ongoing support to humanities scholars.

From a personal perspective, Bolívar has been an ever-present figure in my family. Throughout my childhood I was reminded that I descended from Joaquín Posada Gutiérrez, a general in the *campaña libertadora*. He was one of the last officials to see Bolívar alive as he embarked on his final journey up the Magdalena River toward Santa Marta, and Posada supervised the first exhumation and voyage of Bolívar's remains to Caracas in 1842. His *Memorias histórico-políticas* (1865) are considered the first tragic account of Bolívar and the wars of independence. Also, my uncle Carlos José Reyes Posada worked closely with director Jorge Alí Triana and producer Eduardo Lemaitre on writing the ambitious forty-three-episode series *Bolívar: El hombre de las dificultades* for the television show *Revivamos nuestra historia* (1983), in honor of the bicentennial of Bolívar's birth. Carlos José even acted the part of General Posada Gutiérrez, for whom he is still a dead ringer. This was the first Colombian television show in color, and every Sunday evening my relatives gathered at our house to watch each episode. Consequently, Bolívar seemed more like a distant relative than a national icon. When I embarked on this project I was deeply affected by all the other "Bolívars" out in the world that had so many other stories to tell. Another descendent of General Posada, a figure who has loomed large in my imagination and intellectual development, is my father, Dr. Pablo Reyes Posada. He inculcated in me a deep sense of ethical humanist values that have served as the core of my scholarly pursuits, especially concerning human rights and democratic thinking.

Notes

1. All translations in this volume were made by the author of each essay unless otherwise indicated.

2. While we use the term *criollo* in Spanish here, several authors in this volume use "Creole" as an English translation but sustaining its Spanish connotations. It is important to note that the term "Creole" in former English/French colonies means something very different than in the Spanish-speaking world. The English/French term connotes miscegenation and cultural hybridity (mainly Euro-African), while in Spanish the term *criollo* is used for European (Spanish) people born in the Americas and their culture. It also connotes the elites among the Americans.

References

Aguilar Rivera, José Antonio. 2011. "Men or Citizens? The Making of Bolívar's Patria." In *Forging People: Race, Ethnicity, and Nationality in Hispanic American and Latino/a Thought*, edited by Jorge J. E. Garcia, 57–84. Notre Dame, IN: University of Notre Dame Press.

Aguirre Tobón, Luz Jenny. 2007. "Bolívar no se ha ido de Mulaló." *El País* (Cali), October 14. http://historico.elpais.com.co/historico/oct142007/REG/reg01.html#.

Allatson, Paul. 2006. "Juan Dávila; Queering the Trans-Pacific South." *ArtLink* 26, no. 4:16–20.

Andermann, Jens, and William Rowe, eds. 2005. *Images of Power: Iconography, Culture, and State in Latin America*. New York: Berghahn.

Bicentenario Municipio Yumbo. 2010. "Bolívar y Palomo revivieron sus pasos en Mulaló." Blog post, July 21. http://bicentenarioyumbo.blogspot.com/2010/07/bolivar-y-palomo-revivieron-sus-pasos.html.

Caballero, Manuel. 2006. *Por que no soy bolivariano: Una reflexión antipatriótica*. Caracas: Alfadil.

Calle Vallejo, Carolina. 2012. "Los hijos mulatos de un Bolívar estéril." *El Tiempo* (Bogotá), February 12. http://www.elcolombiano.com/BancoConocimiento/L/los_hijos_mulatos_de_un_bolivar_esteril/los_hijos_mulatos_de_un_bolivar_esteril.asp.

Carrera Damas, Germán. 1970/2013. *El culto a Bolívar: Esbozo para un estudio de la historia de las ideas en Venezuela*. 7th ed. Caracas: Editorial Alfa.

Castro Leiva, Luis. 1984. *La Gran Colombia, una ilusión ilustrada*. Caracas: Monte Ávila Editores.

———. 1991. *De la patria boba a la teología bolivariana: Ensayos de historia intelectual*. Caracas: Monte Ávila Editores.

Chasteen, John. 2006. "Simon Bolivar: Man and Myth." In *Heroes and Hero Cults in Latin America*, edited by Samuel Brunk and Ben Fallaw, 21–39. Austin: University of Texas Press.

Conway, Christopher B. 2003. *The Cult of Bolívar in Latin American Literature*. Gainesville: University Press of Florida.

del Sarto, Ana, Alicia Ríos, and Abril Trigo, eds. 2004. *The Latin American Cultural Studies Reader*. Durham, NC: Duke University Press.

González Aranda, Beatriz. 2013. *Manual de arte del siglo XIX en Colombia*. Bogotá: University of Los Andes Press.

Gramsci, Antonio. 1972. *Selections from the Prison Notebooks of Antonio Gramsci*. Translated and edited by Quintin Hoare and Geoffrey Nowell-Smith. New York: International Publishers.

Guerrero, Javier. 2008. "Simón Bolívar, el zambo." In "Race and Its Others," special issue, *E-misférica* 5, no. 2 (December): 1–3.

Hall, Stuart. 1981. "Notes on Deconstructing the 'Popular.'" In *People's History and Socialist Theory*, edited by Raphael Samuel, 442–53. History Workshop Series. London: Routledge and Kegan Paul.

Hart, Stephen M. 2005. "Blood, Ink, and Pigment: Simón Bolívar as Proteus." *Bulletin of Spanish Studies* 82, nos. 3–4 (May–June): 335–52.

Helg, Aline. 2004. *Liberty and Equality in Caribbean Colombia, 1770–1835*. Chapel Hill: University of North Carolina Press.

Laclau, Ernesto, and Chantal Mouffe. 2001. *Hegemony and Socialist Strategy: Towards a Radical Democratic Politics*. 2nd edition. London: Verso.

Lynch, John. 2006. *Simón Bolívar: A Life*. New Haven, CT: Yale University Press.

Mejías-López, Alejandro. 2005. "(Re)-Imagining Bolívar." Review of Christopher Conway, *The Cult of Bolívar in Latin American Literature* (University Press of Florida, 2003). *A Contracorriente. A Journal on Social History and Literature in Latin America* (Spring): 147–60.

Melo, Jorge Orlando. 2010. "Bolívar en Colombia: Las transformaciones de su imagén." In *Entre el olvido y el recuerdo: Íconos, lugares de memoria y cánones de la historia y la literatura en Colombia*, 103–38. Bogotá: Universidad Javeriana.

Nascimento/Lovera. 2008. *Untitled Mulaló*. Performance, video. http://vimeo.com/29819202.

———. 2014. Interview by Ana María Reyes. Skype, June 12.

Pino Iturrieta, Elias. 2003. *El divino Bolívar: Ensayo sobre una religión republicana*. Madrid: Catarta.

Pividal, Francisco. 1977. *Bolívar: Pensamiento precursor del anti-imperialismo*. Havana: Ediciones Casa de las Américas.

Reyes, Ana María. 1999. "Disrupting the Sensationalistic Gaze: Juan Manuel Echavarría's Photographic Reflections on Violence in Colombia." *Juan Manuel Echavarría*, 1–8. Exhibit catalogue. Bogotá: Valenzuela y Kleiner.

Ríos, Alicia. 2013. *Nacionalismos banales, el culto a Bolívar: Literatura, cine, arte y política en América Latina*. Pittsburgh, PA: Instituto Internacional de Literatura Iberoamericana, University of Pittsburgh.

Safford, Frank, and Marco Palacios. 2002. *Colombia: Fragmented Land, Divided Society*. New York: Oxford University Press.

Salas de Lecuna, Yolanda. 1987. *Bolívar y la historia en la conciencia popular*. Caracas: Universidad Simón Bolívar and Instituto de Altos Estudios de América Latina.

———. 2010. *Manuel Piar: El héroe de múltiples rostros: Una aproximación a la historia desde la perspectiva de la memoria colectiva*. Caracas: Ministerio de Estado para la Cultura.

Schelchkov, Andrei. 2002. "Los estudios latinoamericanos en Rusia (y en la URSS)." *Revista Europea de Estudios Latinoamericanos y del Caribe*, no. 72 (April): 205–20.

Schmidt-Nowara, Christopher. 2011. *Slavery, Freedom, and Abolition in Latin America and the Atlantic World*. Albuquerque: University of New Mexico Press.

Shanahan, Maureen G. 2005. "The Franco-Venezuelan Migrations and Metamorphoses of Simón Bolívar: 1950/2004." In *Democracy and Culture in the Transatlantic World*, edited by Charlotte Wallin and Daniel Silander, 199–207. Växjo, Sweden: Växjo University Press.

Sommer, Doris. 2014. *The Work of Art in the World: Civic Agency and Public Humanities*. Durham, NC: Duke University Press.

Straka, Tomás. 2009. *La épica del desencanto: Bolivarianismo, historiografía y política en Venezuela*. Caracas: Editorial Alfa.

Torres, Ana Teresa. 2009. *La herencia de la tribu: Del mito de la independencia a la revolución bolivariana*. Caracas: Editorial Alfa.

Valencia Murcia, Fernando, and Andrés Correa García. 2005. "Memoria y recuerdos colectivos. El caso de una leyenda en Mulaló. *Revista Sociedad y Economía* (Universidad del Valle), no. 8 (April): 135–158.

Zeuske, Michael. 2013. *Bolívar: History and Myth*. Translated by Steven Rendall and Lisa Neal. Princeton, NJ: Markus Wiener.

Part I

Emergence and Consolidation in the Nineteenth Century

1

Simón Bolívar's Itinerant Portraits

Visual Conquest and the Production of an Icon

EMILY A. ENGEL

Where Bolívar is, there is the republic.
CAMILO TORRES TENORIO

While on military campaign in Alto Peru during the year 1825, Simón Bolívar acquired a full-length portrait of himself painted by the Peruvian artist José Gil de Castro (plate 3). The Liberator later dispatched the painting to his sister in Caracas, María Antonia Bolívar, in the care of Antonio Leocadio Guzmán (O'Leary 1970, 261), with a letter that describes the military portrait by Gil de Castro now in the Venezuelan National Assembly in Caracas. Before the Venezuelan government acquired the painting, María Antonia made the image available for a public viewing that she described in a letter to Bolívar: "Tonight there was a large event in the plaza with your portrait and many in attendance. The portrait was displayed and processed with music and all the town and military figures who chanted praises and acclamations and in the morning there was a mass with artillery presence, in the end, the day was enjoyable, until the old guard came out into the streets" (in Boulton 1964, 75). After the procession of the portrait through the streets of Caracas, María Antonia installed the portrait on the balcony of her house with the windows open for public viewing. In the street, individuals of all classes, races, and ranks participated in a shared devotional practice as they had with royal portraits during the viceregal period. The contextual pageantry surrounding Bolivarian portraiture in the 1820s was a continuation of baroque theatricality in which paintings were activated in a larger multimedia production (Schreffler 2007). In situ, the portrait became a venerated icon honored by supplicants with offerings aimed to ensure a complete transformation of Bolívar into a pan-American agent of political transformation facilitating republican unity.

Historical portraits of political leaders are pictorial monuments that, when publicly activated, conjure and shape shared traditions. In the past, the creation, glorification, and even destruction of political portraits—that is, the formation of icons and iconographic conventions—visualized cultural traditions that provided foundations for national identities and discourse (Guerra 2003). This essay explores the iconogenesis of Bolívar from the point of view of portraits made of the Liberator during his lifetime, a body of 150 drawn, painted, sculpted, and engraved images that later became the iconic foundation for South American republicanism. As several of the essays in this volume demonstrate, theatrical performances, poems, dances, and musical compositions, among other forms of creative expression, produced Simón Bolívar as a cultural sign.

The graphic rendering of Bolívar in portrait imagery resonates in the contemporary visual landscape as evidenced by the proliferation of Bolivarian portraiture analyzed throughout this volume. Art historical analysis opens the possibility to explore the iconicity of Bolívar's earliest portraits from the perspective of established viceregal visual traditions, such as religious images and elite portraits. During Bolívar's lifetime, a succession of ruptures and continuities produced heterogeneous visual responses that presage the emergence of the Liberator as political icon incarnating pan-American political transformation. Between 1799 and 1830, Bolivarian portraits strategically navigated sociopolitical alliances in the wake of far-reaching military campaigns. Bolívar became the face of a movement that was as much ideological as it was militaristic wherein his body came to visualize the principle of political transformation from Spanish imperial domination toward national republican governments.

The story of Bolívar's pictorial transformation from a man into an icon begins after 1816 when casual, anomalous sketches and vaguely imagined portraits are replaced by iconic images intended to materialize the political transition instigated by the proclaimed Liberator of Spanish South America. A British engraver known as M. N. Bate created one of the most influential early portraits of Simón Bolívar (figure 1.1). The image establishes enduring visual attributes that evolved into a Bolivarian iconography: a

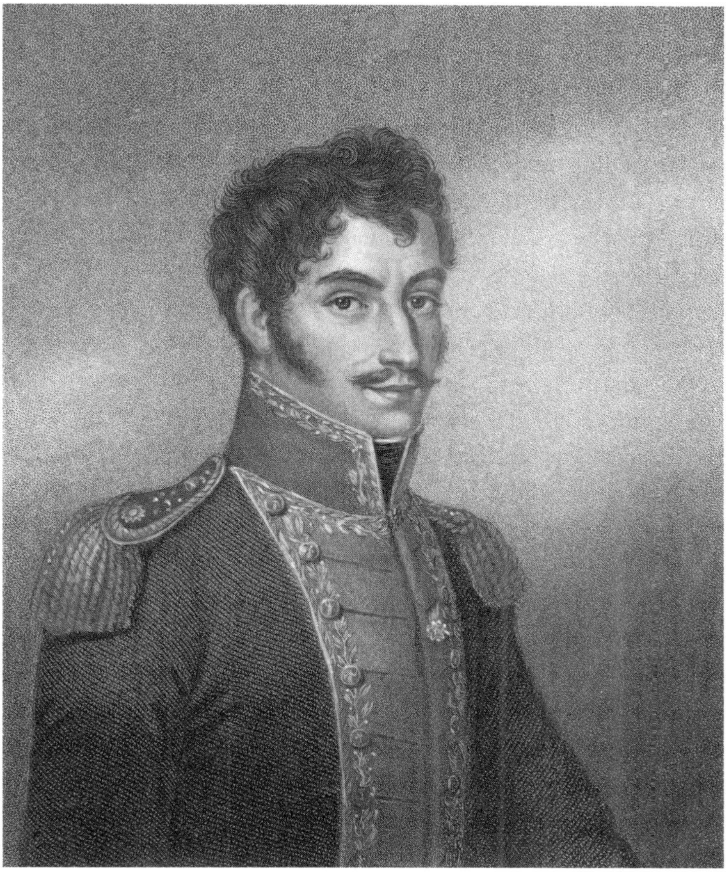

FIGURE 1.1. M. N. Bate. *Simón Bolívar*. 1819. Engraving. 7.87" × 5.039" (20 × 12.8cm). Courtesy of the John Carter Brown Library at Brown University.

three-quarter bust set against an unornamented ground with subtle color variation. Bolívar wears an elaborate uniform establishing his identity as a military hero. In the absence of pictorial setting and detail, a shock of curling dark hair atop his head, bristling sideburns, and a wispy mustache become visually prominent attributes of the portrait. To leave no doubt about the identity of the depicted sitter and the authenticity of the portrayed image, a lengthy inscription enumerates its pedigree: "Simón Bolívar / Supreme Chief of the Republic and Captain General of the Armies of Venezuela and New Granada. / Engraved by M. N. Bate from an original drawing late in the possession of M. Walton Esqr. London Published Feb., 1, 1819, by Messrs.

Colnaghi & Co., Cockspur Street." An unidentified British artist likely drafted the initial portrait as a drawing of Bolívar during his diplomatic travels in London in 1810–11. William Walton, a British printer and vocal critic of Spanish imperial governance, cast this image of Simón Bolívar as the face of a wide-reaching political movement when he published the bust portrait after 1810. The Bolivarian portrait supported Walton's textual efforts to rally British support for Spanish American independence. Walton first addressed the British government in an 1814 treatise, later directing his case to the British people, for whom Bolívar's iconic image signified the military overthrow of the Spanish Empire directed by an able-bodied, youthful general.

At the same time in Bogotá, Bolívar conscripted Pedro José Figueroa to create his official portrait (González-Stephan 2008, 93). From 1819 to 1821, Figueroa painted at least five bust or three-quarter-length portraits of Bolívar in ceremonial blue and red military attire ornamented with gold epaulettes, embroidery, and medals and often sporting a sword with a golden hilt along the left side of his body. One such image, now exhibited in the Quinta de Bolívar in Bogotá, is identified as one of Figueroa's first portraits of the Liberator (plate 4). The 1819 portrait delimits compositional and iconographic protocols that were employed to authenticate later portraits of the Liberator created by artists distanced from Bolívar in time and space: foreground composition defined with very little, if any, contextual detail; a dominating three-quarter-length figure positioned in a grounded, confident pose and ornamented by costume and by pronounced, exaggerated physical features (such as dark-brown tendrils of hair that drift down the sitter's forehead and point to thick, sculptural eyebrows, sideburns, and moustache). Some of Figueroa's portraits are framed by gold-lettered inscriptions that designate Bolívar's place of birth and honorific and military titles and the date of the portrait. Most portraits of Bolívar produced during his lifetime were supplemented by text inscriptions that specified the subject's identity by name and titles, both military and governmental. Over time, the simple composition highlighting the Liberator's body without the trappings of time and place became more prominent. The Bate engraving and Figueroa portraits were copied and circulated in diverse contexts. Text inscriptions guaranteed the reception of the images as representations of Simón Bolívar. They established the identity of the depicted subject, mitigated perceived inadequacies of the visual likeness, and validated the image's authenticity, a period concern stemming from religious visual traditions that demanded historical awareness of an image's artist, iconography, and essence.

When Bolívar commissioned Figueroa to render his likeness as a military officer, he initiated a portraiture campaign that spanned the 1820s. The collaboration between Figueroa and Bolívar established official portraiture as a political strategy that could support military efforts to sever the Spanish imperial hold on South America. Bolívar deployed the painting in official ritual contexts in New Granada following his victorious liberation of the region from Spanish forces. The portrait functioned as a response to Spanish adversaries, caudillo factionalism, and ideological resistance to political transformation (González-Stephan 2008). Around the same time Bolívar enlisted Figueroa to create his official portrait, the Liberator embarked on a public relations campaign designed to shape the intellectual future of emancipated territories, namely to ensure the establishment of national assemblies and electoral processes without backsliding into Spanish governmental models. Bolívar used the weekly newspaper in Santa Fe de Bogotá, *El Correo del Orinoco,* edited by Francisco Antonio Zea, as his mouthpiece (Lynch 2006, 117). The pictorial record parallels this effort, and together the visual and printed content generated by Bolívar and his allies inaugurated the parameters of a Bolivarian cultural agenda upon the moment in which the Liberator claims his title and its accompanying power. As his military campaigns gathered momentum, Bolívar often engaged local artists and pictorial traditions to disseminate his image as an icon of American independence.

Portraiture served as a pictorially discursive medium suited to the task of establishing unity, a stated goal of the South American Liberator in his 1815 "Carta de Jamaica," written during his exile (Bolívar 1815/2003). He envisioned first a Gran Colombia that united northern South America and later a continental coalition of regions joined to ensure stability following the removal and replacement of Spanish control (Ardao 1978). A limited number of portraits in Argentina honored José de San Martín, and Chilean collectors sponsored only a handful of images featuring Bernardo O'Higgins. As representations of fighters cum governmental officials, military portraits visualized the people (generals) and the processes (diplomacy and war) that facilitated South American independence from Spain as it transpired. Even though Bolívar was not the only revolutionary hero whose image was immortalized in portraiture, the proclaimed Liberator was the sole individual whose image became the currency of independence ideology in the 1820s. Hugo Achugar (2009) demonstrates that Bolívar's image appeared on early republican currency in the southern Río de la Plata region, where it supported broader pan–South American efforts to disconnect from centuries of Spanish imperial rule.

Transforming Viceregal Practices

Icons require reference to previous pictorial traditions in order to be visually effective as representational devices. Bolívar, the artists who portrayed his likeness, and his supporters fabricated images that engaged with established visual conventions to give their images cultural currency in a transitional moment. The tradition of portraying military leaders like Simón Bolívar originated in 1722–23 when the Spanish colonial administration appointed five military men to high office in its American holdings, including the viceroys of Peru and New Granada, territories that Bolívar later came to occupy (Eissa-Barroso 2012). This action marked a strategic adjustment in American viceregal governance in response to increasing threats of foreign attack and internal rebellion. It also engendered an adjustment in portrait iconography that opened up the possibility of depicting military leaders wearing uniform dress and posing in their official capacities. Earlier in the viceregal period, portraiture had been reserved for administrative, ecclesiastical, and social elites. Viceroys and their urban associates collected portraits documenting their American exploits in full-length formal poses accompanied by the accouterments of their office explained in laudatory inscribed cartouches. As I have shown elsewhere (Engel 2009), South American viceroy portraits were instrumental in envisioning a shared political ideology represented in the physiognomic likeness of a local authority figure.

With rare exceptions such as the five militarized viceroys, there are few known portraits of military generals who served in South America before the revolutionary period. In correspondence from 1811, Brigadier General Manuel de Villalta outlined glorious moments in the career of the renowned Spanish creole general and diplomat José Manuel de Goyeneche.[1] Villalta describes a now lost portrait of Goyeneche commissioned and displayed in the city of Lima to commemorate the heroic deeds of the military leader as well as to provide an example of patriotic public service. Portraits of military leaders and viceregal officials applied visual principles found in Spanish royal portraits produced in Spain and South America.[2] Natalia Majluf (2013) has argued convincingly that royal portraits provided iconographic and conceptual models exploited by Bolívar in the independence era. Royal portraits acted as allegories of power in Spanish dominated South America, a function coopted first by the viceroys and later by Simón Bolívar.[3]

Military portraits established a new rank in the social hierarchy into which entry could be negotiated in part by way of visual images. Portraits of nobles and other social elites were common in South America from the mid-sixteenth century forward. Men, women, nuns, ecclesiastical authorities, educators, and political figures like the revolutionary Tupac Amaru II posed for or commissioned portraits that demonstrated individual and collective status, wealth, and relationships. Viceregal elites commissioned and displayed portraits to guarantee their social status, and portraits were activated in social settings.

At the turn of the nineteenth century, an artist from Quito painted a formal portrait of Agustín Angulo y Ante, a Spanish businessman with close ties to Bolívar. Angulo stands before an awkward leather-covered table rendered in incomplete perspective, the only furnishing in a dull gray chamber. The subject sports a tailored black suit, a sword hilt peeking out from beneath his jacket by his left hand. This type of iconographical austerity is often termed "neoclassicism" (Stratton-Pruitt 2013, 82–83). Like many late colonial portraits, the painting of Angulo focuses the viewer's attention on the elite subject's place in a network of relations across time and space. Angulo's right hand reaches out to the edge of the canvas proffering a letter addressed to his wife, María Josefa Sáenz del Campo, whom he married in Quito in 1813. Agustín Angulo's wife was the half-sister of Manuela Sáenz del Campo, Bolívar's on-again-off-again companion in the years that followed. Moreover, oversize baroque coats of arms in the top right and left corners of the canvas flank the male figure as iconographic references to Angulo's complex heritage, complemented by swirling phylacteries that detail the names of families from which he descended. Portraits visually articulated social histories as subject to manipulation by sitters, patrons, and viewers; they reveal viable modes of constructing relations by presenting the physical comportment of the sitter, by juxtaposing the public and private components of identity, personality, and appearance, and by establishing social conventions. Portraits visually rendered the complexities of personal heritage with explicit reference to historical positioning and lineage, visible in the inscribed banners in Angulo's portrait.

It is unlikely that Bolívar would have had the opportunity to see the Goyeneche or Angulo portraits, but as an elite, well-traveled individual, he and his supporters were aware of the cultural currency the genre of portraiture held across South America. As the Spanish colonial hierarchy was reconfigured, the status and significance of an individual were no longer assured by pictorial representation. Instead, individuals who identified themselves as worthy of representation commissioned, collected, and displayed their portraits as a way of marking their originating roles in the revolution. Evaluating the intellectual class of New Granada, Anthony McFarlane (2006, 113) states that they pursued "new ways of seeing and understanding their society, and favoured innovation over tradition. . . . [T]hey formed networks . . . that transcended local boundaries and which, in times of political turmoil, could be turned to other purposes." Subtle reconfigurations of the genre of portraiture offered a way to participate in political transition and to demonstrate one's acceptance of or openness to political change and transformation. By the onset of the revolutionary period, military and elite portraits had become part of an established visual lexicon. Bolivarian portraits exploited the ability of the genre to effectively visualize networks of relationships and places navigated by individuals in viceregal society. In the volatile revolutionary environment, the process of creating a portrait (commissioning, sitting, exhibiting) served as a place where individuals and groups could integrate the idiosyncratic with the social.

During the viceregal period, portraiture was regulated and specific, with very little visual or conceptual ambiguity, unlike Bolivarian portraiture, which emerged as a diversity without a coherent pattern. In the revolutionary period, military portraiture became a viable portrait subgenre. Artists commissioned to paint the portraits of military leaders like Simón Bolívar borrowed familiar compositions, iconographies, and conceptual underpinnings from preserved colonial-era imagery. Shared artistic traditions provided artists, patrons, and viewers with legible, coherent portraits that legitimated the political authority of newly minted leaders, while at the same time they underscored the importance of continuity with the viceregal past, which provided the stability and order necessary for complete separation from Spain.

Some early portraits of Simón Bolívar were imagined by artists without access to their subject for geographic reasons; however, most of the 150 portraits made of Bolívar during his lifetime were either observed from life or inspired by images observed from life. Fewer than twenty of the Bolívar portraits made before 1830 are documented to have been created from life. Many copies resulted from these prototypes, as recorded in inscriptions, accompanying texts, and artistic practices (such as artists making copies of their own work observed from life); these are demonstrated as a graph in figure 1.2. Observation from life authenticated Bolívar portraiture as it developed into "an iconic sign system" (Peterson 2005, 69), which became the iconographic foundation for the Spanish American independence movement and later the cult of the Liberator.

Iconicity in Bolivarian portraiture resulted from perceived verisimilitude, as it had with colonial-era sacred icons, such as Our Lady of Guadalupe

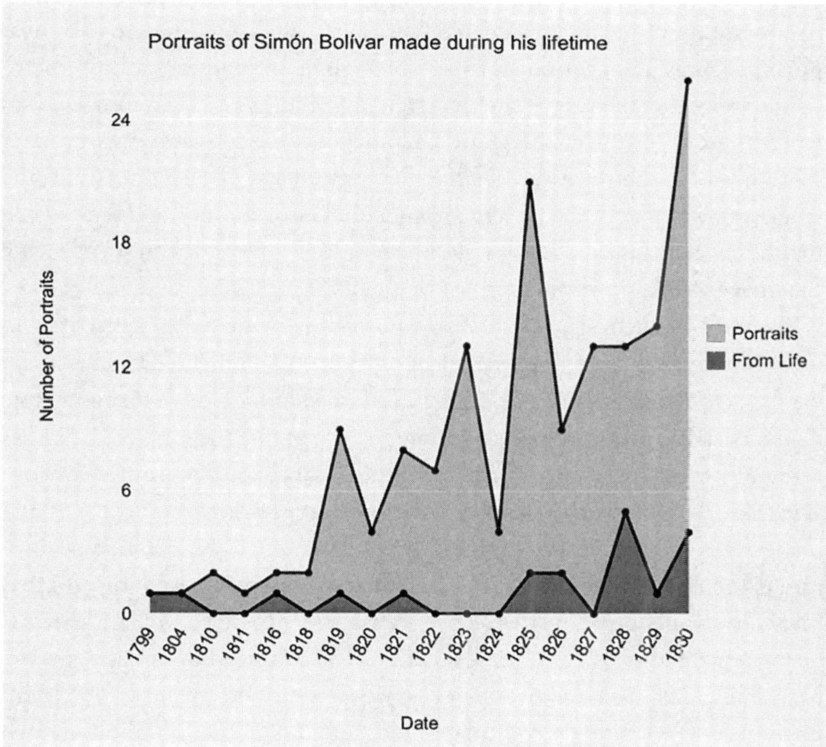

FIGURE 1.2. Graph delimiting the extent of Bolivarian portraits made between 1799 and 1830. Emily A. Engel, 2014.

(Peterson 2005, 68), that required observable parallels between originating images and their later copies. Following the appearance of the miraculous divinity in early colonial Mexico, Our Lady of Guadalupe became one of the most influential sacred images in the Iberoamerican world (Peterson 2014). In religious contexts, the divine origins of an icon established its authenticity as a reliable visual likeness. Artists repositioning themselves as creative agents in viceregal society configured aesthetic strategies to underscore the creative potential of the sacred in rendering American holy icon imagery (Bargellini 2004, 86). Authenticated icons facilitated a visual experience with an otherwise invisible spiritual realm, legitimating cult devotion to them. Like their sacred precursors in which "the exemplary copy produced was perceived as having the potential to embody the same holy properties as the original" (Peterson 2005, 65), Bolivarian portraits became iconic representations of the negotiated positionalities that characterized independence-era Spanish America. The sacred icon of Our Lady of Guadalupe shares visual qualities of iconicity with Bate's and Figueroa's Bolívar portraits: they foreground an image of a single individual with no pictorial context, the likeness of the depicted individual was taken into account when the image was created, and the images were activated in a broader discourse of authenticating a shared ideology. In early Bolívar portraits, the sitter connected with the viewer through direct eye contact, and scant ornamentation focuses the viewer's attention on the subject at hand, endowing the image with a powerful meditative quality.

Even if the likeness presented in a portrait is inadequate, the artist's attempt establishes the referential image as a portrait connected to an individual, but the image remains an empty cultural sign outside of its contextual registers. The portrait visually apprehends the public persona of Bolívar as a liberating military general, an agent of political change, presented for consumption by himself, the artist, and the spectator (Brilliant 1991, 43). A major concern in the historiography of nineteenth-century Bolivarian portraiture is the issue of copy and original, since the visual record indicates that several portraits of Bolívar were replicated freely (Boulton 1982). The first historians to address Bolivarian portraiture scrutinized the images on the basis of likeness; Manuel Arocha (1943), Alfredo Boulton (1959, 1964), and Enrique Uribe White (1967) catalogued portraits of the Liberator created in the nineteenth and twentieth centuries. Their extensive efforts document the unprecedented extent of Bolivarian portraiture, identify iconographic conventions, and categorize the portraits based on artist, style, and place of origin. These early surveys often scrutinized physiognomic accuracy to the point of valorization, diverting attention away from period understandings of portraits as cultural objects meant to depict "an individual known to have lived" (Pointon 2013, 42). Primarily due to technological limitations, the exactitude of Bolívar's likeness was (and continues to be) subordinated in the vast majority of his portraits, in part because the images function as simulacra representing the transformative moment of South American independence.

The emergence of Bolívar as visual icon stands in stark contrast to contemporary European parallels, most notably the visual self-aggrandizement of Napoleon Bonaparte tangibly immortalized in the massive, theatrical portraits painted by Jacques-Louis David. Bonaparte directed court artists to fashion an appropriately regal yet tightly controlled persona in paintings such as Jean-Auguste Dominique Ingres's 1806 portrait of Napoleon on his imperial throne, an image employed by the French dictator in his self-production as an embodiment of political transformation. Bolívar, traveling in a diplomatic capacity throughout Europe in 1804–6, may have visited Paris for Napoleon's coronation (Lynch 2006, 24). During that time an unidentified artist painted his portrait in miniature, identified with a later inscription: "Retrato del General Simón Bolívar de 23 años de edad, en el año de la coronación del Emperador en Paris. El Libertador de Nuevo Mundo nació en Caracas y fue enterrado en 1843." Although Bolívar evidently drew inspiration from Napoleon and particularly crafted a public image for himself, the iconographic simplicity, modesty, and militaristic qualities of early Bolivarian portraiture engender a visible rejection of Napoleonic pomp in favor of an easily duplicated naïve style that reduced existing portrait compositions to minimalist proportions.

Deliberate compositional simplification in the 1820s sets the tone for Bolivarian portraiture into the 1830s. As Simón Bolívar's influence began to wane following the close of independence-era military campaigns, official portraits in public contexts became disconnected from the sitter, as an individual whose political strategies lacked long-term staying power. It is difficult to imagine that Simón Bolívar, a general whose quest for glory has been immortalized, exercised limited control over the commissioning and distributing of such portraits. In his 1876 autobiography, military portraitist José María Espinosa recounts his experience working with the Liberator at the end of his life to create an official portrait. The artist describes a bantering dialogue that emphasizes Bolívar's irritation with the process of posing before a working artist. Despite this image of an impatient leader, Bolívar made himself available to numerous artists throughout his career, first Figueroa, then Antonio Salas and José Gil de Castro, and finally Espinosa and Antonio Meucci. At the end of his life, Bolívar, aware of the possibility he had to shape his legacy before his death, encouraged the further creation of portraits and biographies. Indeed, the greatest number of unique Bolivarian portraits was made in 1829 and 1830, Bolívar's final years; however, later artists drew as much inspiration from these images as they did the earlier, less precisely choreographed precedents. Although artists traveled with officials in Europe to visually commemorate significant historical moments (Pérez D'Ors and Gallagher 2010), the practice did not translate to South America; however, by the end of the viceregal period, the integration of official portraiture into contemporary sociopolitical life became a continental phenomenon that actively shaped shared understandings of leadership, political negotiation, and hierarchical social relations.

Campaigning through Portraiture

Bolívar was celebrated for his staggering endurance in the art of war. Almost ascetic in his daily habits, the Liberator led his generals and soldiers of all ranks through jungles, swamps, and mountains, often breaching political boundaries and shuffling geographic divisions. As Bolívar and his troops traveled, he came to incarnate ideas of liberty and unity in rituals, images, and written texts, concepts that resonated with supporters from Venezuela to Bolivia. These campaign portraits were based on visual traditions present in official, military, and elite portraits from the coterminous viceregal period. When later describing Bolívar's move south into Ecuador and Peru, his trusted aide Daniel O'Leary observed, "There is reason to believe that the Liberator's reputation greatly influenced the deliberations of the people of Quito, and it is certain that only loyalty to his person could induce them to maintain the union with Colombia once they became fully aware of the incompatibility of interests. In addition to this notable proof of regard for the founder of the Republic, the popular assembly accorded honors to him and his comrades-in-arms" (1970, 216). During this time, his friend and portrait painter Antonio Salas visualized Ecuadorian support for Bolívar in at least five portraits created between 1822 and 1826. The large-scale images compositionally elevate the liberating hero to the status of political icon following the pictorial strategies employed by Figueroa while depicting his Augustan reception in Quito (Arocha 1943, 3–12).

As Simón Bolívar traveled through Andean landscapes, his physical presence embodied political change. From Venezuela to Bolivia, maidens showered him with laurels and elites feted him nightly, even as enemies posed a constant threat to his physical being. In travel, Bolívar, the artists who represented him, and his allies engaged a calculated balance of rupture and continuity with visual traditions to endow Bolivarian portraiture with the ability to signify within established and emerging cultural conventions. Roland Barthes has considered this phenomenon in the context of photography, another medium embroiled in questions of visual authenticity; Barthes suggests that the ability of viewers to make meanings from images is dependent upon "coded cultural associations" (1977, 46–51). Repetitive visual reception of Bolívar's likeness, public performance, and discursive media combined to establish "loyalty to his person." Bolívar and his supporters enlisted local support for his political vision to manipulate popular opinion by fashioning the body of the Liberator (whether physical or artistic) as the incarnation of pan-American political transformation. They relied upon regional artists to create images that addressed local constituents and enjoyed elite patronage essential for providing financial support for the portraits.

The early portraits of Simón Bolívar reflect "a compulsion to signify in materialist terms," to borrow a phrase from art historian Alex Potts (2003, 27). All of the early portraits of Bolívar based on observations of the sitter from life were rendered while the military leader and budding politician traveled in Europe, the Caribbean, and South America. For example, informal sketches of the Liberator extend from the earliest created by an unidentified artist in Haiti while Bolívar was in exile and the last drawn by José María Espinosa in Colombia as Bolívar's health declined in 1830. Unlike his peers, the controversial yet victorious Liberator and his allies sought to establish Bolívar's portrait as an icon of sociopolitical transformation through the distribution of portraits throughout the Americas and Europe. Bolívar was the only military officer represented in portrait paintings with any frequency. Most military leaders commissioned one portrait for personal use; multiple copies of military portraits were rarely produced, and institutions did not collect portraits of other generals, for the most part.

Bolívar and his supporters prioritized and utilized portrait imagery to highlight his creative role in the independence movement as well as to shape public opinion on unsettling contemporary shifts in political authority. When Bolívar and his forces were traveling through Alto Peru in September 1825, the city council of Lima sent the Liberator a gold sword and a richly embroidered military uniform as a token of its appreciation of the relations shared between the new political power brokers and the established civic institution (O'Leary 1970, 298). The city council's gift is memorialized in three Bolívar portraits painted by José Gil de Castro in 1825, the so-called Chuquisaca portrait now in Sucre, the portrait today displayed in the Venezuelan National Assembly (plate 3), and the heraldic portrait in the Museo Nacional in Lima that was formerly part of the city council's *pinacoteca* (picture gallery). The three paintings exhibit Gil de Castro's judicious attention to precise detail in his rendering of the uniform gifted to the Liberator; each painting individually captures the glistening surfaces of the metallic embroidery in contrast to the rich black jacket. The artist also renders the piercingly steady gaze of the Liberator to intersect with that of the viewer as he had in previous elite portrait commissions, a point of continuity with the past.

Although Gil de Castro was not an academically trained artist, his portraits capture a modern visual aesthetic that juxtaposes the flattened human subject of the portrait against a solid ground in a manner that responds to the tense historical moment. The times required an overtly simplified visual system to unify the vast diversity of experiences demanding integration in the period following the revolutionary overthrow of a global empire. Luis Eduardo Wuffarden (2001) observes an ambivalence that oscillates between continuity and rupture in Gil de Castro's oeuvre. Wuffarden draws parallels between the artist's aesthetic, which continued to employ pictorial techniques from the viceregal period and neoclassical elements of style, and his role in the South American independence process as a military officer (Gil de Castro was a lieutenant in the Corps of Engineers of the Chilean Army) (Wuffarden 2001, 463).

Gil de Castro, who was likely trained as a portraitist in the Lima guild system, perpetuates the visual formula that characterized earlier viceregal portraiture (elite sitter depicted in an interior setting wearing class-appropriate attire). At the same time, he also documents the relations between the Liberator and regional governing officials. All of the parties involved in the creation of these images—Bolívar as sitter, Gil de Castro as artist, and regional governing institutions as patrons—strategically positioned the portraits as visual indicators of negotiated political relations that reshaped the alignment of power during the independence era.

The Portrait as Itinerant Icon

After Bolivarian portraits had been completed, the finished objects often circulated around the world mapping the diplomatic negotiations and the flow of military operations. Following Gil de Castro's completion of the three portraits in Alto Peru, Bolívar sent one of the paintings (plate 3) to his sister, as described earlier. In a remarkable transformation of viceregal practice in which religious icons and official portraits were celebrated, local partisan authorities sent "Bolívar" in portrait form to visit the people and "hear" their appeals. *El Sol del Cuzco* reported on February 23, 1825, that "the bust of our dictator was placed in the ancient temple of the Sun. The Inca-Kings that lie there lifted up their heads from their sepulchers and, beholding the Liberator of their land, blessed him" (in Thurner 2011, 122). This performative commemoration of the Liberator's victory in the Battle of Ayacucho exacts a pictorial erasure of Spanish imperial forces that have been supplanted by a Bolivarian present (see Neill in this volume).

By the mid-1820s, engravings depict the emerging practice of public procession and celebration of Bolivarian portraits. In one example, a cluster of individuals dressed in feathers representing the indigenous populations of America carry a bust sculpture of Bolívar on a liter. They are surrounded by a group of soldiers who temper the celebratory tone of the image by enforcing a compulsory homage to Bolivarian ideals as represented by the portrait bust. Bolívar and allies to his cause initiated the exceptional practice of transporting a secular portrait across vast geographic regions to activate the physical presence of the Liberator in territories that he himself could not occupy. Portraits of Bolívar thus served as objects of veneration and tangible demonstrations of allegiance as well as representations of the Liberator's benevolent new policies. As New Granadian intellectual and independence martyr Camilo Torres succinctly commented after Bolívar's return from exile in Jamaica, "where Bolívar is, there is the republic" (Lynch 2006, 94). In circulating Bolívar's image, advocates and local governments ostensibly brought liberty, opportunity, and republican values to the people. The engravings depict Bolívar's omnipresence in potent intercessory imagery and the rupture in authority from colonial rule to a transitional state.

Even as Bolívar and other American authorities fueled the fabrication and circulation of Bolivarian portraiture in South America, the trade and exchange of official portraits expanded beyond the boundaries of their control by the second half of the 1820s. Printers in the United States and Europe produced more than thirty interpretations of the M. N. Bate portrait engraving. Bolívar also submitted a portrait of himself by Gil de Castro to the care of General Miller to be delivered in London to Robert Wilson, the father of one of his military aides, Belford Hinton Wilson, a valuable British advocate for the cause of American independence (Sánchez 1916, 12).[4] Here, Bolívar again identifies a Gil de Castro work as the best visual representative of himself, his accomplishments, and his cause. The image's iconic composition, the artist's American painting style, and the demonstrable visual glorification of the sitter rendered the image a fitting cultural ambassador. Wilson used the image to garner financial and ideological support for the South American revolution; he made the painting available to a Mr. Turner, who produced a mezzotint engraving of the portrait in 1827 with a lengthy inscription that advocated the cause of American liberty. This engraving and many others became widely popular in Europe and the Americas. Bolívar's onetime ally Francisco de Paula Santander noted in 1823 that such engravings were exchanged by post in Castillo and Guayaquil (in O'Leary, *Memorias*). Giving a face to the movement, portraits of Bolívar marshaled coherent support for the South American independence process.

Bolivarian portraits not only brought liberation and republican governance to decolonized American territories; the images visualized episodic victories as the movement unfolded. On August 7, 1819, Bolívar and his forces achieved fast and definitive triumph outside Tunja at Boyacá. In John Lynch's analysis, "The victory of Boyacá set the seal of success on Bolívar's authority and his strategy. He took pleasure and pride in the Boyacá campaign, 'my most complete victory'" (2006, 129–30). The military achievement at Boyacá made it possible for rebel forces to enter into the capital of New Granada, where Bolívar and Figueroa then initiated the production of the Liberator as visual icon. Seven years later José Antonio Chaves, the academic rector of the local educational institution, commissioned a portrait of Bolívar by the artist José María Burbano (plate 5). Burbano employed the pictorial style and composition familiarized by Figueroa and later Gil de Castro: a solitary male bust portrait against a solid ground with minimal detail contextualized by a framing inscription. Not painted from life, Burbano's Bolívar blankly stares into the distance while gesturing rhetorically with his left hand. The three-quarter turn of the subject's head on squared shoulders and frontally positioned upper body results in a pictorial dissidence typical of Bolivarian portraiture supplemented by an inscribed text.

Disconnection between the viewer and the subject resulting from technical inadequacies in the art of painting are offset by an inscription that proclaims the interpersonal connections behind the patronage and exchange of the object: "El Colejio Académico de Boyacá al Padre de la Patria y Fundador de la República de Colombia Simón Bolívar año 1826–16 [*sic*]." Chaves and the Boyacá Academy presented the portrait they commissioned to Bolívar in Bogotá, transporting it over 130 kilometers from Tunja, where it was created. The portrait acknowledges Bolívar's predilection for personal portraits by gifting the Liberator a portrait of himself in military dress, visually engaging with portraits Bolívar himself commissioned or sat for. Furthermore, the Burbano Boyacá portrait commemorates an exceptional moment in the evolving history of South America.

Conclusion

The early portraits of Simón Bolívar are significant because they demonstrate the activation of visual imagery as a necessary component in the independence process during a pivotal moment in American history. Portraits of the American Liberator built on existing viceregal traditions while deviating from the past in order to articulate a distinctive iconography of political change. This heterogeneous body of military portraits connoted broad-reaching affiliations with nascent revolutionary ideologies. Bolívar used the images to position himself as an agent of international political change, while his supporters commissioned, collected, and displayed Bolivarian portraits as visual demonstrations of allegiance designed to emphasize the inevitability of his rise to power and the subsequent demise of Spanish imperial domination. Even less ardent allies temporarily displayed Bolivarian portraits as they negotiated their social positions in the liminal space between imperialism and nationalism. Visual and sociopolitical ruptures and continuities produced heterogeneous visual responses resulting from relational insecurities, technological deficiencies, fractured political environments, and inconsistent resonance with cultural imaginaries. Collectively, Bolivarian portraits produced during the Liberator's lifetime articulated the foundation for the transition of the hero into an icon in the second half of the nineteenth century.

Upon Bolívar's death in 1830, regions that had aligned with the Liberator's ideological positions and governmental strategies publicly celebrated his exemplary life. When Bolívar physically exited the political stage, his portraits maintained the presence of the anti-imperial ideology he espoused in his military and political career. An Ecuadorian decree of that year mandated that Bolivarian portraits be installed in all government buildings, honoring the Liberator and establishing his enduring visible legacy in the South American republics. In death, as he had in life, Bolívar continued to operate as a political icon imagining the history of authority as something malleable, ever-changing, and contingent. By 1842, when Bolívar's remains were repatriated to his homeland, Bolivarian portraiture from the 1820s was positioned to transform into republican iconography in northern South America, in particular Colombia and Venezuela, while in the south the iconic images soon faded into symbols of the independence era.

Notes

Epigraph: Camilo Torres, after Bolívar returned from exile in Jamaica; in Lynch 2006, 94.

1. Archivo de la Municipalidad de Lima, 1. Cabildo y Junta Municipal (Administración) 1638–1846, 1.14 Correspondencia External (1782–1828), Caja No. 2, Militares, Doc. 56: Expediente iniciado por el brigadier general Manuel Villalta dirigida al Cabildo para elevar un retrato del general Goyoneche en la Sala Consistorial. 1811. 10 fs. No image is available for this now lost portrait.

2. Louis Marin in his classic analysis of royal portraiture as political device (1988) inspired Alejandro Cañeque (2004) and Diane Bodart (2011), among others, to consider the performative qualities of Spanish royal portraits in European and Latin American contexts.

3. Evidence presented by Jaime Rodríguez (1998) suggests that South American independence was not an anticolonial movement but rather part of the dissolution of the Spanish monarchy. Bolívar's endorsement of royal imagery as pictorial inspiration for his own portraiture supports Rodríguez's claim for a broader reconfiguration of power in transatlantic terms.

4. Bolívar's outreach in England was one of his most controversial and contradictory political maneuvers; the place of the Wilson painting and subsequent Turner engraving requires further research.

References

Achugar, Hugo. 2009. "Foundational Images of the Nation in Latin America." In *Building Nineteenth-Century Latin America*, edited by William Acree and Juan Carlos González Espitia, 11–31. Nashville, TN: Vanderbilt University Press.

Anderson, Benedict. 1991. *Imagined Communities: Reflections on the Origin and Spread of Nationalism*. New York: Verso.

Ardao, Arturo. 1978. *Estudios latinoamericanos: Historia de las ideas*. Caracas: Monte Avila.

Arocha, Manuel. 1943. *Iconografia ecuatoriana del libertador*. Quito, Ecuador: Romero.

Barbón, María Soledad. 2006. "'El Júbilo de la Nación Índica': Indigenous Celebrations in Lima in Honor of Charles IV (1790)." *Jahrbuch für Geschichte Lateinameirkas* 43:147–65.

Bargellini, Clara. 2004. "Originality and Invention in the Painting of New Spain." In *Painting a New World: Mexican Art and Life, 1521–1821*, by Donna Pierce, Rogelio Ruiz Gomar, and Clara Bargellini, 79–91. Denver: Denver Museum of Art.

Barlow, Paul. 1997. "Facing the Past and Present: The National Portrait Gallery and the Search for 'Authentic' Portraiture." In *Portraiture, Facing the Subject*, edited by Joanna Woodall, 219–38. Manchester, England: Manchester University Press.

Barthes, Roland. 1977. *Image, Music, Text*. Translated by Stephen Heath. New York: Hill and Wang.

Bodart, Diane. 2011. *Pouvoirs du portrait sous les Habsbourg d'Espagne*. Paris: Comité des travaux historiques et scientifiques, Institut national d'histoire de l'art.

Bolívar, Simón. 1815/2003. "The Jamaica Letter: Response from a South American to a Gentleman from This Island." In *El Libertador: Writings of Simón Bolívar*, edited by David Bushnell, translated by Frederick H. Fornoff, 12-30. New York: Oxford University Press.

Boulton, Alfredo. 1959. *Miranda, Bolívar y Sucre: Tres estudios iconográficos*. Caracas: Fundación John Boulton.

———. 1964. *Retratos de Bolívar*. Caracas: Fundación John Boulton.

———. 1982. *El rostro de Bolívar*. Caracas: Macanao.

Brilliant, Richard. 1991. *Portraiture*. Princeton, NJ: Princeton University Press.

Cañeque, Alejandro. 2004. *The King's Living Image: The Culture and Politics of Viceregal Power in Colonial Mexico*. New York: Routledge.

Carlyle, Thomas. 1840. *On Heroes, Hero-Worship, and the Heroic in History*. London: Chapman and Hall.

Chicangana-Bayona, Yobenj Aucardo. 2011. "Imagens, conceitos e cultura política: A pintura sobre a independência da Colômbia na primeira metade do século XIX." *Tempo* 31:145–76.

Coleman, Patrick, Jayne Lewis, and Jill Kowalik. 2000. *Representations of the Self from the Renaissance to Romanticism*. Cambridge: Cambridge University Press.

Eissa-Barroso, Francisco. 2012. "'Of Experience, Zeal, and Selflessness': Military Officers as Viceroys in Early Eighteenth-Century Spanish America." *The Americas* 68 (3): 317–45.

Engel, Emily A. 2009. "Facing Boundaries: Identity and Authority in South American Portraiture, 1750–1824." PhD diss., University of California, Santa Barbara.

Espinosa, José María. 1876/1936. *Memorias de un abanderado*. Bogotá: Editorial Minerva.

Freedberg, David. 1989. *The Power of Images: Studies in the History and Theory of Response*. Chicago: University of Chicago Press.

Freund, Amy. 2011. "The Citoyenne Tallien: Women, Politics, and Portraiture during the French Revolution." *Art Bulletin* 93 (3): 325–55.

Garrido, Margarita. 2009. "Nueva Granada entre el orden colonial y el republicano: Lenguajes e imaginarios sociales y políticos." In *Las independencias hispanoamericanas: Interpretaciones 200 años después*, edited by Marco Palacios, 105–15. Bogotá: Norma.

González-Stephan, Beatriz. 2008. "Tecnologías par alas masas: Democratización de la cultura y metáfora militar (Venezuela siglo XIX)." *Iberoamericana* 8 (30): 89–101.

Guerra, François-Xavier. 2003. *Inventando la nación: Iberoamérica siglo XIX*. Mexico City: Fondo de Cultura Económica.

Hart, Stephen. 2005. "Blood, Ink, and Pigment: Simón Bolívar as Proteus." *Bulletin of Spanish Studies* 72 (3–4): 335–52.

Harth-Terré, Emilio, and Alberto Márquez Abanto. 1964. *Pinturas y pintores en Lima virreinal*. Lima: Librería e Imprenta GIL.

Hobsbawm, Eric. 1983. "Introduction: Inventing Traditions." In *The Invention of Tradition*, edited by Eric Hobsbawm and Terence Ranger, 1–14. Cambridge: Cambridge University Press.

Lynch, John. 2006. *Simón Bolívar, A Life*. New Haven, CT: Yale University Press.

Majluf, Natalia. 2013. "De cómo reemplazar a un rey: Retrato, visualidad y poder en la crisis de la independencia (1808–1830)." *Histórica* 38 (1): 73–108.

Marin, Louis. 1988. *Portrait of the King*. Minneapolis: University of Minnesota Press.

McFarlane, Anthony. 2006. "Science and Sedition in Spanish America: New Granada in the Age of Revolution, 1776–1810." In *Enlightenment and Emancipation*, edited by Susan Manning and Peter France. Lewisburg, PA: Bucknell University Press.

O'Leary, Daniel. 1970. *Memorias del General Daniel Florencio O'Leary: Narración*. Edited by Robert McNerney. Austin: University of Texas Press.

Paulding, Hiram. 1835. *Un rasgo de Bolívar en campaña*. New York: J. de la Granja.

Pérez D'Ors, Pablo, and Michael Gallagher. 2010. "New Information on Velázquez's Portrait of Philip IV at Fraga in the Frick Collection, New York." *Burlington Magazine* (October) 652–59.

Peterson, Jeanette. 2005. "The Reproducibility of the Sacred: Simulacra of the Virgin of Guadalupe." In *Exploring New World Imagery*, edited by Donna Pierce, 43–78. Denver: Denver Museum of Art.

———. 2014. *Visualizing Guadalupe: From Black Madonna to Queen of the Americas*. Austin: University of Texas Press.

Pointon, Marcia. 2013. "Slavery and the Possibilities of Portraiture." In *Slave Portraiture in the Atlantic World*, edited by Agnes Lugo-Ortiz and Angela Rosenthal, 41–69. Cambridge: Cambridge University Press.

Potts, Alex. 2003. "Sign." In *Critical Terms for Art History*, edited by Robert S. Nelson and Richard Shiff, 20–34. Chicago: University of Chicago Press.

Rishel, Joseph J., with Suzanne Stratton-Pruitt. 2006. *The Arts in Latin America, 1492–1820*. New Haven, CT: Yale University Press.

Rodríguez O., Jaime E. 1998. *The Independence of Spanish America*. Cambridge: Cambridge University Press.

Sánchez, Manuel Segundo. 1916. *Apuntes para la iconografía del Libertador*. Caracas: Lit. del Comercio.

Schreffler, Michael. 2007. *The Art of Allegiance: Visual Culture and Imperial Power in Baroque New Spain*. University Park: Pennsylvania State University Press.

Stratton-Pruitt, Suzanne, ed. 2013. *Journeys to New Worlds: Spanish and Portuguese Colonial Art in the Roberta and Richard Huber Collection*. Philadelphia: Philadelphia Museum of Art.

Thurner, Mark. 2011. *History's Peru: The Poetics of Colonial and Postcolonial Historiography*. Gainesville: University Press of Florida.

Uribe White, Enrique. 1967. *Iconografía del Libertador*. Caracas: Lerner.

Wuffarden, Luis Eduardo. 2001. "Gil de Castro, El pintor de los libertadores." In *La independencia en el Perú de los Borbones a Bolívar*, edited by Scarlett O'Phelan Godoy, 455–77. Lima: Pontificia Universidad Católica del Perú.

2

Dancing with the Enemy

Diplomacy in the Revolutionary Era

JUAN FRANCISCO SANS

Simón Bolívar's well-documented passion for dance has often been the object of misinterpretation and accusations of frivolity. His reputation as a gifted dancer has even been used to demystify the hero and to put his integrity into question. But Bolívar was undoubtedly a man of his time. As in the case of most contemporary heroes like Bonaparte or the duke of Wellington, dance was an essential and performative part of public life. Such political and military figures used dance not only as a leisure activity but also strategically—to assess a situation, subdue the enemy, foster camaraderie within their troops, calm a terrorized population, and consolidate power relations. Historical testimonies reveal that dance was a political tool during Bolívar's times, the Independence War (1810–21), and the República de Colombia (1821–30). In the contested contexts of independence and the early republic, Bolívar and some of his contemporaries used dance strategically and to great effect.

The Dance of the Patria Boba and the República Aérea

Balls and soirées have historically been excellent occasions for political display. Despite this, there are few studies about the close relationship between dance and power, and none that show how seduction, persuasion, or coercion in dance played crucial roles in the fate of the people. Yet there is evidence that the culture of dance and its diverse functions was carried over from the viceregal era and was refashioned for the new republics during the early nineteenth century political periods known as the Patria Boba (Foolish Fatherland, in Colombia) and República Aérea (Flighty Republic, in Venezuela). Henri LaFayette Ducoudray-Holstein, a Napoleonic soldier who joined Bolívar's campaign, describes the culture of dance in Caracas and Bogotá in the final years of the Spanish rule: "Before the revolution, it was not unusual to see ladies at a ball or other festivals wearing more than 200,000 [U.S.] dollars [an estimated $4.7 million today] in watches, diamonds, pearls, etc., in their dresses, without appearing to be overloaded" (1829, 45). Dance became then an indisputably political practice within which the ostentatious display of power and wealth constituted an essential element. These spectacles of wealth and status continued well into independence. On May 11, 1859, Nicomedes Pastor Díaz, a member of the Senate of Spain, vehemently denounced the political machinations circulating around the ballroom: "It is necessary that we protest day after day against this sort of diplomatic orgy, in which the borders of a nation are determined in between quadrilles, in which a toast decides the fate of a city, and in which entire provinces become payment or treatment when courting" (Pastor Díaz 1996, 336).

Before the independence wars, the American colonies had the custom of organizing balls, dances, and soirées in the main cities of the viceroyalty of Nueva Granada and the Capitanía General de Venezuela. These events were attended by la crème de la crème of the political class, the future founding fathers of independence. No sooner had independence been declared than many of these events continued just as before. In his *Recuerdos sobre la Rebelión de Caracas* (1829), José Domingo Díaz criticizes his peers from the Caracas city hall for their celebrations after Venezuela declared its independence on April 19, 1810. Díaz accuses them of being spendthrifts, gamblers, and licentious, ostentatious good-for-nothings who spent about three million pesos of Her Majesty's funds on feasts, balls, and public festivals (26). Similarly, in Colombia, when the Junta Suprema de Santa Fe de Bogotá was installed on December 22, 1810, Camilo Torres Tenorio, one of the independence heroes, hosted a splendid dress ball after the popular feasts (Henao and Arrubla 1920, 278). These examples show that during the early years of the war, life continued more or less as usual in the areas far from the front despite some inconveniences and shortages caused by the conflict. However, when the war got worse, what came was the weeping and gnashing of teeth.

In times of war, citizens as social actors are forced to pay tribute to whichever side holds political power at a given moment, and during the Bolivarian wars, terrain shifted rapidly from the royalists to the patriots. A ball constituted, therefore, an excellent occasion to commit the population, especially the most influential and wealthy people, to the new regime. The event became the perfect context for both releasing the heightened emotions generated by the war and establishing new power relations. When one of the factions in power planned a ball, whoever decided not to attend it would be considered an enemy, and that would bring consequences. In her 2001 study of music during the independence war in Venezuela, Véronique Hébrard explores precisely the kind of society established during conflicts (37). The fact that people attended these celebrations did not necessarily mean that they changed their loyalties; instead, they were motivated by fear of retaliation to make at least a temporary show of deference. Hébrard characterizes these events as "imposed musical manifestations," that is to say, "officially supported practices through which the authorities at a given time decide to mark out a political project and context at a sound level" (30). The civilian population had to choose between the warring sides, risking the burden of otherness imposed by the enemy. The inevitable social repositionings that occur at the end of hostilities—amnesty, revenge, migration, and exclusion—are processes that are crucial to analyze in order to understand how human beings behave under crisis conditions. In such a volatile context, elites and others used the ball as a site of negotiating social position and reestablishing a certain degree of balance and order within chaos.

Perhaps the most infamous "imposed musical manifestations" were the balls organized by royalist general José Tomás Boves during the time of the War to the Death decreed by Simón Bolívar in 1813. Historical novels in Venezuela have since made Boves's balls famous—for their cruelty. A century later Darius Milhaud's *Bolívar* opera (1943), which Maureen Shanahan discusses in this volume, dramatized one of Boves's balls. Boves infamously compelled entire populations to participate in these events and then executed his enemies halfway through the balls as a warning. This would immediately drive people into terror and submission. Similar practices by other royalist generals have been documented by historians William Duane (1968), Felipe Larrazábal (1865, 319), and José Manuel Restrepo (1858, 238). However, it would be naïve to think that the patriots did not use similar methods when it came to teaching a lesson to the common people in order to win them over to the patriot cause. Díaz, for example, writes about a ball given by patriot general Juan Bautista Arismendi in the ominous days of 1814 to celebrate a massacre of royalists (1829, 391).

These events were meant to break the will of the defeated, who could hardly be expected to change their minds after all the atrocities they had gone through. But they were also intended to intimidate or persuade the majority of the population to follow a coerced elite. The host of a ball demanded the participation of the most influential people in town—landlords, merchants, liberal professionals, craftsmen, and so forth—to convince the rest of the population that the elite supported the new status quo. Wars are largely won by swaying public opinion, and an event of this nature provided the most convincing proof during that era that things had gone back to normal. After all, who hosts a ball in the middle of a public disturbance? Apparently, the sine qua non condition of dance is social peace, and that is precisely the symbolic strength of hosting a dance in the middle of a warring conflict: to make people believe that everything is fine, even when it is not. Misinformation is vital to win the support of the civilian population, which desperately clamors for a return to peace, civic calm, and stability, no matter the price. The political function of the ball can only be explained if we also understand that they served as intelligence and counterintelligence operations vital to keeping information under control as well as vehicles for demoralizing the enemy and bending the will of the population into submission. These kinds of social events thus became symbolic battlefields.

At this point, it is worth remembering the exceptional story told by Ducoudray-Holstein about the anything-but-glamorous arrival of the patriot general José Francisco Bermúdez in Caracas on May 19, 1821: "[It] resembled a funeral. In the streets were a mass of miserable wretches, some begging for a cent for charity. Prostitutes mingled among the ranks of the soldiers, [and] amidst the ringing of bells, [there was] the sound of cannons" (1829, 280). In such a forsaken, devastated city, common sense would suggest that Bermúdez should have taken care of the urgent medical, housing, and sanitation needs of the people, and that he should have consolidated a government as best he could. However, the first thing Bermúdez did was to give a ball that Ducoudray-Holstein characterized as a reversal of class and racial hierarchies: "one could not find even four ladies of distinction, all were people of color or blacks"(280). The festivities continued for the next three days "at the expense of the ruined inhabitants" (280), meaning the elites and creoles. Balls thus functioned as propaganda for a new social hierarchy, as means of property appropriation, and as a measure of political loyalty. Finally, when Bolívar signed the War Regularization treaty with Spain, the ball acquired yet another connotation: as a diplomatic vehicle.

War Is Like Fandango

A nineteenth-century Spanish proverb says, "Life is like fandango, and he who does not dance it is a fool." The fandango, a popular eighteenth-century Spanish dance, became synonymous with making a fuss or display either positively, as in celebrating a triumph, or negatively, as in a heated debate. War, like the fandango, required everyone to declare a position. For the armies that fought the War of Independence, officers and troops alike, dance played a very important role as a favorite source of distraction and relaxation in the middle of the horrors of conflict. This kind of leisure was common even during the bloodiest years of the war. Among the most famous soirées were those organized by patriot general José Antonio Páez, who at every opportunity offered dance as solace to civilians and his troops and along the way had a great time himself. However, it was Simón Bolívar in the flesh who most excelled in his fondness for balls, many of which he held during the course of his military campaign, as described by Ducoudray-Holstein: "Whenever he stays two or three days in a place, he gives a ball or two, at which he dances in his boots and spurs, and makes love to those who happen to please him for the moment" (1829, 325).

Dance was also used in this period to assert the victor's symbolic power. An anonymous aide-de-camp of San Martin published a text in the *Revista de Buenos Aires* as "Entrevista en Guayaquil (1822)" describing the circumstances of a ball that took place during the famous meeting that year between Generals José de San Martín (hero of the Argentine and Chilean independence) and Simón Bolívar to decide who would lead the independence of Peru. The most illustrious people of the city attended. The text evidences the high tensions and power displays that took place during the event. However, we would like to focus our attention on how dance was used as an exceptional stage on which the future of the growing South American republics was decided. The account describes the Guayaquil ball both as a real display of elegance, seduction and politics and as an overturning of racial and class orders, a tour de force functioning as a competition over who could win more points in the approval of the Ecuadorian people:

> At nine p.m. that same night we went to the ball we had been invited to. The gathering was brilliant in the number, beauty, and elegance of the ladies and the sumptuous salon was perfectly adorned and illuminated; as for the men, most of them were commanders and officers from the Colombian army and the General Staff of the Liberator [Simón Bolívar]; a good number of them were mulattoes and knew nothing of the refined manners of a distinguished society. We were shocked by the way they treated the ladies, their lack of courtesy and composure, not quite understanding why the presence of the Liberator, who treated them as servants, would not impose respect from them, until we noticed with surprise that when he too went dancing, he did exactly the same as his subordinates. (66)

As in Bermúdez's narrative, the derogatory reference to blacks and mulattoes expresses an anxiety about the revolution's perceived reversal of social hierarchies while revealing the writer's attitudes. The text's injurious expressions about Simón Bolívar and his people, especially mulattoes, evidence a common prejudice of the elite of the period who attributed non-elites with poor behavior as being rowdy, uncivilized men with no morals. These expressions do not match the historical truth and can only be considered as part of the political propaganda.

As the victory of the patriotic cause seemed imminent, dances became even more extravagant, making people forget for a moment that they were still in the middle of a conflagration. War is no impediment for vanity, and hence these balls often differed little from those of the viceregal era described by Ducoudray-Holstein. Richard Bache, an exceptional witness of the time, puts it this way: "Official soirées are quite splendid, and for them ladies wear elegant and expensive dresses adorned with opulent laces, gold or silver embroidery, artificial flowers, and lavish jewelry" (in Benedittis 2002, 173). As might be expected, many people disapproved of such profligate spending since it exacerbated the dramatic contrast between the lives of officers and the lives of the troops and common people. The sumptuousness in the midst of the widespread scarcity and privation provoked severe criticism. One unidentified disgruntled contemporary complained, "It was said that with the money spent on social gatherings they could have paid our salaries" (in Benedittis 2002, 328).

The flamboyant victory celebrations at the elite and popular levels functioned as displays of public support as well as vehicles for distracting a war-weary populace. According to the Act of the Junta Assembled in La Guaira on May 28, 1820, for the Publication and Celebration of the 1812 Constitution (in Hébrard 2001, 32), the royalist authorities of the Venezuelan port city of La Guaira decreed eight consecutive days of dances and comedy as well as a general illumination of the city, all aimed to show the strength of the royal authority. Bearing in mind the old Roman practice of *panem et circensis,* the followers of both causes did their best to distract the masses. As usual, many of these city festivals, like the elite balls, took place at public expense, causing people to feel coerced to give their best efforts to fulfill the government's decrees.

Dances worked not just as a way to ease frayed nerves in a violent environment. They also served as a means to carry out revenge, intimidate others, pinpoint enemies, coerce people into loyalty or submission, negotiate alliances, or generate public support through distracting spectacles. They were part of a political, ideological, and intelligence strategy used to strengthen the position of one of the warring factions and to persuade the population. Although historians have systematically ignored such events, casting balls as mere protocol of no real importance, the historical record reveals that they played an important role in negotiating power relations within the inherent instability of war.

La République S'Amuse

Deep-seated problems confronted the government of the new republics when the war was over and independence was secured: organizing the state; guaranteeing social stability, governability, and public security; developing the economy, commerce, and industry; taking care of the urgent needs of the people, which were many after the war; rebuilding cities and institutions; and finally, designing a physical and moral restorative plan. It was as titanic an enterprise as the war itself. Dances were still common during this period of relative peace. They were used as political and diplomatic instruments but with a subtler and more suggestive character, full of nuances that were hard to grasp sometimes but still politically imperative.

By 1822, some dramatic changes had already taken place compared to the kinds of dances that were popular before the revolution (Duane 1968, 102). Old Spanish colonial dances like the fandango, bolero, ondú, and zorongo were displaced by two new genres: the waltz and the contra dance. These two dances established a choreographic landscape in which the vices of old viceregal politics finally gave way to a new elite. When and how Bolívar managed to learn the steps of these new dances remains a real mystery, busy as he was with the liberation of Colombia. But if we are to believe his good reputation as a dancer, we must infer that somehow he found the time to do so. All of Bolívar's contemporaries agree, without exception, that he was an extraordinary dancer. One said, "He comported himself as a perfect gentleman in everything he did. He danced the waltz marvelously. He was moderate and self-restrained, and he spoke with grace and precision" (in Benedittis 2002, 327). One of the Liberator's frequent dancing partners, Jeanette Hart from the United States, describes more than eloquently how skillful he was: "The last piece that the band played and we danced together was a waltz; everybody stopped dancing, left the center of the salon for us alone and stood around, just watching us. . . . The General moved as if the chords of that waltz were coming out of his own body, it was something like an inborn talent" (in González Henríquez 1989). This description contrasts radically with the unflattering impressions regarding Bolívar and his people in "Entrevista en Guayaquil (1822)" published in the *Revista de Buenos Aires*; it also shows why Bolívar's specialty, the waltz, became the most popular genre in South American salons for the rest of the nineteenth century.

In a very famous passage of his memoir, patriot general Daniel Florencio O'Leary states that Bolívar "did a lot of exercises; after a very busy day that would have been more than enough to exhaust even the strongest of men, I have seen him . . . work for five or six hours, or dance just as long, with all the passion that he felt for dancing" (in Henao and Arrubla 1920, 298). Some of Bolívar's generals were also famous for the same reason. General Francisco de Paula Santander, vice president of the República de Colombia, took pride in his dance skills, so much so that his name was associated with some complex forms of the quadrille reportedly of his own creation: "The arrangement and execution of a quadrille required the highest level of strategic expertise; General Santander was really good at it, which was probably why the required quadrilles, those with complicated moves, were known as santandereanas" (Cordovez Moure 1893/2006, 25–26).

During the most glorious years of the República de Colombia (1822–28), the country celebrated October 28, Saint Simon's Day and the saint's day of the president Liberator, with great splendor. This day became the best time for people to show their loyalty to the head of state, although other saints' days could also be cause for celebration. In any event, to display loyalty, nothing could be better than a ball. All around Colombia people celebrated the day in the most ostentatious ways, eager to please their ruler as evident in contemporary accounts. The *Suplemento de la Gaceta de Colombia* published on December 17, 1826, reports on a lavish saint's day celebration in Trujillo: "The event finished at night with a splendid ball and refreshments which said Colonel Blanco hosted in his residence." The *Gaceta de Colombia* from October 31, 1829, also mentions a sumptuous dance hosted in Bolívar's honor: "Such a memorable day ended with a magnificent soirée attended by the most select residents of the capital. More brilliant than the rich and elegant dresses were the gentility and joy of the ladies, who embellished it with grace and charm." Of course, many of these honorific banquets carried the scent of serfdom and servility as many sought to curry favor with the new leadership.

Almost any event was an opportunity to render homage to Bolívar. In Bogotá there were all kinds of receptions to celebrate his return to the capital in 1826. A honeyed note entitled "Gifts to the President Liberator in Bogotá," published in the *Gaceta de Colombia* on November 26, 1826, describes an incredible number of feasts that took place one after the other. Bolívar danced through all of them:

> Although no gift would be honorable enough for General Bolívar, we have the pleasure to make public the presents that this capital has extended to him with its finest wishes. The government gave him an extraordinary feast at the palace on November 14, when he arrived. The following day there was another one in His Excellency's villa. On the evening of the 17th Mr. Antonio de Velasco, director of the military music band, gave him a prominent concert at the palace when they played the Tancredi opera, arranged by Velasco as an instrumental piece, for the first time. On the 21st it was Colonel Campbell, chargé d'affaires of S.M.B. [Bolívar], who gave him a magnificent feast. Then on the 22nd there was yet another magnificent feast hosted by Mr. Francisco Montoya. On the morning of the 23rd Mr. Segismundo

> Leidersdorf gave him a splendid lunch, while in the evening S.M.B.'s chargé d'affaires hosted another ball. On the 24th Misters Juan Manuel and Manuel Antonio Arrublas gave him an elegant and splendid feast. Then yesterday, November 25th, the Liberator left this capital and will eat and sleep at the estate of His Excellency Mr. Vice President, where we know a grand reception has been planned. Today he will be received by Mr. Luis Montoya in his estate in Boita, where he will stay for the night.

The *Gaceta de Colombia* devoted a number of reviews to the many official or private balls that took place mostly in Bogotá. They were always attended by distinguished diplomats, officials from powerful countries, and entrepreneurs who had already arrived in the new republic in search of the substantial profits ensured by commercial contracts. Oddly enough, many of these reviews were identified with the title "unofficial dispatch" as if announcing a war update. On August 15, 1824, the anniversary of the Battle of Boyacá, the *Gaceta de Colombia* reported about "an elegant ball at the palace whose attendance was both great and magnificent." On April 24, 1825, the same newspaper announced that "last week was very active, with feasts and balls held by the most illustrious society." Again, on October 31, 1829, the *Gaceta de Colombia* described the arrival of José Larrea y Loredo, the plenipotentiary minister of Peru, who came to Santa Fe de Bogotá to negotiate peace between Peru and Colombia: "He was received on the 15th by the Liberator in his palace, where they ate together, and then at night there was a ball." These events had become now the theater of operations where what were deployed were not belligerent forces but diplomatic skills.

Toward the end of the 1820s the political environment had become gloomy. Conspiracies were on the rise, which was one of the reasons Bolívar imposed a dictatorship. On September 25, 1828, there was an assassination attempt against him at the presidential palace in Bogotá. The note in the *Gaceta de Colombia* from October 5, 1828, offers details about the assassins' preliminary plans, which reveal that they expected to carry out the assassination precisely during a ball:

> The first intention of the traitors was to carry it out on the night of August 10, during the masquerade ball organized by the city hall to celebrate the anniversary of the Liberator's arrival after his victory in Boyacá. . . . They nevertheless united at the ball all wearing the same

> disguise. The occasion may have been tempting, since the Liberator walked through the different salons by himself and among the people in masks. It was tempting, indeed, but the good star of Colombia saved H.E. [His Excellency], who retired to the palace before the plotters planned to arrive. What would have come of the reunion, what of the city, of the entire Republic if to the grievousness of the crime [against Bolívar] we would have had to add such serious circumstances [for the nation]?

As the conspiracy plots increased, so too did the banquets for Bolívar. It could not be otherwise, since just as during the war, the postwar message to the population had to be loud and clear; so too the republic should display leisure and pleasure, thus showing that everything was under control. However, contradictions came to the surface in the *Gaceta de Colombia* on December 31, 1829. On the same page that describes six days of festivities hosted by Colonel José Félix Blanco before a portrait of the Liberator in the city of Girón, Pamplona province, one can read that the Antioquia province did not recognize the supreme authority of the Liberator.

Public displays of support for Bolívar's rule were quite common during such a critical period, and these necessarily included a dance as a corollary. When he started his dictatorship on June 28, 1828, it became imperative to support the measure with convincing demonstrations of loyalty. That is why in Petare, a village close to Caracas, the town council issued an official pronouncement supporting the Liberator's decision. In the document the president of the town council addressed the most prominent families and other notables of the area, informing them that Bolívar had set himself up as the supreme chief of Colombia in order to fight the reign of anarchy and to guarantee stability in the republic. The community members agreed, therefore,

> that on the night of the 26th there will be a *tablado* [stage] at the square to show a portrait of the American hero and supreme chief of Colombia. Then there will be a concert with songs, and soon after a public ball and the corresponding illumination for three nights: at the church there will be a solemn thanksgiving mass singing the Te Deum on the 27th, which will be attended by this body [the town council] and other notables; and that the people will be invited to indulge themselves in all kind of legal celebrations that might be suggested by

> their patriotic enthusiasm, as called by the heads of families and other distinguished people for tomorrow night, when we will agree on all the other activities that we consider necessary to honor the republic and its benefactor. (Bolívar 1828, 257–58)

Ultimately, due to the declaration of supreme power, Bolívar fell into disgrace and had to leave power in May 1830. However, on his way to exile through Colombian territory he continued to receive all kinds of homage and banquets that generally led to dance. In "Partida del Libertador" (1866), Juan B. Ortiz provides an account of an ill and debilitated Bolívar, who, when passing through the city of Honda and despite his precarious health, accepted the homage brought to him by the city's most illustrious people: "The members of the town council, the public employees, and the most distinguished neighbors had prepared a ball that night, and Bolívar, though exhausted and weak, was very pleased and thankful for such kindness, unexpected for a man in his situation" (98).

Conclusion

The interaction between dance and power was particularly crucial for South America from the time of the independence wars against Spanish rule that took place all around the continent through the second and the third decades of the nineteenth century. After the cessation of conflict, the people from these lands faced the challenge of building republics on the liberated territories. Here we have chosen to study Simón Bolívar, as one of the main protagonists of the period, and his Colombian political project. In spite of his heroic profile, he made time for relaxation, leisure, vanity, gallantry, and love affairs; in other words, he pursued the very human impulse shared by many of his contemporaries to turn to the delight of dancing as a very important activity even during the fiercest of conflicts. Indeed, despite the odds, dancing was not an exceptional activity during the crisis but quite the opposite: it was used as an effective and ideal propaganda tool to attract support and to measure loyalties, to exert power and dominance, to negotiate agreements or to impose a regime. Contemporary accounts bring attention to the ways that popular history intersects with and mutually constitutes the great gests of heroic history. When the lives of ordinary people were in danger as a consequence of war, they found a chance to balance tribulation with pleasure. It is in this sense that dancing played an important symbolic role and was used—consciously or unconsciously—by the parties involved in the conflict as a means to serve their political interests.

Note

This article is an adapted version of a previous work entitled "Baile y poder en la Colombia de Bolívar," published in *Ensayos. Historia y Teoría del Arte* 22:136–68, Instituto de Investigaciones Estéticas, Universidad Nacional de Colombia.

References

Benedittis, Vince de. 2002. *Presencia de la música en los relatos de viajeros del siglo XIX*. Caracas: Fondo Editorial de Humanidades y Educación, Universidad Central de Venezuela.

Bolívar, Simón. 1828. *Colección de documentos relativos a la vida pública del Libertador de Colombia y del Perú, Simón Bolívar*. Vol. 15. Caracas: Imprenta de G. F. Devisme.

Cordovez Moure, José María. 1893/2006. *Reminiscencias de Santafé y Bogotá*. Bogotá: Fundación Editorial Epigrafe.

Díaz, José Domingo. 1829. *Recuerdos sobre la rebelión de Caracas*. Madrid: Imprenta de D. León Amarita.

Duane, William. 1968. *Viaje a la Gran Colombia en los años 1822–1823*. Vol. 1. Caracas: Instituto Nacional de Hipódromos.

Ducoudray-Holstein, Henri La Fayette Villaume. 1829. *Memoirs of Simon Bolivar, President Liberator of the Republic of Colombia: and of His Principal Generals; Secret History of the Revolution*. Boston: S. G. Goodrich.

"Entrevista en Guayaquil (1822) de los Generales San Martín y Bolívar." In *Revista de Buenos Aires: Historia Americana, Literatura, Derecho y Variedades* 15 (1868): 62–68.

González Henríquez, Adolfo. 1989. "La música costeña colombiana en la tercera década del siglo XIX." *Boletín Cultural y Bibliográfico* 26, no. 19:3–23. http://www.banrepcultural.org/blaavirtual/.

Hébrard, Véronique. 2001. "Alteridad e historia durante la guerra civil venezolana a través de las prácticas musicales y de la canción patriótica (1812–1823)." *Escritos. Revista Universitaria de Arte y Cultura* 13:27–50.

Henao, Jesús María, and Gerardo Arrubla. 1920. *Historia de Colombia para la enseñanza secundaria*. Bogotá: Librería Colombiana, Camacho Roldán y Tamayo.

Larrazábal, Felipe. 1865. *Correspondencia general del libertador Simón Bolívar: Enriquecida con la inserción de los manifiestos, mensajes, exposiciones, proclamas, &. &*. New York: Imprenta de E. O Jenkins.
Ortiz T., Juan B. 1866. "Partida del Libertador (Honda-1830)." In *Museo de cuadros de costumbres y variedades*, vol. 2, 94–99. Bogotá: Foción Mantilla.
Pastor Díaz, Nicomedes. 1996. *Obras políticas*. Barcelona: Anthropos; Madrid: Fundación Caja de Madrid.
Restrepo, José Manuel. 1827/1858. *Historia de la revolución de la República de Colombia en la América Meridional*. Vol. 1. Besanzon (*sic*) [France]: Imprenta de José Jacquin.

3

Bolivarian Imagery and Racial Ideology in Early Nineteenth-Century Cuba

PAUL NIELL

A lithograph by A. Leclerc of 1819 depicts South American revolutionary leader Simón Bolívar in a bust-length portrait and identifies him in French as "Chief sub-General of Venezuela" (figure 3.1). His military standing is communicated by epaulettes adorning a sharp uniform, while beneath the portrait an allegorical vignette of a seminude female Indian with bow, arrow, and quiver reclines against a rock as a ship departs in the background. Behind the rock, a protruding alligator identifies the allegorical figure as the embodiment of America, a visual practice dating to the sixteenth century (Rabasa 1993). The Indian woman supports a liberty pole upon which rests a liberty cap, co-opting the French and North American signifiers that circulated widely in the Atlantic world. This imagery in combination, including the bust of Bolívar, offers the Amerindian as an emblem of liberation and the South American revolutionary as a hero in the struggle for independence from Spain (Ades 1989; Acevedo 2000; Carrera 2006; Widdifield 1996, 2001).

The Leclerc print exhibits the Bolivarian movement's appropriation of Amerindian imagery as a vehicle of mythology, offering Bolívar as the liberator of an "authentic" America reimagined in non-Spanish terms (Anderson 1983). A similar conjunction of images appears in the portrait *Simón Bolívar, Libertador y Padre de la Patria* by Pedro José Figueroa, oil on canvas, from the same year (plate 1). In this painting Bolívar stands with his right arm around the shoulder of the allegorical female Indian who, in this case, is fully clothed with pearls and jewelry, perhaps evoking the civilizing promise

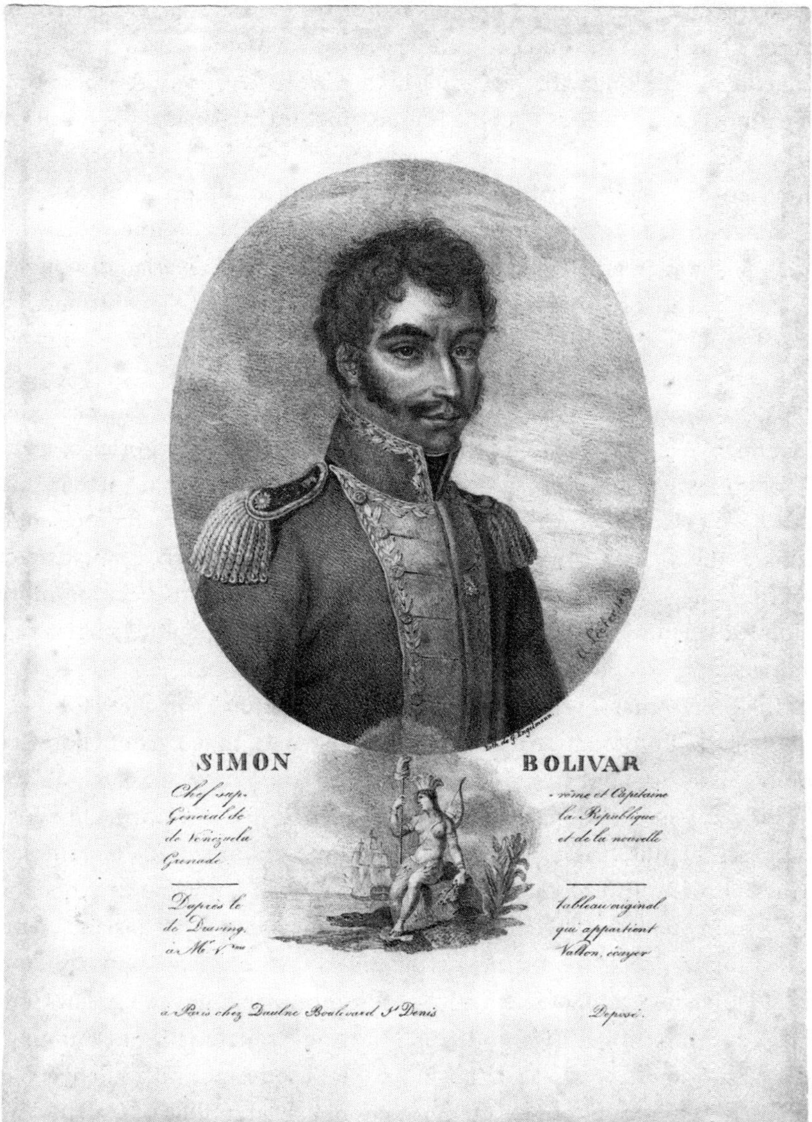

FIGURE 3.1. A. Leclerc. *Simón Bolívar*. 1819. Lithograph. 15 ¾" × 10 ½" (40 × 26.75cm). Collection Museo Nacional de Colombia. Photography © Museo Nacional de Colombia / Ángela Gómez Cely.

of an American republic. Such imagery operated in what Hugo Achugar has termed "a visual city," before and after national revolutions (2009, 11). He argues that nation states and hegemonic groups have systematically manipulated the visual along with the textual in the construction and consolidation of national consciousness. Yet the multiethnic and multiracial composition of the societies under Bolivarian Revolutionary persuasion produced a tension between an essential image of the nation and the problem of social assimilation in disparate areas. In other words, the ability of Amerindian imagery to signify a non-Spanish, American identity in Bolivarian discourses was complicated by the difficulties that revolutionary movements and national republics faced in constructing a homogeneous national language amid social heterogeneity.

The fraught issue of the emancipation of slaves following Bolivarian independence in Venezuela and the Caribbean-bordering territories of Gran Colombia with the profusion of *pardo/a* (Spanish-African mixed) and *moreno/a* (black African) identities in this region suggest such representations of the *india/o* (Indian) as a racialized figure as much as an abstract political allegory. The issues at stake in these translations become more complex when we examine the imagery in comparable cultures of slavery and race that existed on the Spanish Caribbean island of Cuba.

The Bolivarian movement's production of Amerindian imagery for revolutionary and protonational purposes in Venezuela, then part of Gran Colombia, likewise appeared in Cuba. The 1823 conspiracy of Soles y Rayos de Bolívar (Suns and Rays of Bolívar) emerged in association with José Francisco Lemus, originally from Havana and a colonel in the Colombian army of Bolívar in South America. Lemus mobilized a movement to liberate Cuba from Spanish rule with the aid of Masonic lodges on the island (Gott 2004, 49; Thomas 1998, 101–2). Cuban rebels under Bolivarian persuasion would join an invading force from South America led by Venezuelan General José Antonio Páez (1790–1873), but it never materialized (Cunninghame-Graham 1929, 227–32). This movement used Amerindian imagery as a cultural sign, evident in its attempt to establish a republic of Cubanacán, co-opting an Amerindian word for Cuba. The Spanish authorities exposed, investigated, and suppressed the conspiracy in July and August 1823, the process of which is detailed through historical accounts and primary documents in the 1929 book *Historia documentada de la conspiración de los Soles y Rayos de Bolívar* by Roque E. Garrigo.

In Bolivarian imagery pertaining to the Amerindian in Cuba and South America during the 1810s and 1820s, conceptions of national liberation and emancipation in each context became entangled with local constructions of race and shaped by disparate conditions. Amerindian imagery became a trope in the manufacture of difference from Spain. Yet symbols of things pre-Hispanic could also mediate between questions of independence and race, which included the emancipation of African slaves.

The racial politics of early nineteenth-century Cuba developed from a number of conditions particular to the Hispanic Caribbean. The outbreak of the slave rebellion on the neighboring island of Ste. Domingue in 1791, later known as the Haitian Revolution, destroyed French dominance in Atlantic sugar production and compelled Cuban planters to petition the Spanish Crown for authorization to further develop Cuba's sugar economy. Spain relaxed centuries-old restrictions on the African slave trade to allow for unfettered slave imports, which rapidly increased the population of African descent in Cuba. Thus Cuban planters faced the contradiction of profiting from a French economic calamity in ways that had the potential to lead to their own demise. By the first decades of the nineteenth century, Creole planters, wealthy from the sugar industry and perhaps content with the Spanish Crown's numerous accommodations, abstained from the independence movements of the mainland and preserved their loyalty to Spain. By 1791 the slave population of the island had reached 85,000 and more than tripled by 1827 to 287,000 (Gott 2004, 46; Pérez 1995, 86). The total population of African descent was actually much higher with the proliferation of *libertos/as* (free people of color) and their offspring. Phobias over this growing number of blacks on the island led to the founding of a special council staffed by Creole and peninsular (Spanish-born) elites, the Junta de Población Blanca (Council of the White Population) to find ways to increase the number of whites (Gott 2004; Marrero 1983; Pérez 1995; Thomas 1998; Tomich 2005).

In revolutionary and postrevolutionary Venezuela and the Caribbean areas of Gran Colombia the politics of race were configured somewhat differently than in Cuba. By the 1770s, slavery was an important feature of this broader region with a majority population of African descent (Helg 2004; Safford and Palacios 2002). Even Simón Bolívar was said to have had African traces in his bloodline, although no clear evidence exists for this claim (Chasteen 2006). His tutor Simón Rodríguez addressed various assertions that Bolívar was a *zambo* (man of African and Amerindian descent), yet this contention may speak more to negotiations over the essence of national identity (Briggs 2010, 52–53). Born to a family of landed elites, Bolívar expressed desires to see the emancipation of slaves as part of his revolutionary vision. However, the actual process of slave liberation proceeded slowly and in stages, with slavery persisting until the late nineteenth century. He nevertheless touted the equality of all, and at least two men of African descent served as his generals. Yet Bolívar's complex position on race is suggested by his decision to execute his Afro-Venezuelan generals José Padilla and Manuel Piar for insubordination, while white generals received lesser sentences for the same crime.

On the issue of the nation's government, Bolívar abhorred the thought of what he referred to as a *pardocracia,* or rule by blacks (Chasteen 2006; Helg 2004; Lynch 1986, 2006). Thus two important differences emerge between the political situation in Cuba and the captaincy general of Venezuela and the viceroyalty of New Granada in the beginning of the nineteenth century: first, the majority of Creole elites pursued loyalty in the former and independence in the latter; second, representatives of the Spanish state and Cuban elite sought to aggressively disavow people of African descent from public memory, as race became more sharply delineated. In Venezuela and New Granada, by contrast, blacks were co-opted into the revolutionary cause, while an ambivalent attitude prevailed toward the African's place in the prospective nation and regarding the fate of slavery.

These divergent constructions of race between the northern South America and Cuba are registered in similarities and differences in the uses of Amerindian imagery in each context. In the former, the deployment of the allegorical Indian could relate to what Natalia Majluf (1995) has termed an "early Creole Indianism" in the context of Peru. Here, Creole leaders appropriated the pre-Columbian past to forge popular support for nationalist ideology (Brading 1991, 293–301; Earle 2007; Majluf 1995, 22–49; Widdifield 1996). Majluf argues that the Indian became a sign of victimization in order to underscore the oppression of Spanish rule. However, in terms of the mythology of Bolívar, the construction of a glorious Incan past emphasized not only non-Spanish origins but also the greatness of the Liberator as inheritor of Incan sovereignty.

In Cuba the movement known as Soles y Rayos de Bolívar began as a Masonic lodge seemingly founded by a colonel in the Bolivarian army, José

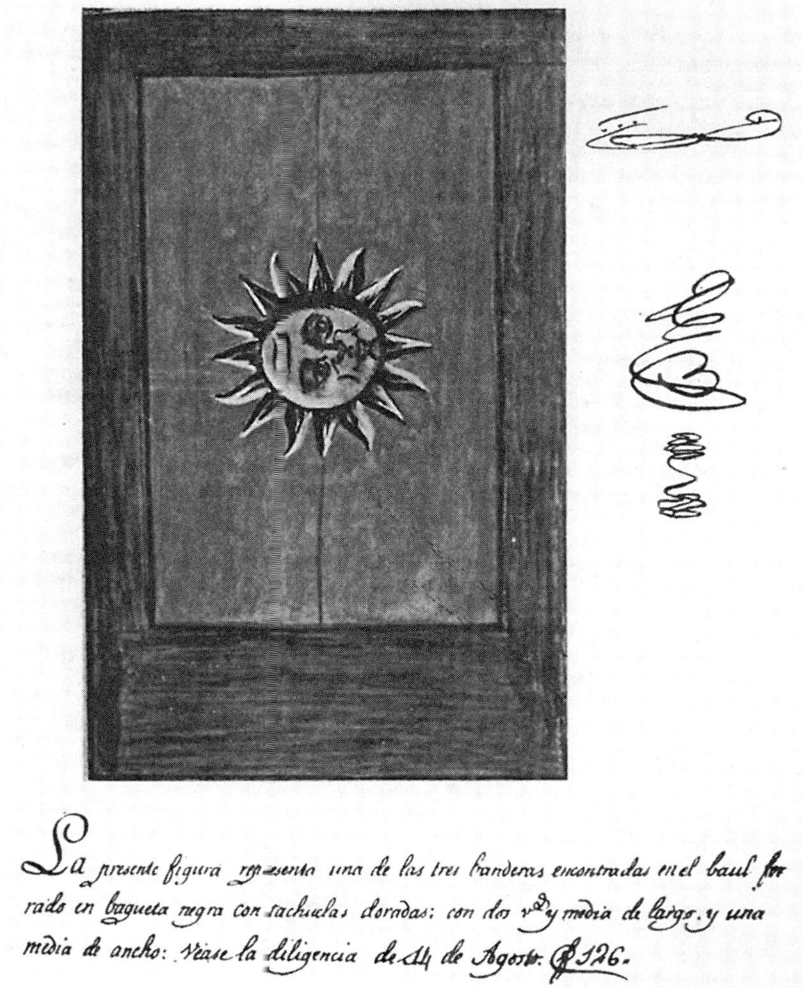

FIGURE 3.2. *Bandera* of Soles y Rayos de Bolívar. Ca. 1826. Textile. Dimensions unknown. Reproduced in Garrigo 1929, after p. 206. In the public domain.

Francisco Lemus. He arrived in Havana in 1820 from the United States, where he had been negotiating in Washington for U.S. acknowledgement of the Republic of Colombia (Torres-Cuevas 2004, 76–77). The lodge in Havana possessed two grades, the first, Rayos and the second, Soles. It produced at least one *bandera* (flag) consisting of a sun surrounded by sixteen rays (figure 3.2), the solar motif perhaps inspired by appropriations of

Inca imperial imagery (Earle 2007, 64–67). The now lost flag is only known through its publication in an early history of Soles y Rayos (Garrigo 1929). The movement Soles y Rayos de Bolívar, apparently limited to Cuba, sought to establish an independent republic of Cubanacán. It therefore seems to have drawn upon various indigenisms from the broader Bolivarian movement and perhaps other mainland developments such as those in New Spain, the region that is now modern Mexico. The flag of Soles y Rayos appears to construct a metaphor of Bolívar as the Incan sun god with Cuba as one of its rays. The image suggests an effort to encourage the island to find its own indigenous sovereignty and perhaps to tie Cuba ideologically to Gran Colombia.

Prior to the emergence of Soles y Rayos in Cuba and its appropriation of the idea of pre-Hispanic antiquity, various populist movements on the island had already begun to fashion revolutionary signs of the Amerindian figure. In 1810 a group of *libertos* enrolled in black militias in Cuba, joined a white independence movement led by a group of Freemasons, and devised a flag with the figure of an Indian woman garbed in a tobacco leaf. The group likewise invoked the rebellious cacique Hatuey who had resisted the Spanish in sixteenth-century Cuba (Gott 2004, 49). In the slave conspiracy of 1812 allegedly led by free black carpenter José Antonio Aponte, authorities seized a *libro de pinturas* (book of pictures), now lost, in the suspect Aponte's apartment in Havana. Trial records reveal that authorities found among the images a flag symbolizing the motherland, "which is pictured as an Indian woman" (Palmié 2002, 102). Similarly, the Cuban poet José María Heredia, born in Santiago de Cuba in 1803 and exiled from the island in 1823 for his connections to Soles y Rayos de Bolívar, produced romantic works that contain sympathetic views toward the Indian oppressed at the hands of the Spanish and perhaps inspired during his stay in New Spain/Mexico in the early 1820s (Heredia 1970). The poem "En el Teocalli de Cholula" ("In the Pyramid God-House Teocalli of Cholula") recounts the slaughter of the innocent residents of the indigenous city of Cholula by Spanish conquistadors. Following his exile from Cuba in 1823, Heredia produced "A Bolívar" in 1827, a poem heavily inflected with pan–Spanish American ideas. The work condemns a tyrannical Spain and immortalizes Bolívar along with Colombian, Peruvian, and Ecuadorian independence and sovereignty (Heredia 1970).

While such imagery in Cuba could carry radical associations for elites and the masses and might suggest a reworking of Bolivarian ideas from the mainland, many Creole elites on the island would have reacted unfavorably to the Indian as a revolutionary sign. The Haitian Revolution, which erupted in 1791, effectively reshaped the Creole racial imagination in the Hispanic Caribbean. In early nineteenth-century Cuba, insular geography, proximity to Haiti, and the ratio of whites to blacks created heightened anxieties among the Cuban Creole elite toward people of African descent on the island. Indeed, historians have speculated that their apprehensions inspired loyalty to Spain among an insular elite not eager to destabilize the social and political order (Pérez 1995). For these Cuban Creoles, civic uses of Amerindian imagery in the 1820s and 1830s seem to have represented Creole place and distinction from peninsulars rather than radical solidarity. Thus while the Creole elites in Cuba enjoyed greater wealth and exhibited a sense of belonging to a distinctive Atlantic-world city and American region within the Spanish Empire, they refrained from rebellion and began to increasingly distance themselves physically and conceptually from populations of African descent on their own island.

The Bolivarian-inspired notion of an independent Cubanacán seems to have had a dynamic relation to the issue of slavery and slave emancipation in Cuba for both rebels and colonial authorities. In documents pertaining to the conspiracy published as appendixes to Garrigo's 1929 book, the links between Soles y Rayos and slavery in Cuba are discussed in various ways in accounts by royal authorities and proclamations by alleged conspirators. Spanish officials framed the conspiracy as not only an insurrection against the Crown but also a nightmarish, Ste. Domingue–style slave insurrection. Official documents stressed the existence of subversive codes in the movement resulting in the meetings of "all the black and mulatto natives of the Island and the freedmen" (Garrigo 1929, 125). Captain General Francisco Dionisio Vives, who reigned in Cuba 1823–32, dispatched a report to the Ministry of the Interior denouncing "the conspiracy discovered in this Plaza aimed at upsetting the legitimate government, separating this island from Spain, and attempting to incorporate it into the Republic with the name of Cubanacán" (182). He warned that "for slaves and free people of color, upon the outbreak of any revolution, there is no other end than the extermination of one of the two parties [white or black], as happened on the island of Santo Domingo" (185). Vives couches Soles y Rayos in Cuba in terms resonant of the Haitian Revolution, continually asserting that their activities would have the devastating effect of "arousing the ambition of the negroes" (185).

In proclamations supporting the movement by the supposed ringleader of Soles y Rayos, José Francisco Lemus, the issue of emancipation is treated somewhat differently. In an exhortation of 1823, Lemus addresses his fellow "Cubanacanos," celebrating "Salud, Independencia, Libertad" (Health, Independence, Liberty) (in Garrigo 1929, 127). He champions "our political emancipation" and counts Cubanacán as part of the fraternity of the "new republics of Paraguay, Chile, Lima, Buenos Aires, Colombia, and Mexico" (128). In several instances, Lemus makes reference to slaves and slavery. In noting the "virtuous character of free men," he writes, "let us treat those unfortunate slaves with tenderness, alleviating their dreadful fate until the representatives of our country propose the means of their happy redemption, without prejudice to individual interests: they are children of God himself" (130). Other passages regarding slaves seem to suggest a general denunciation of imperial absolutism and the tyrant Ferdinand VII, sympathizing with those unfortunates still under the "slavery" of the absolute monarch.

Lemus urges Cubanacanos to embrace the facets of an enlightened republic, including "public administration with men of capacity and virtue . . . public education . . . liberty and *las luces* [enlightenment]" (131). He then attacks Spaniards for "sustaining our degradation and slavery" (132). Lemus does mention the importance of including *pardos*, *negros*, and people of all classes in the island's liberation; however, this rhetoric of national assimilation says little in itself about what he actually planned to do with slavery in Cuba and suggests a similar ambivalence as that seen in Bolívar's approach to slavery in Gran Colombia. Lemus's ambiguity on the issue, from these few documents, could be interpreted as an effort to distance the movement from slavery itself in a possible attempt to attract more white followers, some of whom appear to have been members of the planter class. On the other hand, Captain General Vives's denunciation of Soles y Rayos emphasizes its potential connection to the Haitian Revolution perhaps to turn the Havana elite resolutely against it, to stain it beyond sympathy. These documents suggest that as with developments in South America,

Soles y Rayos de Bolívar in Cuba seemed more resolute about achieving independence and vague toward the emancipation of African slaves.

The conflation by Vives of the independence movement with slave rebellion and the imprecision of Lemus on the issue of emancipation suggest important political negotiations regarding the movement of Soles y Rayos de Bolívar in Cuba. In part, Cuban planters and Spanish officials would likely have known that Bolívar spent significant time in Haiti in 1816, receiving aid for his invasion of Venezuela from Haitian president Alexandre Pétion. Providing military and financial support, Pétion requested that in return Bolívar was to abolish slavery in the territories he liberated in Venezuela (Fischer 2013; Lynch 2006). This Bolívar-Pétion alliance and promises of abolition in South America would certainly have repulsed the Cuban planter elite, whose livelihoods and sense of insular security compelled them to maintain the status quo.

The production of Amerindian imagery in the broader Bolivarian movement interacted with similar elite appropriations in New Spain and the Caribbean with respect to defining a sense of Creole place and American antiquity. Yet the signification of this imagery was far from universal and was reconditioned according to local racial ideologies. If Amerindian imagery carried revolutionary significance in Cuba in association with a Bolivarian and/or populist movement, it would need to be emptied of such significance for the Creole and peninsular elite, whose racist phobias may have driven a persistent loyalty to Spain. For loyalist Creoles in Havana, the Indian could be transformed into a sign of civic pride in support of loyal subjectivity and seemingly negate the African presence in Cuba. These negotiations appear lucidly as academic artists arrived in Havana in the early nineteenth century and as local patrons contracted works abroad to be shipped to the Caribbean city. French expatriate painter Jean-Baptiste Vermay arrived in 1815 from Paris by way of New Orleans and provided a director for a drawing school known as the Academy of San Alejandro, opened by the Creole and peninsular elite-controlled Economic Society in 1818 as a drawing school. Literary scholar Sibylle Fischer has persuasively argued that this academy's conceptualization responded to racial agendas as an early nineteenth-century attempt to construct an elite cultural bastion against people of African descent who seem to have dominated the production of the visual arts in Havana (2004, 57–76).

By March 1828, Vermay created two grand history paintings to be displayed within a civic monument known as El Templete. In his scene *The First Mass* (figure 3.3), the Dominican friar Bartolomé de las Casas stands beneath a ceiba tree and conducts a Christian Mass as Spaniards gather around in various expressions of reverence. In the lower right-hand corner of the scene, the Spanish conquistador Diego Velásquez with his back to the viewer touches an Amerindian man on the shoulder as though shepherding him into the new faith. Here, the Indian appears as a sign of Creole pride of place in a fictive scene emphasizing the civilized nature of Cuba's Amerindians. This visual statement supported claims to the reason and "enlightened" sociability of nineteenth-century Creoles (Niell 2011, 2013). The Indian-conquistador vignette, furthermore, serves to disinherit the African in the foundational moments of Cuba's history and becomes a form of racial cleansing to metaphorically whiten the nineteenth-century population, responsive to the surge in Africans due to the slave trade.

The efforts seen in Vermay's paintings for El Templete in Havana to define the Creole community in terms of the Spanish-Indian encounter can be instructively compared to large-scale public works that propagated the myth of Bolívar. Venezuela's Panteón Nacional, established by 1874 and configured as a Latin basilica, has paintings along the length of its central vaulting from the 1930s and '40s by Tito Salas (1887–1974) (plate 6). A large composite mural known as the *Apoteosis de Bolívar*, finished by 1942 and composed of multiple episodes, depicts Bolívar's crossing of the Andes accompanied by indigenous Andeans (plate 6). The scene may allude to an Amerindian presence in Bolívar's armies at that time. In one portion of the larger mural, a flag-bearing allegory of victory moves across the battlefield with a group of men of various skin tones, some possibly representing *llaneros*, Venezuelan or Colombian herders often known to be Afro-Venezuelan (Pineda 1974, 219–30). In the actual apotheosis scene, the spirit of Bolívar is conveyed to the heavens in a chariot drawn by horses and guided by a number of male figures whose skin colors range from light brown to black. These scenes from the 1930s construct the image of a multiracial nation, as do those of Martín Tovar y Tovar (1827–1902) at the Casa Natal del Libertador in Caracas that likewise include people of African and Amerindian descent (Pineda 1974, 194–216).

While twentieth-century nationalist imagery in Venezuela celebrates the inclusion of a multiracial population in the national narrative, the pro-

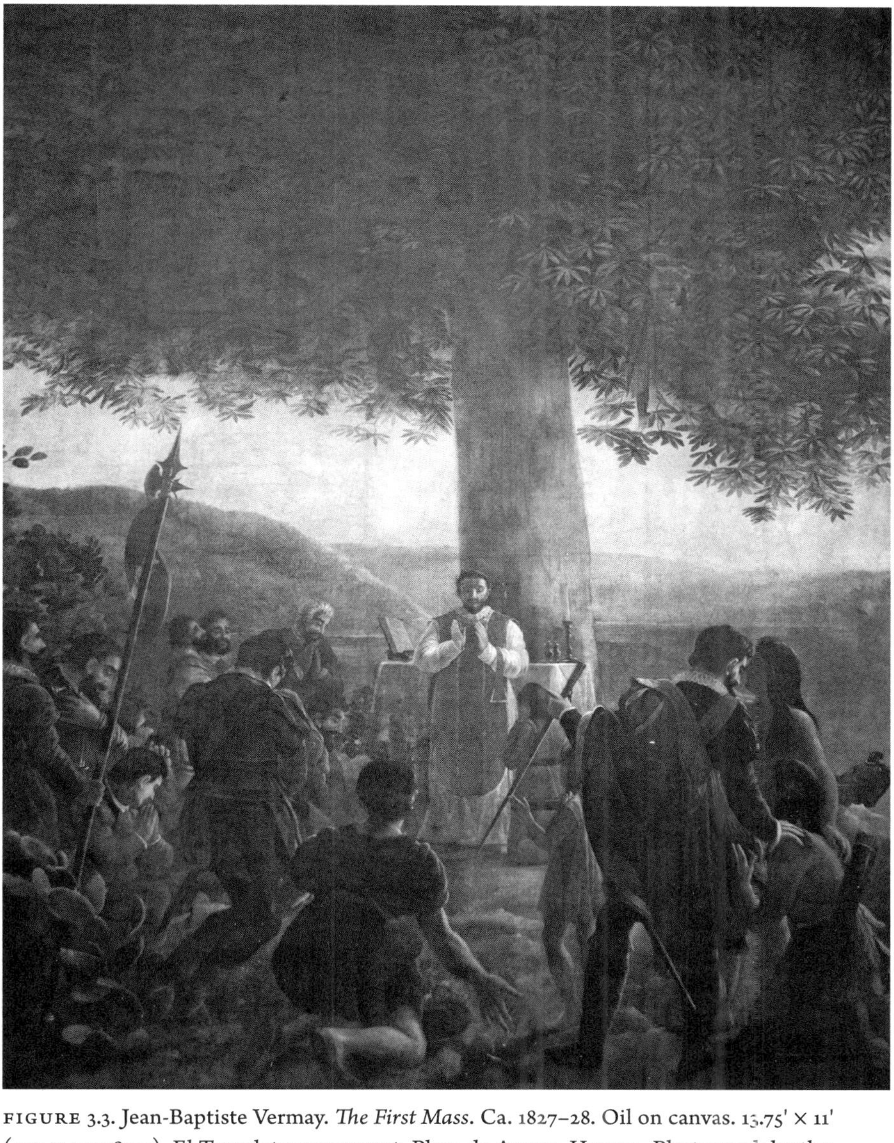

FIGURE 3.3. Jean-Baptiste Vermay. *The First Mass*. Ca. 1827–28. Oil on canvas. 13.75' × 11' (419 × 335.38cm). El Templete monument, Plaza de Armas, Havana. Photograph by the author. Permission of the Oficina del Historiador de la Ciudad de La Habana.

duction of civic imagery in early nineteenth-century Havana continued the trend of employing Indian figures to assert Creole place. Indeed, Cuba would not attain independence until 1902. A fountain sculpture from the 1830s reasserted the non-African nature of Creole place, as begun by Vermay's paintings in El Templete. *The Fountain of the Indian*, also known as *Noble Havana*, sculpted by Italian academician Giuseppe Gaggini (1791–1867), arrived in Havana in the late 1830s from Genoa, Italy. The acting Cuban-born intendant Claudio Martínez de Pinillos, conde de Villanueva, financed the work and its shipment to Havana. Destined for a space on the southern end of the Paseo de Extramuros directly in front of the colonial military parade ground, the Campo de Marté, the fountain stood just outside the Puerta de Tierra (Roig de Leuchsenring 1963, 18–20; Niell 2013). Atop a classicizing base complete with dolphin figures, a sculpture of an Indian woman provides an allegory of the city. The figure wears a feathered headdress and a skirt, has a bare torso, and holds a shield emblazoned with the arms of the city in her right hand while cradling an overflowing cornucopia in her left. In its principal icons, this allegory of Havana reveals an appropriation and retooling of the long tradition of geographic, revolutionary, and nationalist references found in the image of Bolívar by Leclerc from 1819. A dedicatory inscription on the fountain reads, "Por el Conde de Villanueva" (By the Count of Villanueva), affirming the patronage of Martínez de Pinillos. Here the intendant, an economic ally of Creole planters, financed an Indian figure that would stand for the commercial pride and American identity of a plantocracy, not the revolutionary leanings of individuals from the lower social echelons. Furthermore, the elevation of an Indian figure during a time when "Indian" as a racial category had virtually disappeared from legal discourses in Cuba suggests a process of racial whitening of the Indian to offset anxieties among elites about the growing population of African descent (Childs 2006, 56–57).

The complex uses and significations of Amerindian imagery in this era in the Atlantic world and with respect to Bolivarian movements underscore the need to consider both the locus of enunciation and the impact of local racial ideologies. The embodiment of the nation as the allegorical Indian could serve to activate the racialized dimensions of national identity formation and could simultaneously serve as a sign of non-Spanishness. Cuba's contested politics of slavery and race drove a rejection of Bolivarian ideology by the majority of the Creole elite and effectively recast the use of

Amerindian imagery in civic contexts to disavow not only a fledgling independence movement but also the African as a potentially national figure. In Gran Colombia, Bolívar himself manifested ambivalence toward the full racial questions of the nation as registered in his actions and discourses. Yet here as well, the Indian appears as a mediator between Spanish and Creole, white and *casta*. The appearance of this figure in Bolivarian imagery reveals a preliminary negotiation on the acceptable visual means to construct the nation, a process that had further developed by the early twentieth century, as evidenced in the paintings of Martín Tovar y Tovar and Tito Salas.

Acknowledgments

My sincere thanks to the editors of the volume for their helpful critiques and to Eusebio Leal Spengler of Havana for his vital research assistance.

References

Acevedo, Esther. 2000. "Entre la tradición alegórica y la narrativa factual." In *Los pinceles de la historia de la patria criolla a la nación mexicana 1750–1860*, edited by Jaime Soler, 114–31. Mexico City: Consejo Nacional para la Cultura y las Artes.

Achugar, Hugo. 2009. "Foundational Images of the Nation in Latin America." In *Building Nineteenth-Century Latin America: Re-Rooted Cultures, Identities, and Nations*, edited by William G. Acree Jr. and Juan Carlos González Espitia, 11–31. Nashville, TN: Vanderbilt University Press.

Ades, Dawn. 1989. *Art in Latin America: The Modern Era, 1820–1980*. New Haven, CT: Yale University Press.

Anderson, Benedict. 1983. *Imagined Communities: Reflections on the Origin and Spread of Nationalism*. London: Verso.

Brading, David A. 1991. *The First America: The Spanish Monarchy, Creole Patriots, and the Liberal State, 1492–1867*. Cambridge, England: Cambridge University Press.

Briggs, Ronald. 2010. *Tropes of Enlightenment in the Age of Bolívar: Simón Rodríguez and the American Essay at Revolution*. Nashville, TN: Vanderbilt University Press.

Carrera, Magali M. 2006. "Affections of the Heart: Female Imagery and the Notion of Nation in Mexico." In *Woman and Art in Early Modern Latin America*, edited by Kellen McIntyre and Richard E. Phillips, 47–72. London: Brill Press.

Chasteen, John. 2006. "Simón Bolívar: Man and Myth." In *Heroes and Hero Cults in Latin America*, edited by Samuel Brunk and Ben Fallaw, 21–39. Austin: University of Texas Press.

Childs, Matt D. 2006. *The 1812 Aponte Rebellion in Cuba and the Struggle against Atlantic Slavery*. Chapel Hill: University of North Carolina Press.

Cunninghame-Graham, R. B. *José Antonio Páez*. Philadelphia: Macrae-Smith, 1929.

Earle, Rebecca. 2007. *The Return of the Native: Indians and Myth-Making in Spanish America, 1810–1930*. Durham, NC: Duke University Press.

Fischer, Sibylle. 2004. *Modernity Disavowed: Haiti and the Cultures of Slavery in the Age of Revolution*. Durham, NC: Duke University Press.

———. 2013. "Bolívar in Haiti: Republicans in the Revolutionary Atlantic." In *Haiti and the Americas*, edited by Carla Calargé, Raphael Dalleo, Luis Duno-Gottberg, and Clevis Headley, 25–54. Jackson: University Press of Mississippi.

Garrigo, Roque E. 1929. *Historia documentada de la conspiración de los Soles y Rayos de Bolívar.* Havana: Imprenta El Siglo XX, A. Muñiz y Hno.

Gott, Richard. 2004. *Cuba: A New History*. New Haven, CT: Yale University Press.

Helg, Aline. 2004. *Liberty and Equality in Caribbean Colombia, 1770–1835*. Chapel Hill: University of North Carolina Press.

Heredia, José María. 1970. *Poesías completas*. Edited by Angel Aparicio Laurencio. Miami, FL: Ediciones Universal.

Landers, Jane. 2010. *Atlantic Creoles in the Age of Revolutions*. Cambridge, MA: Harvard University Press.

Lynch, John. 1986. *The Spanish American Revolutions, 1808–1826*. New York: W. W. Norton.

———. 2006. *Simón Bolívar: A Life*. New Haven, CT: Yale University Press.

Majluf, Natalia. 1995. "The Creation of the Image of the Indian in 19th-Century Peru: The Paintings of Francisco Laso (1823–1869)." PhD diss., University of Texas, Austin.

Marrero, Leví. 1983. *Cuba: Economía y sociedad (1763–1868)*. Vol. 9, *Azúcar, ilustración y conciencia (1763-1868)*. Madrid: Editorial Playor.

Niell, Paul B. 2011. "El Templete and Cuban Neoclassicism: A Multivalent Signifier as Site of Memory." *Bulletin for Latin American Research* 30, no. 3:344–65.

———. 2013. "Rhetorics of Place and Empire in the Fountain Sculpture of 1830s Havana." *Art Bulletin* 95, no. 3:440–64.

Palmié, Stephan. 2002. *Wizards and Scientists: Explorations in Afro-Cuban Modernity and Tradition*. Durham, NC: Duke University Press.

Pérez, Louis A. Jr. 1995. *Cuba: Between Reform and Revolution*. New York: Oxford University Press.

Pineda, Rafael. 1974. *La pintura de Tito Salas*. Caracas: E. Armitano.

Rabasa, José. 1993. *Inventing America: Spanish Historiography and the Formation of Eurocentrism*. Norman: University of Oklahoma Press.

"Real Cédula de 21 de octubre 1817, sobre aumentar la población blanca de la Isla de Cuba." Archivo Nacional de Cuba, Asuntos Políticos, legajo 16, exp. 14, 1817.

Roig de Leuchsenring, Emilio. 1963. *La Habana: Apuntes históricos*. Havana: Editora del Consejo Nacional de Cultura, Oficina del Historiador de la Ciudad de La Habana.

Safford, Frank, and Marco Palacios. 2002. *Colombia: Fragmented Land, Divided Society*. New York: Oxford University Press.

Thomas, Hugh. 1998. *Cuba or the Pursuit of Freedom*. New York: De Capo Press.

Tomich, Dale. 2005. "The Wealth of Empire: Francisco Arango y Parreño, Political Economy, and the Second Slavery in Cuba." In *Interpreting Spanish Colonialism: Empires, Nations, and Legends*, edited by Christopher Schmidt-Nowara and John M. Nieto-Phillips, 54–85. Albuquerque: University of New Mexico Press.

Torres-Cuevas, Eduardo. 2004. *Historia de la masonería cubana: Seis ensayos*. Havana: Imágen Contemporánea.

Widdifield, Stacie G. 1996. *The Embodiment of the National in Late Nineteenth-Century Mexican Painting*. Tucson: University of Arizona Press.

———. 2001. "El índio re-tratado." In *Hacia otra historia del arte en México de la estructuración colonial a la exigencia nacional (1780–1860)*, 1:241–56. Mexico City: Conaculta.

4

Simón Bolívar's Centennial Anniversary

Music for a Triumphal Parade

JUAN DE DIOS LÓPEZ MAYA

Bolívar engraved his exploits
in the golden pages of history
and there Boyacá and Carabobo and Junín
are proclaiming his glory.

You, Guzmán, with our Homeland on the edge
of an abyss of shame, held back its fall,
saved it, and filled it with riches.
Your ambition is to make our country happy.

[Chorus]
Today two heroes admire the Andes
that together in time [they] will go forward.
They are Oh Homeland! your greatest glories.
Hail Bolívar! Hail Guzmán!

"HIMNO PARA EL CENTENARIO DEL LIBERTADOR," 1883

The return of Simón Bolívar's remains to Caracas in 1842 is widely considered to be the beginning of the formation process of the Bolivarian cult, which was consolidated in 1883 with the Apotheosis of Bolívar and the centennial celebration of his birth. In its early days the cult of Bolívar was closely associated with the Roman Catholic Church and its rituals and institutions, but with the arrival of Antonio Guzmán Blanco to power in 1870, the cult underwent a radical change, becoming a secular religion controlled by the

Venezuelan government. Music played a major role in the establishment and secularization of the cult, and Guzmán Blanco's centennial celebrations functioned as a culminating moment in this process. Here I trace the previously underrecognized role of music in forming and consolidating the cult of Bolívar. I show how Guzmán Blanco confiscated and secularized the Church's sites and ritual practices around Bolívar, a process in which music played a major role and shifted from liturgical to secular and militarized forms. Drawing upon archival evidence of the centennial committee, I also show how Guzmán Blanco's regime recruited military bands, famous composers, amateur musicians, and choral groups in commissioning, performing, and disseminating a wide-ranging and varied Bolivarian repertoire. This evidence is critical in showing how and why music remains central to the cult of Bolívar. This new civic religion functioned to replace the Church with the Liberal reforms of Guzmán Blanco, who sought to transfer power from the Church to the state through the veneration of Bolívar.

The Church and the Bolivarian Cult

Between the time of Bolívar's death in 1830 and the rise of Guzmán Blanco and the Liberal Party (discussed more fully in Tomás Straka's essay in this collection), the cult of Bolívar emerged as a cultural practice largely controlled by the Roman Catholic Church. Simón Bolívar died on December 17, 1830, in the small country home Quinta de San Pedro Alejandrino, near the Colombian city of Santa Marta. At the time of Bolívar's death and the dissolution of his main project, to unify much of South America as Gran Colombia, Bolívar's popularity was at its lowest level. Some sectors of the Venezuelan public harshly criticized him and accused him of being an autocrat. But in 1840 the situation changed dramatically when the formation of the Liberal Party forced the Conservative government in power to face an organized opposition for the first time. As Germán Carrera Damas has shown (2008), the Conservatives, who were aligned with the Church, then claimed a revolutionary and ideological lineage tied to Bolívar that served as a response to the newly organized criticism and a way to enhance their legitimacy.

In 1842, at the initiative of José Antonio Páez's government, Bolívar's remains were transferred to Caracas, where they were honored in a predominantly religious context. To mark the occasion, Mozart's *Requiem* (composed in 1791) was performed in a ceremony on the anniversary of Bolívar's death, December 17 (Toro 1843). During the course of that week, three religious works by well-known Venezuelan composers, written especially for the occasion, were also performed (Calcaño 2001). On December 23 the remains were transferred from the Iglesia San Francisco in Caracas to the Catedral Metropolitana de Santa Ana, where they were deposited in the Bolívar family mausoleum and remained for thirty-six years (Calcaño 2001). Once Bolívar's remains were deposited in the Catedral Metropolitana, the Church transformed them into a kind of holy relic and made the cathedral a place of pilgrimage, thus providing the Church with direct control over commemorations and rituals dedicated to Bolívar. Every year the Church held special masses; Te Deums (an early Christian hymn of praise in Latin that has been set to music by many composers), requiems (Catholic masses for the dead and compositions created for them), and all kinds of religious compositions were performed every year to honor Bolívar's memory. During this entire period, the principal date associated with the Liberator was October 28, Saint Simon's feast day and thus Simón Bolívar's name day, a Catholic tradition consisting of celebrating the homonymous saint's day instead of the individual's actual birthday. These religious practices remained in place for almost thirty years and forced the government to share control of the cult of Bolívar with the Church as long as the Church remained the depository of the sacred remains.

The Guzmán Blanco Era

The tension between Conservatives and Liberals finally led to the Federal War (1859–63), the Liberal victory, and a new generation of political leaders, the most prominent of whom was undoubtedly Antonio Guzmán Blanco. He was the son of Antonio Leocadio Guzmán, one of the founders of the Liberal Party, and had demonstrated outstanding military leadership during the conflict. As the son of a renowned political leader, Guzmán Blanco sought to build his own leadership agenda to avoid being eclipsed by the reputation of his father. His remarkable performance during the Federal War helped him to become the most important minister in the government of President Juan Crisóstomo Falcón (1863–68). A new political crisis led to the overthrow of Falcón and the dissolution of his government in 1868.

Finally, after a brief war, Guzmán Blanco came into power in 1870, launching one of the most controversial eras of Venezuelan history.

Guzmán's administration is credited with having pacified the embattled Venezuela, giving it a modern infrastructure, providing the country's larger cities with public buildings, railroads, electricity, and telephone service, and implementing a new legal framework that was consistent with positivist and liberal beliefs of the era. However, Guzmán Blanco is also remembered for his autocratic behavior, his abuse of power, and his ruthlessness with his political enemies, encouraging an exaggerated cult of personality around himself and Bolívar and enriching himself by embezzling public funds. He had control of power for eighteen years, between 1870 and 1888, and held the presidency on three occasions, known in history as the Septennial (1870–77), the Five-Year (1879–84), and the Acclamation (1886–88). Congress (then a bicameral body), dominated by his supporters, awarded him with the official title of "Illustrious American, Peacemaker, and Regenerator of Venezuela" in 1873 (Arráiz Lucca 2007), but his detractors sarcastically nicknamed him "the Enlightened Despot" and "the Civilizing Autocrat."

Starting in 1863, as his influence on the country's political and economic development grew, Guzmán Blanco made the transformation of the Bolivarian cult into a secular and state spectacle one of his top priorities. He sought to wrest control of the cult away from the Church to serve his purposes, and to do so, he had to strip the cult of its Catholic references and replace them with secular significations. To achieve his goals Guzmán Blanco commissioned the leading architects, sculptors, painters, writers, poets, and composers in multiple symbolic projects aimed at creating an iconographic apparatus for the glory and worship of Bolívar. Starting in 1870 the government took a series of actions that progressively weakened the Church as the intermediary and administrator of the Bolivarian cult. The effect was to transfer control of the cult to the state and particularly to the figure of Guzmán Blanco, who linked his own image to the Liberator, thus augmenting his reputation and legitimacy. The Apotheosis of 1883, the secular ceremony celebrating Bolívar's ascent into the heavens and the annals of history, was the culmination of this process. In the 130-some years since then, the fundamental characteristics of the cult and its rituals and practices have changed little.

Secularizing and Militarizing the Cult of Bolívar

Guzmán Blanco used the occasion of Saint Simon's feast day in 1872 to quite literally take the cult out of the cathedral and into public spaces while at the same time transforming the spectacle from a church event with liturgical music to a state and military event with martial and secular music. Guzmán Blanco's new program included a concert at the Federal Palace with the assistance of the government staff and the diplomatic corps, a procession past the landmarks in the city center, a parade of cultic objects belonging to the Liberator, and a solemn session of the Venezuelan Academy of Literature. Guzmán Blanco led the procession carrying the most emblematic relic of all: the Liberator's sword (*La Revista* 1872). (The history and symbolic values given to this sword are the subject of the essay in this volume by Alejandro E. Gómez Pernia.) This event was the precedent for what would eleven years later become known as the Apotheosis of the Liberator, now an annual national ritual.

Guzmán Blanco initiated other symbolic transformations intended to secularize the cult, expand the number of sites commemorating Bolívar, and thus increase the public domain of the cult's rituals. The image of the Liberator received augmented public visibility when the old Plaza Mayor (Caracas's main square), the central site of Spanish urban tradition whose main use was as a marketplace, was transformed into Plaza Bolívar, a space now dedicated to leisure activities. In the center of the square Guzmán Blanco's regime placed a towering equestrian statue of the Liberator, which was inaugurated in November 1874 (Calcaño 2001, 267). Thereafter, Plaza Bolívar became the epicenter of the country's political life; La Casa Amarilla, the seat of the executive branch, City Hall, the Capitol, and the Catedral Metropolitana are all located around it.

As the symbolic heart of the city and nation, Caracas's Plaza Bolívar established a model for town and urban centers around the country, not only as a center of political life but also as a center of regular military music performances celebrating the Liberator. Plaza Bolívar soon became the setting for the popular *retreta,* an outdoor concert that Caracas's martial band still gives every Thursday and Sunday. In this way, the new space had a voice of its own that over the years created a strong historical and emotional identification between Plaza Bolívar and the band. By the early twentieth century, almost every city and town in the country created its own Plaza Bolívar that featured a statue and a *retreta*. The *retreta* arose from the tradition of the marching band, the most characteristic musical group of the nineteenth century. Shortly after the establishment of the federal government in 1863, the old military bands of the colonial era were reenvisioned and assigned a new task outside the barracks: to entertain a public accustomed to meeting and strolling along the wide avenues, parks, and other newly created public spaces. To successfully accomplish this mission, the bands had to modify their traditional repertoire of marches and anthems. They developed a new repertoire composed of three genres: Venezuelan popular dance pieces, opera highlights, and patriotic character pieces (music dedicated to national heroes and national holidays). This program expanded the nationalist symbolism dedicated to Bolívar as a military hero.

Guzmán Blanco's next step in improving Bolívar's visibility as a central national icon was to transfer Bolívar's remains from the Catedral Metropolitana to the Pantéon Nacional. The Panteón was formed by appropriating and secularizing the church of Santa Trinita, which had a privileged location in the northern part of the city. Caracas is in a valley, and the northern part of the city is higher than the rest, meaning that the Panteón Nacional can be seen from almost anywhere in the city center. In 1874, Guzmán issued a decree ordering the church's transformation into a pantheon to hold the remains of the Liberator, the heroes of independence, the so-called liberal heroes of the Federal War, and other eminent personalities. The consecration of the Panteón took effect two years later, when on Saint Simon's Day in 1876 Bolívar's remains were placed in the altar of the former church (Zawisza 1997). Since then the Panteón Nacional has been the main stage of patriotic celebrations, effectively displacing the Church and leaving it quietly in the background. The next and perhaps most important stage in the consolidation of the Bolivarian cult was the centennial celebration of Bolívar's birth; the commemoration occurred in 1883, during Guzmán Blanco's second presidential term.

The Centennial Commission

The extensive preparations for the centennial celebration began some two years in advance of the actual events, signaling Guzmán Blanco's plan to use the anniversary as a major display of his consolidated power and as a vehicle tying his vision of modernism, liberalism, and progress to Bolívar's legacy.

On September 3, 1881, Guzmán Blanco issued a decree ordering the commemoration and establishing the guidelines for its implementation (Centenario de Bolívar 1883). The decree created a commission whose members represented the secular and symbolic scope of the project. Guzmán entrusted the leadership of this commission to his father, Antonio Leocadio Guzmán, who had been a revolutionary hero. Fernando Bolívar and Pablo Clemente, distinguished public men and also Bolívar's nephews, provided legitimacy and authenticity to the project and the Liberal Party. Four other members represented military authority and the liberal values of reason and modern sciences: Andrés Level, navy officer, mathematician and also the founder of the Department of Statistics at the Universidad Central de Venezuela (Fernández Heres 1997); Aristides Rojas, historian, physician, journalist and pioneer of naturalism and popular science (Sujo Volsky 1997); and Manuel Vicente Díaz and Agustín Aveledo, founding members of the Society of Sciences and the Association of Engineers (Fernández Heres 1997). These illustrious men represented a well-balanced combination of the glorious past symbolized by Antonio Leocadio Guzmán, the figure of Bolívar in the person of his nephews, the ideals of progress, and turn-of-the-century liberalism, represented by four distinguished local academic personalities.

The decree also provided a list of international delegations that should be invited, including all of the American republics, Haiti, the United States, France, Switzerland, Britain, and the governments of those European nations (Belgium and the Netherlands) that had participated in the transfer of the remains of the Liberator from Santa Marta to Caracas (Centenario de Bolívar 1883). Guzmán Blanco envisioned the centennial as an important vehicle in the state confiscation and secularization of the cult of Bolívar as well as in propagandizing Venezuela's modernity and illustrious history to the international community.

The Centennial Program as Secular Agenda

A close analysis of the centennial plans and program reveals how the government sought to secularize the cult of Bolívar and demonstrates the significant role of music in this process. On October 20, 1881, the centennial commission presented the proposed program of festivities (Castellanos 1983). The monumental ten-day program included events that began on

July 23 and culminated on August 2. To set up the operational part of the celebrations, several subcommittees were appointed and were responsible for specific activity areas representing the different guilds in Caracas. The music delegation was chaired by José María Velásquez, president of the Guild of Musicians of the Federal District. The other members of the music delegation, Manuel Azpúrua, Rafael Saumell, Rogerio Caraballo, and Manuel Hernández, were all well-known composers and board members of the Music Academy of the National Institute of Fine Arts, founded by presidential decree in 1877. Velásquez played a leading role in the musical events of the centennial, as we will see.

The planning booklet also contains detailed instructions to participants and establishes a protocol for each one of the acts (Centenario de Bolívar 1883). It is in this section, which is a kind of theatrical script, where we realize the importance the commission assigned to music in staging the event. The program required that the Triumphal Parade had to be on July 24, a fundamental change in the nature of worship. Instead of October 28, Saint Simon's day, the celebration was changed to the date of Bolívar's birth, snatching from the Church its previously central role in commemorating Bolívar. In some early documents the Triumphal Parade is even described as a "civic procession," which both alludes to the original religious procession and displaces it with a secular form.

During the Septennial (1870–77), Guzmán's first tenure as president, he had serious clashes with the Church over political power. In 1870 Guzmán Blanco deported the archbishop, causing the Vatican to intervene by appointing a special ambassador to mediate the conflict, but the government denied his entry to the country (Castillo Lara 1998). In response, in 1873, the Congress proposed the creation of a national church independent of Rome. Convents and seminaries were closed, and their property was confiscated (Arráiz Lucca 2007). In 1877, the government and the Vatican finally reached an agreement to prevent a definitive schism; thereafter, relations improved but remained tense. Curiously, what sparked the conflict was the archbishop's refusal to sing a Te Deum at the cathedral during a celebration of the government's military victories. The archbishop refused to sing the Te Deum as a way of demanding amnesty for certain Conservative political prisoners who had been accused of conspiring against the government. But Guzmán Blanco saw this demand as an unacceptable intrusion of the Church into government affairs (Castillo Lara 1998). After the tensions during the Septennial, the Bolivarian centennial was an occasion for reconciliation between Guzmán Blanco and the Church. The program thus required that the festivities begin at six o'clock in the morning of July 23 with bells pealing from every church in the country, followed by the celebration of a Solemn Mass and the singing of a Te Deum. But this was the extent of the Church's participation in the centennial events since all other events were secular.

Despite the Mass and Te Deum marking the opening of the centennial, the Triumphal Parade and all other events were decidedly secular, and all were to be accompanied by newly commissioned music for band, symphony, and voice. The apotheosis concert celebrating Bolívar's secular deification by borrowing from antiquity was planned for the Teatro Municipal, originally named Teatro Guzmán Blanco. The first lady chaired a committee of prominent "ladies and misses" who presented an offering of charity to public hospitals, hospices, and orphanages. There was a ceremonial unveiling in the Panteón of a statue of Francisco de Miranda, honored as Bolívar's predecessor in the campaign for independence. Other celebrations included a popular feast to honor the people of Caracas; the opening of the first railway line between Caracas and La Guaira, the country's main port; and the opening of the Great National Exhibition of arts and industry. The program's varied festivities reveal that Guzmán Blanco sought to recruit all levels and classes of society into this radically new secular Liberal vision of Bolivarianism. The protocol or sequencing of events reveals the social hierarchy while also engaging all sectors of society in the cult: the government staff, the diplomatic corps, the clergy, ladies and misses, the guilds, and the common people. Each had a specific role to fill in this "grand opera" led by President Guzmán Blanco as master of ceremonies.

The Musical Program's Operatic Scale

If Guzmán Blanco cast himself as a kind of operatic impresario and envisioned the centennial as a grand operatic spectacle, it meant that the musical program arranged by the commission had to be extremely demanding in terms of the number and types of new compositions scheduled for performance. Indeed, an opera company was formed in Caracas in 1883 to brighten the centennial celebrations, and it received the direct support of President Guzmán Blanco. It debuted on July 1, 1883, with a performance of Verdi's *Ernani* in the Teatro Municipal (Castellanos 1983). No doubt alarmed by Guzmán's heady ambitions, the centennial musical delegation had to coordinate performances by secular and military musicians rather than rely on Church choirs and musicians. On January 6, 1883, the secretary Andrés Level sent a memo to the president's father and leader of the commission, Antonio Leocadio Guzmán, calling his attention to this matter and notifying him of the need for orchestras and bands to fulfill the program's requirements (Level 1883a). On January 17, musicians' guild president José María Velásquez, a member of the music delegation, submitted a proposal for setting up the orchestras, which was quickly accepted on January 20 by the commission (Guzmán 1883a; Velásquez 1883).

The very serious problem that the musical delegation faced was where to find enough well-trained musicians, orchestras, and bands to meet the program's packed schedule of performances as well as Guzmán Blanco's desire to showcase a modern Venezuela. Although the government could recruit the Federal District's military band and bugle and drum band, there was a problem. As Andrés Level reported on January 29 to the members of the commission, President Guzmán Blanco believed that Caracas's martial band was not worthy of the centennial celebrations (Level 1883b). To avoid risking the disapproval of the president, the commission turned to Dr. Pedro Ramos, a renowned lawyer and musician in Caracas,[1] and requested that he, along with Velásquez, make arrangements to correct the deficiency. On February 24, Ramos presented a proposal co-authored with Federico Villena outlining the organization of orchestras for the ten-day program (Ramos and Villena 1883).

Ramos's proposal not only created a plan for preparing bands and orchestras but also identified renowned composers and the works he commissioned from them. Indeed, many of those he named were the Romantic-era greats of Venezuela's musical history and the first who tied national pride to classical music. Ramos's proposal included the first mention of Federico Villena in the centennial materials. Villena, a composer who was later to develop an important career in Caracas in the 1880s and 1890s, was then commissioned to deal with the bands and to write an allegorical composition to be interpreted during the apotheosis ceremony. In addition to Villena, the musical delegation recruited other nationally and internationally prominent Venezuelan composers to compose works especially for the centennial. Teresa Carreño, a child prodigy who became an international sensation as a pianist, singer, composer, and conductor, created "Himno a Bolívar" (Calcaño 2001). Manuel Azpúrua, renowned for his waltzes, composed "Gran fantasía militar," and Jesús María Suárez, another prominent composer and a member of the Music Academy at the Fine Arts Institute, contributed his "Himno marcial" (Quintana 1998). Unfortunately, most of these works have been lost.

The musical repertoire was so important to President Guzmán that he intervened personally by attempting to recruit prestigious foreign orchestras, which itself triggered a budgetary crisis and a quick reaction from Pedro Ramos. In a report signed by Undersecretary Pedro Sotillo on March 27, Sotillo states that President Guzmán had entered into discussions with Fermín Toledo, president of the Concert Association of Puerto Rico. Toledo had offered to move to Caracas along with his orchestra to take part in the festivities. The report emphasized that Toledo was a prestigious musician, as a member of the Royal Academy of Fine Arts of San Fernando and laureate student of the Royal Conservatory of Music, both in Madrid (Sotillo 1883). Toledo's orchestra consisted of sixty-five *profesores* (the designation for orchestral musicians) and had a wide and select repertoire. Guzmán, who had expressed doubts about the quality of his own government's military bands, evidently wanted to hire an internationally recognized orchestra to brighten the musical offering.

In an apparent attempt to ward off the prospect of a costly foreign orchestra at a national commemoration, Pedro Ramos developed a counterstrategy. The day after Guzmán's conversations with Toledo, on March 28, Ramos, who presumably had heard about the negotiations with the Puerto Rican orchestra, sent a letter to the minister of the interior. In it Ramos reported that he had created a new budget that offered some ingenious solutions designed to reduce the costs (Ramos 1883). Ramos, in the first instance, asserted that it would only take an average of thirty-five *profesores* to set up a national orchestra, as he planned to recruit a large number of amateur musicians. In addition, he informed the minister of the interior that for the interpretation of Villena's composition, a chorus of twenty voices and some members of the martial band could be used. The band would, of course, perform for free (or as part of their military duties) because the government could require their participation.

The success of Ramos's plan depended heavily on the figure of the "amateur musician," a peculiarity of the nineteenth-century musical world.

Music was a very important component of nineteenth-century Venezuelan education. Numerous references to schools included music as a mandatory part of their curricula; some even had their own orchestras, among them the Colegio Independencia,[2] founded in Caracas in the early 1830s (Calcaño 2001). In addition, female education in the schools routinely included mandatory musical subjects. Guzmán Blanco's Decree of Free and Mandatory Public Instruction of 1870 was an initiative to expand primary education that called upon the federal government to create and fund a federal system of primary education schools, among which were many schools dedicated to the education of girls. These schools maintained a tradition of including music as an obligatory subject. As a result, in 1883, the city had a remarkable number of good amateur musicians.

Ramos's cost-saving proposal to call on amateur musicians was approved by the commission, and the offer from the Puerto Rico Concert Society was finally rejected. The argument presented by Antonio Leocadio Guzmán and now part of the historical record was the high cost of the Puerto Ricans in contrast to local musicians: "Measures were taken to organize the Centennial orchestras plus various gentlemen and ladies of this city have gladly agreed to celebrate some concerts" (Guzmán 1883b). In addition, on June 22, several bands from the provinces expressed their willingness to travel to Caracas to reinforce the martial band (Salas 1883).

As for the repertoire, we know that the Foreign Ministry asked the invited nations to submit their respective national anthems and any allegorical compositions they considered relevant. The latter were a remarkable success, as the embassies of Brazil, Colombia, Paraguay, and Belgium flattered Venezuela with works by their most prominent composers written especially for the occasion. These works, together with those by Venezuelan composers, contributed to creating a repertoire tailored to the centennial and thus relieved the urgent need for adequate music demanded by the program. Thus, by early July, everything seemed to be going smoothly toward the realization of the festivities.

The Apotheosis

As recorded by Ramón Hurtado Sánchez (1883), the official chronicler of the centennial, the planned events for the ten days of festivities unfolded successfully, and music functioned to forge social harmony and cohesion at all occasions. The reconciliation agreement between the Church and Guzmán Blanco was symbolically sealed on July 23 at nine o'clock in the morning when a battalion of the Presidential Guard accompanied by their band marched from the Government House to the doors of the cathedral. The band played the national anthem while the president, his cabinet, and the diplomatic corps entered the Catedral Metropolitana.[3] Another symbolic reconciliation occurred the same day when a statue of Francisco de Miranda was unveiled with great fanfare in the square facing the Panteón. Miranda, who preceded Bolívar in the campaign for independence, was betrayed by Bolívar with the help of other patriots; they arrested Miranda in 1812 and handed him over to Spanish authorities. This event, considered one of the darkest pages in Bolívar's biography, was adroitly handled by the Centennial Commission by placing the statue of Miranda only a few feet away from the Liberator's remains, with enough proximity to suggest the revolutionary continuity yet not too much to disturb their spirits (Salcedo Bastardo 1997).

In the opening hours of the ceremonies, the military band asserted the predominance of Guzmán's regime over the Church, with music representing Guzmán's good governance as generating abundance and benevolence. At the end of the day the government offered the people of Caracas a popular feast in an outdoor esplanade at the San Carlos fortress near the Panteón. Twenty head of cattle were slaughtered for the occasion, and during the banquet a band and an orchestra entertained the populace (*Presupuesto* 1883). President Guzmán Blanco attended the feast, shared the meal, and enjoyed music with the people (Hurtado Sánchez 1883). For Hurtado Sánchez, the feast was symbolic because it reminded him how the armies camped outdoors and took their meals during the Independence War. In his closing comments about the banquet, Hurtado emphasizes the government's message of social unity and the role of music in bringing it about: "Everything here is harmony and brotherhood, bands and the orchestra cheer up the feast, and the Government is today the inseparable friend of the people" (53).

Contemporary newspapers and other chroniclers reported on subsequent events and the role of the musical program in adding ceremonial flourish and generating national pride in the secularized Bolivarian cult. By all accounts, the planned program for the second day, July 24, also went smoothly. *El Siglo* (Caracas) reported on July 27, 1883, that a salvo of artillery was the signal for the huge entourage to meet in the west wing of the capitol. Eighteen groups representing the country's industries, commerce, arts, sciences, and public workers marched downtown with the flags of the republics of the Americas (Guardia 1883). The program required the band to perform five marches during crucial moments of the parade: the departure of the entourage from the capitol, the arrival at the presidential residence, the entrance to the Panteón Nacional, the departure from the Panteón, and the arrival at Plaza Bolívar. *La Opinión Nacional* of August 4, 1883, reported that Villena selected five scores for this purpose: "El Libertador," "Fiesta nacional," "Bocaccio," "Alegraos pueblos," and "Saludos al Presidente—Honor al Mérito." Two orchestras completed the musical offering, one inside the Panteón and another next to the statue of the Liberator in Plaza Bolívar. This method of using a band performance to mark the major landmarks of a procession is typical of Holy Week festivities and is still practiced in many cities in Latin America and Spain.

After leaving the Panteón and returning to Plaza Bolívar, the delegations made an offering to the statue, and the parade concluded. At eight o'clock at night the apotheosis began at the Teatro Municipal with a selection of works by Verdi, Donizetti, Bellini, and Mozart (Hurtado Sánchez 1883), a clear sign of how deeply rooted the love for opera was at the time. To close the concert the work *El Centenario* by Villena was performed. The score required a huge and innovative composition for the martial band, the band of bugles and drums, and a chorus of mixed voices.

This is the first documented instance of the use of multiband templates in Venezuela, a programming coordination that metaphorically represents unity. In 1886 Villena wrote a work of the same nature entitled *Batalla de Carabobo* intended for three military bands, a drum and bugle band, an orchestra, a mixed choir, and four soloists (Villena 1886).[4] Other contemporary composers wrote works in this format. The modality could be defined as patriotic program music, with musical programs that integrate bands, orchestras, and voices to show the sophistication and prestige that bands had reached by then. Merging bands from the military world with orchestras, choirs, and soloists associated with opera and theater is also symbolic of the union of military and civil domains and a clear reference to the ruling classes consolidated during Guzmán's era. The principal example of this notion, quoted in the epigraph, is "Himno para el Centenario." The score has not been located yet in any archive; however, we have the lyrics, in which an anonymous author synthesizes the centennial message.

Musicologists hold out Federico Villena as an exceptional figure during the republican era (1830–1900), when most composers were considered amateurs with little technical training (Calcaño 2001, 319). During much of the twentieth century it was assumed that the Venezuelan musical life of the nineteenth century had been decadent and not up to date relative to Europe. This strongly Eurocentric view was shared by, among others, José Antonio Calcaño and Juan Bautista Plaza, who are today regarded as founders of national musicology. We have overcome this prejudice since research over the past thirty years has shown a nineteenth-century Venezuela of intense musical activity and has deepened our understanding of the complex and rich Venezuelan musical life of that time.

Conclusion

Guzmán Blanco's administration managed to consolidate the Bolivarian cult through the centennial festivities and establish Blanco as the high priest. As a close analysis of the centennial's planning documents, program, and contemporary reviews shows, the organizers produced a dramatic musical proposal whose purpose was to support the ritual and liturgical component for what has since become the official religion of Venezuela. The government made use of music as a fundamental tool for the transmission of its message. This message had two versions and two recipients. The first variant had a domestic target; it came to associate the image of Bolívar with Guzmán, who proclaimed his administration the achievement of the Liberator's dream. As Guzmán Blanco declared in a speech on January 1, 1883, at the Federal Palace, "It is providential that Venezuela will submit to the Liberator as an offering of love, a republic such as he had dreamed and conceived and struggled to achieve. The Republic we have today and [that] we bring to the Centennial was the heavenly vision of the Liberator" (in Castellanos 1983). This view of the unfinished independence and the accomplishment of the Bolivarian dream has been consistently used since then throughout Venezuelan history by the political leadership. The second variant of the message has an external target that might be called "the international community." It tells the world that Venezuela has been pacified and has resolved its internal problems and now is headed down the road to self-development and to adding its own voice to the concert of nations. The most visible icon of progress and unity was the railroad. In Guzmán Blanco's speech on July 24, 1883, at the Panteón Nacional, he famously claimed that Bolívar, looking into the future, contemplated "this country constituted, organized, and prosperous, celebrating its centenary with the opening of railways, as clear evidence that we are already on the horizons illuminated by the sun of a truly great civilization" (in Castellanos 1983, 233).

Although this speech by Guzmán Blanco is etched in Venezuelan memory while the centennial's musical repertoire has largely been lost, music elevated the national spirit and provided the symbolic language for the Bolivarian cult with its vision of a heroic past and utopian future. Ramón Hurtado Sánchez, the official chronicler, must have been aware of the important role that music played in the government's strategy, when a few pages before concluding his chronicle, full of musical references, he affords himself a romantic consideration: "Without music any celebration would be mute and charmless: the word dignifies, it is true, but music is the language of the soul and expresses its expansion" (1883, 86).

Notes

The epigraph is my translation of the anonymous 1883 "Himno para el Centenario del Libertador," archived in Caracas at the Archivo General de la Nación, sección Centenario del Libertador (hereafter referred to as AGN SCL), legajo 3, folio 60r.

1. Venezuelan lawyers are addressed with the courtesy title "Dr." The "musician lawyer" was common in nineteenth-century Venezuela, the most emblematic being Felipe Larrazábal (1816–73), lawyer, politician, journalist, virtuoso pianist, and composer. He was a founding member of the Liberal Party, a judge of the Federal High Court, founder of several newspapers, a biographer of Bolívar, and composer of *Trio in A Major, for Violin, Cello, and Piano*. This work was the most representative work of the Venezuelan chamber music repertoire throughout the nineteenth century.

2. Guzmán Blanco himself and Felipe Larrazábal attended this school (Straka 2010).

3. The national anthem was an old patriotic song from the times of the Independence War that was officially decreed by Guzmán Blanco in 1881.

4. The Battle of Carabobo was the military action that definitively sealed the

independence of Venezuela in 1821. Its grand celebration on June 24, 1886, during the acclamation period, allowed Guzmán's administration to establish the current Venezuelan patriotic holiday calendar: April 19, June 24, July 5, July 24, and December 17.

References

Aponte, Pedro Rafael. 2009. "The Invention of the National in Venezuelan Art Music, 1920–1960." PhD diss., University of Pittsburgh. http://d-scholarship.pitt.edu/10289/.

Arráiz Lucca, Rafael. 2007. *Venezuela 1830 a nuestros días.* Caracas: Alfa.

Attali, Jacques. 1995. *Ruidos, ensayo sobre la economía política de la música.* Mexico City: Siglo XXI.

Calcaño, J. A. 2001. *La ciudad y su música.* Caracas: Ediciones de la Biblioteca de la Universidad Central de Venezuela.

Carrera Damas, Germán. 2008. *El culto a Bolívar: Esbozo para un estudio de la historia de las ideas en Venezuela.* 6th edition. Caracas: Alfa.

Castellanos, Rafael Ramón. 1983. *Caracas en el Centenario del Libertador.* Caracas: Congreso de la República.

Castillo Lara, Lucas G. 1998. *Personajes y sucesos venezolanos en el Archivo Secreto Vaticano (siglo XIX).* Caracas: Academia Nacional de la Historia.

Centenario de Bolívar. 1883. Caracas: Imprenta al Vapor de la Opinión Nacional.

Fernández Heres, Rafael. 1997. "Agustín Aveledo." In *Diccionario de historia de Venezuela,* 1:314. Caracas: Fundación de Empresas Polar.

Fundación Polar. 1997. *Diccionario de historia de Venezuela.* 2nd edition. Caracas: Fundación Empresas Polar.

Guardia, H. M. de la. 1883. *El primer Centenario del Libertador en Caracas.* Caracas: Imprenta Editorial.

Guillen, Y., A. Medina, and T. Quintero. 2008. *Noticias musicales en el diario La Opinión Nacional.* Caracas: Universidad Central de Venezuela.

Guzmán, Antonio Leocadio. 1883a. *Al ciudadano José Maria Velásquez,* January 20. AGN SCL, folder 1.

———. 1883b. *Ciudadano Ministro de Relaciones Exteriores,* June 15. AGN SCL, folder 4.

Hurtado Sánchez, Ramón. 1883. *Las fiestas del primer Centenario del Libertador Simón Bolívar.* Caracas: Imprenta Editorial.

Level, Andrés. 1883a. *Memorándum para el Ilustre Prócer Antonio Leocadio Guzmán,* January 6. AGN SCL, folder 1, folios 47RV, 48RV, 49RV, 50R.

———. 1883b. *Memorándum para el Ilustre Prócer Antonio Leocadio Guzmán,* January 29. AGN SCL, folder 1, folios 24R, 24V, 25R.

López Maya, Juan de Dios. 2008. "*El Río de las Siete Estrellas* de Evencio Castellanos: Una visión política de la historia de Venezuela." Review. *Musicaenclave* 2, no. 2 (May–August). http://www.musicaenclave.com/vol-2-2-mayo-agosto-2008/.

Pino Iturrieta, Elías. 2006. *El Divino Bolívar.* 3rd edition. Caracas: Alfa.

Plaza, Juan Bautista. 1965. "La música colonial venezolana al dia con la europea." *Revista Nacional de Cultura* 27:45–49.

Presupuesto para el Banquete Popular, July 18, 1883, AGN SCL, folder 4, folio 7R.

Quintana, Hugo J., ed. 1998. *La lira venezolana.* Caracas: Fundación Vicente Emilio Sojo.

Ramos, Pedro. 1883. *Sr. Ministro de R.R.,* March 28. AGN SCL, folder 3, three unpaginated folios.

La Revista. 1872. "Crónica: Fiestas del 28 de octubre de 1872." October 30, pp. 63–65.

Ramos, Pedro, and Federico Villena. 1883. *Al Señor Presidente de la Junta del Centenario del Libertador,* February 20. AGN SCL, folder 2, folios 3RV, 4RV, 5R.

Salas, José Antonio. 1883. *Ciudadano Ministro de Relaciones Interiores,* June 2. AGN SCL, folder 4, folio w/n.

Salcedo Bastardo, José Luis. 1997. "Francisco de Miranda." In *Diccionario de Historia de Venezuela,* 3:173–79. Caracas: Fundación de Empresas Polar.

Sotillo, Pedro. 1883. *Informe,* March 27. AGN SCL, folder 2, folios 14R, 15R.

Straka, Tomás. 2010. *Instauración de la República Liberal Autocrática.* Caracas: Fundación Rómulo Betancourt.

Sujo Volsky, Jeannine. 1997. "Arístides Rojas." In *Diccionario de Historia de Venezuela,* 3:985–86. Caracas: Fundación de Empresas Polar.

Toro, Fermín. 1843. *Descripción de los honores fúnebres consagrados a los restos del libertador Simón Bolívar.* Caracas: Imprenta de Valentín Espinal.

Velásquez, José María. 1883. *Gremio de Músicos,* January 17. AGN SCL, folder 1.

Villena, Federico. *Batalla de Carabobo: Himno a la caridad en honor a San Vicente de Paul.* Manuscript score. Biblioteca Nacional de Venezuela, Caracas.

Zawisza, Leszek M. 1997. "Panteón Nacional." In *Diccionario de Historia de Venezuela,* 3:488–89. Caracas: Fundación de Empresas Polar.

5

The Birth of the Myth

The Liberals and the Cult of Bolívar (1840–1900)

TOMÁS STRAKA

The most solemn moment in the history of the Apoteosis de Bolívar (1883), a civic festivity commemorating the transfer of Bolívar's remains to the Panteón Nacional,[1] was, at the same time, the most democratic. An old Afro-American woman who had been born a slave placed a wreath over the grave of Simón Bolívar, the most famous of her masters. She was more than a hundred years old and for the first time in her life wearing shoes and an elegant dress. At the last minute she was about to faint. Then the aide-de-camp of General Antonio Guzmán Blanco took her by the hand (Esteller Camacho y Clemente 1928). That episode would become a legend. The image of high-ranking officers helping a former slave made a deep impression among the diplomats, politicians, officers, and priests who attended the ceremony. Thus the former slave Matea Bolívar, whose birth year some claim as far back as 1765 (d. 1886), became the talk of the town. Many legends arose about this episode. According to one, it was Guzmán Blanco himself who extended his hand to help her, although in fact, he assisted Matea's onetime owner and the Liberator's niece Valentina Camacho Bolívar, who was also weakened with old age, as she put her own wreath on the grave of her illustrious uncle (Castellanos 1983, 235).

In another legend, Negra Matea, as she is popularly known,[2] made a triumphal entry into Panteón Nacional arm in arm with Guzmán Blanco, while the truth was that by that time she could no longer walk and the president sent for her in a landau. The historical consensus concerning stories of Matea's participation in the Apotheosis and in the earlier inauguration of the Panteón on October 28, 1876, is that they had a propagandistic function intended both as a populist symbol and a way to legitimize Guzmán Blanco's regime. Although she supposedly had been the governess of the Liberator, he never mentions her in any document, causing historians to question not so much whether she was a slave of the Bolívar family but whether she was his nurse. In any case, Guzmán Blanco's propaganda was effective: in Venezuelan historical memory Matea became the nanny par excellence of Bolívar. Her fame has even supplanted that of Hipólita Bolívar ("my mother Hipólita," in words of the Liberator), about whom there is abundant documentary evidence.

It is not my purpose here to ascertain the historicity of Negra Matea. If we recall this episode it is because we consider it an emblematic example of the Bolivarianism promoted by the Liberal Party, renamed the Great Yellow Liberal Party as of 1870. My aim here is to show that in order to build a nation-state, the Liberals introduced one set of memory politics (a kind of *mutatis mutandis*, or *Vergangenheitspolitik*)[3] in which the cult of Bolívar played a central role. Likewise, the party also sought a source of legitimacy in history by trying to show that its program was the continuation of the Bolivarian project. Venezuelan Liberals' idea of the Bolivarian project was different from that of the Colombian Conservative Party, which used the memory of the Liberator to promote its agenda (Melo 2008). Indeed, although the Venezuelan Liberals had in general unfriendly relations with the Colombian Conservatives, both groups claimed to be heirs of Bolívar. This demonstrates that the multiple uses and manipulations of the image of Simón Bolívar by different and even opposing political groups in Latin America had already started in the nineteenth century. The Venezuelan Liberals created the Bolivarian political historicism before they came to power, and once in power they turned this historicism into state policy. Most of the symbols, values, and images of Bolívar that persist in Venezuelan culture were produced from the 1840s, when the party was founded, until 1913, when Juan Vicente Gómez broke with the last remaining members of the party in his administration.

Liberal Historiography and the Birth of Historicism

The history written by politicians, journalists, and historians of the Liberal Party is known in Venezuela as Liberal historiography. Its authors, such as

Francisco González Guinán, Laureano Villanueva, Rafael Villavicencio, Luis Level de Goda, brothers Felipe and Miguel Tejera, José María Rojas, and even his brother Arístides generated a version of Venezuelan history focused on justifying the thesis of the Liberal Party. In effect, the Liberals had to convince Venezuelans of the need for and the legitimacy of their program and reforms, such as the secularization of society, promotion of foreign investments, and enactment of a modern legal code. For that purpose they elaborated a historical discourse based on their ideas about the past, society, and the people of Venezuela. It was a discourse that expressed the typical convictions of the Creole elites in Latin America in the middle of the nineteenth century: the idea of progress, the superiority of North Atlantic culture ("civilization," as they claim), and subsequently the superiority of the white race over mestizo, Indian, and Afro-descent peoples. They sought to transform Venezuela into a "European" nation with the values of a modern citizenry and a capitalist economic system.

In this context, independence was reinterpreted according to Liberal ideology. In the 1820s the first Liberals of Caracas began to attribute independence with the aim of establishing a system of political and economic liberties encompassing freedom of religion, federalism, and civilian control of the military. While not entirely accurate, they established a link between the Liberal Party and the Padres de la Patria (Fathers of the Homeland), or Próceres (Independence Heroes). Thus, independence became not only the foundational legend of the nation but also the origin of the Liberal project. When positivism replaced romanticism in the 1880s, those emerging ideas gave Liberals a new impetus. Their generation, inspired by the emerging social sciences, concluded that independence and liberalism were manifestations of the laws of history, which pushed society toward progress. For example, in 1900, in his investiture speech at the National Academy of History, Rafael Villavicencio gave a lecture about order and progress as the two forces that move history. Villavicencio said Liberals were the promoters of progress and that in Venezuela this started in 1811, when the country became an independent republic. At that time, it enacted a "system of popular government, republican, federal, representative, alternative, and responsible," in other words, "a masterpiece of liberalism" (1900/1966, 51). The Liberal Party thus claimed to be the continuation of independence.

Bolívar is the emblematic case of this type of historical—and political—discourse. By 1825 he was president of Colombia (known as Gran Colombia in the historiography of the twentieth century), dictator of Peru, and protector of Bolivia (then named the Republic of Bolívar). He ruled from Potosí to Panama, and the cult of his personality was already emerging. In Caracas he had been named "the Liberator" in 1814. The early liberal groups of Bogotá and Caracas of the 1820s—opponents of Bolívar's centralism and presidentialism—as well as European liberal thinkers like Jeremy Bentham and Benjamin Constant accused him of wanting to become another Napoleon (Aguirre Elorriaga 1941; Filippi 1983; Guerrero 2005; Parra Pérez 1957).

Nowadays several historians maintain that Bolívar was more republican than liberal or that he was the father of Latin American conservatism (Straka 2010; Urueña Cervera 2006). The Conservative Party of Colombia has claimed him as its founder even though Mariano Ospina Rodríguez, its actual founder, was part of the anti-Bolivarian conspiracy of 1828. In any case, the theses of the Conservative Party are very similar to those ideas Bolívar held at the end of his life when he advocated for order, centralism, and an alliance with the Church. Meanwhile, in Venezuela, the memory of the Liberator took on other significations. The relationship with the Father of the Homeland was traumatic for Venezuelans because they rejected the union with Gran Colombia and many of Bolívar's political ideas, such as his centralism and his proposal of a presidency for life, but at same time they were proud of his military triumphs, power, and fame. The reconciliation with him started in 1833, when Juan Vicente González, considered the most important author of Venezuelan romanticism, began publishing emotional homages and articles about Bolívar in the newspapers, especially on his name day, October 28, the saint day of Saint Simon. October 28 was celebrated as a patriotic holiday until the 1940s, after which the holiday was moved to Bolívar's birthday, July 24.

Indeed, when the fall of coffee prices produced an economic and political crisis in 1840, the Venezuelan elite divided into two parties, and the name of Bolívar came back into the political arena (Pino Iturieta 1993). One group organized the Liberal Party around *El Venezolano,* a newspaper directed by Antonio Leocadio Guzmán. The other group began to be called the Conservative Party by the Liberals. The ideological differences between the two parties were less than in other places in Latin America, particularly in Colombia. Many historians argue that there was no difference between the two parties, but this is not strictly true. The Liberal Party had a democratic discourse—popular education, universal suffrage, the sale of public lands—and defended the idea of revolution, the abolition of slavery, federalism, state intervention in the economy through promoting policies, immigration, foreign investment, and secularization. The Conservatives postulated a market economy, the careful separation of powers, and gradual change.

It is not surprising that the majority of Venezuelans were liberal, in particular *castas,* as people of color were called in the colonial regime; in contrast, businessmen, a new bourgeoisie born of the capitalist reforms of the 1820s and 1830s, and the former nobility, who lost their titles under the republic as of 1811, in general were conservative. This social division was very significant in a country that had suffered the worst racial war in South America, the Guerra de Colores (War of Colors), the name given to the racial war that occurred in the context of the Independence War, especially in 1812–14, and one of bloodiest in the Caribbean. Thus, the Liberal discourse divided Venezuelan citizens into two groups: *el pueblo* (the people) versus the *oligarquía* (oligarchy). In Liberals' version of history, the oligarchy was heir to colonial values in opposition to progress, while Liberals were heirs to independence. A summary of Liberal ideas can be read in the 1893 "Manifiesto del Partido Liberal a la nación" (Manifesto of the Liberal Party to the nation), which synthesizes the major theses of this group (Partido Liberal 1893/1960).

Antonio Leocadio Guzmán (1801–84) was a major figure in forming the Venezuelan Liberal Party's discourse and agenda. His father was a Spanish officer, and for that reason, during the War of Independence he studied in Spain, where he witnessed the Spanish Liberal Revolution of 1820. In 1822, he returned to Venezuela and quickly joined the Liberal group opposed to the union between Venezuela and Gran Colombia. The historian Elena Plaza has called this movement "liberal separatism" (2011). On one side, it opposed the formation of Gran Colombia and particularly the authority of Vice President Francisco de Paula Santander despite his liberalism. On the other hand, it promoted a radical program of reforms: federalism, more freedom for the press, religious tolerance, and civilian control of the military. In the following years, Guzmán was a separatist; later he went to Peru to offer a crown to Bolívar. In that country he was a secretary to the Liberator; he then returned to Caracas as a Bolivarian. During the so-called Cosiata rebellion against Gran Colombia's centralized authority in Bogotá in 1826 led by José Antonio Páez, Guzmán was again a separatist; when Venezuela finally separated from Colombia, he served as a minister for Páez. Notwithstanding that affiliation, Guzmán broke with the government in 1840.

Guzmán probably held the same admiration for Bolívar as most Venezuelans did, meaning admiration for his deeds but not for many of his ideas. However, there were other reasons to be Bolivarian—powerful reasons—that motivated his break with Páez in 1840. José Antonio Páez was the head of what was then called the Conservative Party. He had been the main caudillo in Venezuela since 1820, and between 1826 and 1830 he led its separation from Colombia, becoming a symbol of anti-Bolivarianism. That image has persisted until today. Hugo Chávez in his *Aló Presidente* television program of October 25, 2009, systematically accused Páez of betrayal. Because by 1840 Páez was popular for his acts of heroism, battles won, and other adventures, the Liberals needed their own legend to oppose him, motivating Guzmán to reclaim the image and memory of Bolívar.

Guzmán was part of a new literary wave praising Bolívar in the discourse of the Liberal Party. Juan Vicente González, who was also a founder of the party, launched this new wave. Indeed, in 1842, *El Venezolano* collected and published his articles about Bolívar in a volume entitled *Mis exequias a Bolívar* (My last rites for Bolívar). This book is considered a milestone in building the Bolivarian cult. Although González soon separated from the Liberal Party to become the main propagandist of the Conservatives, his forms of Bolivarianism—such as celebration of the October 28 Saint Simón name day—remained the domain of the Liberals (see López Maya in this volume). Felipe Larrazábal, another romantic writer, musician, and historian, also joined the Liberal Party. Years later he would edit *Correspondencia general del Libertador Simón Bolívar* (1865), considered the first great biography about the hero. The book also became important in building the cult of the Liberator not only because it made accessible unknown or little-known documents but also because its romantic and emotive style appealed to many Venezuelans. Similarly, Guzmán wrote several historical articles in which he exalted the Liberator and, not coincidentally, highlighted his own relationship with him. In an effort to promote the links between Bolívar and the Liberal Party, Guzmán foregrounded his brief service as a secretary to Bolívar. In 1873, the Congress even awarded Guzmán the title of Ilustre Prócer (Illustrious Hero) normally reserved for veterans of the Independence War.

González, Larrazábal, Guzmán, and other writers who imitated these masters (as discussed more fully in Harwich Vallenilla 1988), generated and perpetuated a set of literary titles and images. For these writers Bolívar was a man sent by Providence: the clairvoyant of Casacoima, the Venezuelan town where Bolívar had a vision of the future as chronicled by González; the visionary of El Chimborazo, the Andean peak where Bolívar spoke with Chronos and had another prophetic moment described in a probably apocryphal poem nevertheless attributed to him, "Mi delirio sobre el Chimborazo"; the Prophet of Jamaica; the invincible man of Pativilca, or "the patient of Pativilca," the Peruvian town where Bolívar contracted malaria yet, according to the exhortatory legend of his gallantry and courage, insisted on pursuing his campaign, "To Triumph!"; as well as the classical hero of the Crossing of the Andes and other such appellations. However, even when Bolívar was alive, the cult of his personality was already important; his followers called him "the second Washington," "the Sun of Colombia," and even "Simon Maccabeus" in reference to the Old Testament leader of Judea.

In the same way as the U.S. and French Revolutions imitated ancient Greece and Rome, the founding fathers of Latin America imitated the neoclassical style of these revolutionaries. The next generation inherited the neoclassical forms and combined them with the values of romanticism. At the same time, during the first half of the nineteenth century, a guiding national principle that Luis Castro Leiva (2005) has called "Bolivarian historicism" also emerged, characterizing the Liberator's thinking as irrevocable law that should be obeyed by every Venezuelan citizen. Therefore, the legitimacy of any political agenda or movement, cultural values, and even Venezuela's national existence depended upon a discursive relation to Bolivarian ideas, even as their ideological signification was contingent upon the power that interprets them.

The Creation of National Symbols

The move from Bolivarianism as a cult of a few political groups to an official national cult was relatively quick. The first step was Bolívar's symbolic return to Venezuela. In 1842, the Liberator's remains were transferred from Santa Marta, Colombia, to Caracas, providing an opportunity to seal Bolívar's reconciliation with his homeland. For this important occasion the Páez government modeled its ceremony on the *retour des cendres* (return of ashes), as the spectacular return of Napoleon's remains and his burial in

Paris in 1840 was called (Castillo Herrera 2012; Pérez Rancel 2002; Salvador González 2001). Although Páez suggested repatriating Bolívar's remains as early as 1833, the fact that Liberals were using his memory for their propaganda probably accelerated this return. Germán Carrera Damas has shown that since that moment in 1842, the Liberator has been an essential element of national unity (2013, 52–57). Nevertheless, the official cult of Bolívar had to wait until the Liberals came to power in 1848 to become state policy.

The transformation of the cult of Bolívar into official policy was contingent upon the Liberal Party's rise to power. In 1846 José Tadeo Monagas, an independence hero and important caudillo of eastern Venezuela, won the elections. He had been supported by Páez in a conflictive context. A peasant rebellion had broken out in support of Antonio Leocadio Guzmán, candidate of the Liberal Party. Quickly Páez defeated the uprising, and Guzmán—who in fact did not organize the rebellion—was charged with conspiracy and jailed. However, once in power, Monagas rapidly broke with Páez and made an alliance with the Liberals. Guzmán was pardoned and released. But not only that—Monagas soon appointed Guzmán as minister of internal affairs and justice and in 1849 promoted him to vice president. During the ten years following Guzmán's promotion, several key elements of the Liberal political platform were enacted into law, including the abolition of slavery, the sale of public lands, and state control over the interest on loans. In 1858, when Monagas reformed the constitution in order to stay in power, all political classes—Liberals and Conservatives—rejected Monagas's dictatorial move and came together into what became known as a *fusión* to overthrow his government that same year.

However, the problems had just started; the alliance had a short life and began what became more than a decade of civil wars, the longest of which was the Federal War from 1859 to 1864. In those years the republic almost disappeared, the economy was in ruins, some regions attempted to secede from the union, and the social and racial issues of the Guerra de Colores returned to the fore. In the end, the Liberals took power and initiated the reconstruction of the country on new foundations. When they won the Federal War in 1864 and tried to establish a democratic and federal regime, the new president, Juan Crisóstomo Falcón, was unable to control the regional caudillos, and his government fell in 1868. Two years later, in 1870, Antonio Guzmán Blanco, son of Liberal Party founder Antonio Leocadio Guzmán, subdued Caracas by forging a great alliance of caudillos. Thereafter, he remained the main caudillo of Venezuela and ruled for twenty years as dictator, initiating a Liberal revolution.

No previous Venezuelan leader had accumulated as much power as Guzmán Blanco. Endowed by the Congress with the title Ilustre Americano (Illustrious American), Guzmán Blanco launched a regime that was both fiercely authoritarian and politically revolutionary. To assert his dominance, Guzmán Blanco erected statues of himself, renamed plazas and buildings in his honor, placed his portrait in all public buildings, printed official publications with his image, and, in short, promoted a cult of personality. At the same time, he imprisoned, banished, and even executed his political enemies. He also sought to incorporate Venezuela into the capitalist system, helped to raise the wealth of the rising bourgeoisie, attracted investment, modernized the legal code, increased public works, diminished the social role of the Church, improved the educational system, and so made efforts to build a modern nation-state. Venezuela thus went through a Liberal revolution under Guzmán Blanco's rule, the impact of which continued for a century and a half. Finally, the ideological uses of history that González, Larrazábal, Guzmán, and other literary liberals initiated developed into a real politics of memory under Guzmán Blanco. His regime infused the Liberal historiography into Venezuelan culture at all levels and in closely interlinked systems: the historiography published by the state, the fine arts academies, the school system, the press, public holidays, and national propaganda. As a result, his regime created a systemic national imaginary that remains to this day.

In his speeches Guzmán Blanco consistently linked himself to Bolívar. Every time he inaugurated a public work—a square, a statue, a bridge, a railway—or enacted a new law, he claimed he was continuing Bolívar's project. Throughout his regime Guzmán Blanco characterized himself and liberalism as championing an independence ethos while his enemies continued the old colonial order. In 1870, Guzmán Blanco stated, "Since 1840, Venezuela has been divided into two parties, one of which has been fighting for liberty, while the other is armed with its authority. This [latter] party is heir to the colonial order, and the other is the child of the republic; the first party walks toward the future, the second is anchored in the past" (265).

The climactic point of Guzmán Blanco's Bolivarianism was the centennial of the Liberator's birth, which was commemorated in 1883 with a landmark celebration known as the Apotheosis. Throughout the country there were balls, speeches, parades, fireworks, and even bullfights in tribute to Bolívar. At the same time, the government inaugurated the Caracas–La Guaira railway line, at that moment the most extensive engineering project in the country's history, as well as the electrification of the Palacio Federal and its surrounding neighborhoods and the first telephone lines in Caracas. The festivities included an exhibition modeled on World Fairs held in London and elsewhere; the aim was to display Venezuela's industrial and cultural achievements (Calzadilla, Dávila, and Galindo 2009).

For Guzmán Blanco the festivities were an opportunity to propagandize his government and his personality as worthy of the Liberator. The centennial commemorative medal presented overlapping profiles of Guzmán Blanco and Bolívar as though they were standing side by side gazing together into a shared vision of Venezuela's future. In his speech on July 24, 1883, Guzmán Blanco proclaimed, "[When] Bolívar was at El Chimborazo, at the depths of despair, looking toward the future, what he contemplated at the end of the century was this Fatherland, rebuilt, organized, and prosperous, celebrating his Centenary even as the inauguration of the railways makes evident, that we are entering horizons illuminated by the Sun of a truly great civilization" (1883/2001, 201). With rhetorical flourishes pronounced as part of official functions that then became ritualized into annual events, Guzmán Blanco marshaled Bolivarian historicism in the service of legitimizing the Liberal regime.

The Guzmanato, as his regime became known, created an entirely new iconography around Bolívar and Venezuelan history, new spaces dedicated to the cult of Bolívar, and even new historical figures such as Negra Matea. In 1872, Guzmán Blanco inaugurated Caracas's new Palacio Federal, known as the Capitolio due to its dome, which provided an august setting for paintings narrating the official history of the nation. Initially, in 1873, Martín Tovar y Tovar, the most renowned Venezuelan painter of the time, was commissioned to produce thirty portraits of the founding fathers and the Liberal leaders Juan Crisóstomo Falcón and Guzmán Blanco (Plaza 1883), as well as subsequent commissions. In this context Tovar y Tovar painted for the Palacio Federal his best-known works, such as the monumental *Signing of the Declaration of Independence* (1883), the ceiling painting of the *Battle of Carabobo* (1887), and the canvases of the *Battle of Boyacá* and *Battle of Junín* (both in 1895). These pictures as well as the works of Arturo Michelena and Cristóbal Rojas, together known as the "great masters" of Venezuelan academicism, exerted an enormous influence on the Venezuelan imaginary.

In 1877, Guzmán Blanco inaugurated the Salón Elíptico (Oval Room) of the palace, similar to the U.S. Capitol rotunda. Tovar y Tovar became a kind of Venezuelan John Trumbull; indeed, Tovar y Tovar's *Signing of the Declaration of Independence* seems to be influenced by Trumball's *Declaration of Independence, 4 July 1776* (1826). In order to create a social imaginary of the nation and its independence, the government encouraged the study of fine arts. It not only provided grants to young painters to study in Paris but also established the Fine Arts Academy in Caracas in 1887. The Venezuelan academicians were among the best reputed in Latin America since the quality and style of their work matched the European academic artists of that time. They won prizes in Paris and achieved international renown for their portraiture.

Over the next 150 years, the images produced by Tovar y Tovar, Michelena, and others commissioned by the state have been reproduced in bills, textbooks, newspapers, lithographs, and photo engravings, effectively naturalizing the Guzmanato's Liberal historiography as Venezuelan history. Arturo Michelena's *Miranda en La Carraca* (1896), probably the most famous picture of the academy, had an enormous impact when it was unveiled in the Teatro Municipal of Caracas during the centennial apotheosis commemorating the death of the Precursor, as Francisco de Miranda is known in Venezuela. Today this picture continues as one of the most acclaimed pieces in the Galería de Arte Nacional. In the minds of many Venezuelans, this image of Miranda in La Carraca, the prison in Cádiz, Spain, where he was jailed and died in 1816, establishes both Miranda's reputation for heroism and the misery of his final days. Another remarkable image is *La muerte de Girardot en Bárbula*, a canvas painted by Cristóbal Rojas in 1883. Based upon this picture, in Venezuela the hero normally is represented as Rojas imagined him: falling on the battlefield with a flag in his hand.

The same is true for Negro Primero, the lieutenant Pedro Camejo, a former slave whose bravery brought him great fame. According to *Venezuela heroica*, a compilation of episodes of the Independence War written in epic style by Eduardo Blanco and published for the first time in 1881, Pedro Camejo died a romantic death in the Battle of Carabobo. Although Camejo did die at Carabobo, today we know that the story narrated by Blanco is in essence fictional. There is no documentary evidence of the episode he describes. In fact, recent research has shown that Blanco's narration is full of legends, fantasies, and inaccuracies (Pulido 2011). Nevertheless, the book was a popular success at the time of its publication, and schools still teach its version of the battle.

Blanco's narrative was probably the source of Tovar y Tovar's image of Camejo in the Battle of Carabobo ceiling painting, which gave a face to the legend. The image has become an icon that, like Bolívar, has been incorporated into the pantheon of the cult of María Lionza, an influential Afro-indigenous religion. Indeed, the cult's altars represent Camejo just as Tovar y Tovar painted him. The same cult depicts another Afro-Venezuelan who died fighting against the Spanish, Negro Felipe, but rather than any claims to historical exactitude, Negro Felipe is represented with the same face and uniform as Negro Primero except that Negro Felipe's coat is black rather than red. The representations of Bolívar, Negro Primero, Negro Felipe, and other revolutionary figures in the María Lionza cult and other forms of popular culture have been analyzed elsewhere and are beyond the scope of this study (Ríos 2013; Salas de Lecuna 1987; Torres 2009). Certainly, Tovar y Tovar's depiction of Negro Primero in the Carabobo painting and thus official history was a gesture of recognition to people of color, as was Negra Matea's participation in the Bolívar Apotheosis festivities.

But the images and historical figures created by the artists and propagandists Guzmán Blanco commissioned were not the only contributions of his *Vergangeheitspolitik* to the national symbols of Venezuela (Martín Frechilla 1999). In 1872, Guzmán Blanco ordered the reconstruction of Caracas's Plaza Mayor and, two years later, inaugurated the renovated space as Plaza Bolívar with a replica of Adamo Tadolini's equestrian statue of the Liberator of Lima at the center. Since then, Bolívar has remained at the heart of power and the center of the republic. Like so many monuments of the era, it immortalizes Guzmán Blanco at the same time. The pedestal is engraved, "General Antonio Guzmán Blanco erected this monument in 1874" (Calzadilla 2004; Salvador González 2009). Plaza Bolívar, with its gardens, fountains, walkways, and proximity to the main boulevard to the Capitol (named, of course, Guzmán Blanco Boulevard), quickly became the most fashionable neighborhood for the elite of Caracas to parade in their most stylish clothing.

In the next century, cities, towns, and villages throughout Venezuela erected similar plazas with their own statues or busts of Bolívar, in some cases with replicas of the one in Caracas. In 1874 Guzmán Blanco decreed the formation of another symbol: the Panteón Nacional, inspired by the Pantheon of Paris. For this purpose the Church of Santa Trinita in Caracas was secularized and renamed, and the mausoleum of Bolívar was moved there. The mausoleum is a monument sculpted by the celebrated Pietro Tenerani between 1843 to 1851 that had initially been placed in the cathedral of Caracas. Thus, the Panteón Nacional was inaugurated as the final resting place for the remains of the heroes of independence and of the Federal War (Próceres de la Independencia y los Próceres de la Federación) in yet another example that equated Liberals with the founding fathers. Finally, in 1879, Guzmán Blanco renamed the Venezuelan currency, then known as the venezolano, as the bolívar. The profile of the Liberator etched on the coins that was made by the famous French engraver Albert Desiré Barré remains on Venezuelan coinage and has been a true national symbol for two centuries.

Finale

In the last third of the nineteenth century, thanks to the historiography and especially the new and powerful iconography produced by the Liberal Party's men of letters (historians, journalists) and artists, a new identity arose. Even today we can see how the effort of two generations—the romantics who wrote the essential values of the cult of Bolívar and the positivists who turned the cult into state policy—created some of the most important images and beliefs of the present historical memory of Venezuelans. Historical figures like Negra Matea and Negro Primero, images like *Miranda en La Carraca* and *La muerte de Atanasio Girardot,* and sites like Plaza Bolívar and the Panteón Nacional were all produced during this period.

Although today only historians can identify the strong political meanings of those works, we must remember that all of them were created with propagandistic and ideological aims. Artists painted the founding fathers and Liberal politicians at the same time. Tovar y Tovar painted the heroes of independence as well as the portraits of Falcón and Guzmán Blanco for the Palacio Federal. The Panteón Nacional was conceived of as a big mausoleum to Bolívar, the other *próceres,* and the heroes of the Federal War. In a word, the Liberal Party strove to represent itself as the heir of independence.

This does not mean Liberals had no other motivations, such as building the nation-state or sincerely admiring the Liberator and other heroes. However, the ideological and propagandistic aspect of this policy of memory was an important part of its configuration. Since the romanticism of the 1830s that provided the basis of the historic discourse of Bolivarianism, historiography and policy have been joined together. Nevertheless, the Liberals created most of the national symbols of Venezuela—and by this they contributed to the creation of the nation. The cult of Bolívar has thus been the main result of their policies.

Notes

1. "Apotheosis" was the name of a kind of civic festivity celebrated from 1870 to 1900 in which the remains of founding fathers were transferred to the Panteón Nacional. The president and other authorities led the procession, and at the new grave they held solemn ceremonies and gave speeches. Similar ceremonies occurred around the country in every church, school, and square. Some of the most famous apotheoses were those held in honor of other national heroes: Juan Crisóstomo Falcón (1876), José Antonio Páez (1888), Antonio José de Sucre (1895), José Gregorio Monagas (1895), and Francisco de Miranda (1896). In the cases of Sucre and Miranda, because their remains had disappeared, they received two cenotaphs in the Panteón Nacional. In 1900 the remains of Sucre were found and transferred to the Cathedral of Quito.

2. Traditionally, when a historical figure was Afro-Venezuelan, "Negro" or "Negra" has been added before the name, for example, Negro Miguel, Negro Primero, Negra Matea, Negra Hipólita. In spite of the affirmative-action policies enacted by Hugo Chávez's government such as the antidiscrimination law, the state continues using the words "Negro" and "Negra" in its agencies; one of these is the Misión Negra Hipólita, which is focused on protecting addicts and the homeless.

3. *Vergangeheitspolitik* is the category denominating the policies developed in West Germany after World War II to face its Nazi, militaristic, and even Prussian past. These policies involved measures concerning historical curricula in schools, cultural heritage management, public opinion, policies of amnesty to former Nazi officers, and so forth. Other countries have similar policies that focus on their own contextual issues and historical memories.

References

Aguirre Elorriaga, Manuel. 1941. *El abate de Pradt en la emancipación hispanoamericana (1800–1830)*. Rome: Universitatis Gregorianae.

Blanco, Eduardo. 1881/1972. *Venezuela heroica*. Caracas: Monte Avila.

Calzadilla, Pedro Enrique. 2004. "Las ceremonias bolivarianas y la determinación de los objetos de la memoria nacional en Venezuela." *Tierra Firme*, 86: 221–28.

Calzadilla, Pedro Enrique, Mireya Dávila, and Luis Galindo. 2009. *La exposición nacional de 1883: Memoria, identidad y nación*. Caracas: Centro Nacional de Historia.

Carrera Damas, Germán. 1970/2013. *El culto a Bolívar. Esbozo para un estudio de la historia de las ideas en Venezuela*. 7th ed. Caracas: Editorial Alfa.

Castellanos, Rafael Ramón. 1983. *Caracas 1883 (centenario del natalicio del Libertador)*. Vol. 1. Caracas: Academia Nacional de la Historia.

Castillo Herrera, Luis Fernando. 2012. "Entre el respeto y la veneración: Imagen y cuerpo del libertador Simón Bolívar." *CONHISREMI* 8: 94–116.

Esteller Camacho y Clemente, Antonia. 1928. "Matea Bolívar." *Revista Bolivariana* 16:447–51.

Filippi, Alberto. 1983. *Bolívar y Europa en las crónicas, el pensamiento político y la historiografía: Siglos XIX y XX*. Caracas: Presidencia de la República.

Guerrero, Carolina. 2005. *Republicanismo y liberalismo en Bolívar, 1819–1830: Usos de Constant por el padre fundador*. Caracas: Universidad Central de Venezuela.

Guzmán Blanco, Antonio. 1870. "Exposición que dirije el Jeneral Guzmán Blanco, al Congreso de Plenipotenciarios de los Estados." In *Rejenerador i Pacificador de Venezuela, Jeneral Guzmán Blanco*. Caracas: Imprenta de El Demócrata.

———. 1883/2001. "Discurso pronunciado por el General Guzmán Blanco en el Panteón Nacional el 24 de Julio para inaugurar las fiestas del Centenario de Bolívar." In *Hojas sueltas venezolanas del siglo XIX*, edited by Haydée Miranda Bastidas and David Ruíz Chataing. Caracas: Universidad Central de Venezuela.

Harwich Vallenilla, Nikita, 1988. "La génesis de un imaginario colectivo: La enseñanza de la historia en el siglo XIX." *Boletín de la Academia Nacional de la Historia* 282:349–87.

Larrazábal, Felipe. 1865. *Correspondencia general del Libertador Simón Bolívar, enriquecida con la inserción de manifiestos, mensajes, exposiciones, proclamas, &&&, publicados por el héroe colombiano desde 1810 hasta 1830 (precede a esta colección interesante una vida de Bolívar)*. New York: Eduardo O. Jenkins.

Castro Leiva, Luis. 2005. "El historicismo político bolivariano." In *De la patria boba a la teología bolivariana*. 1991. Reprint, *Obras de Luis Castro Leiva*, vol. 1. Caracas: Fundación Polar/UCAB.

Martín Frechilla, J. J. 1999. *Cartas a Guzmán Blanco, 1864–1887: Intelectuales ante el poder en Venezuela*. Caracas: Universidad Central de Venezuela.

Melo, Orlando. 2008. "Bolívar en Colombia: La transformación de su imagen." *Boletín de la Academia Nacional de la Historia* 363:7–40.

Parra Pérez, Caracciolo. 1957. *La monarquía en la Gran Colombia*. Madrid: Ediciones Cultura Hispánica.

Partido Liberal. 1893/1960. "Manifiesto del Partido Liberal a la nación." Reprint, *Liberales y conservadores, textos doctrinales*, 2:157–65. Caracas: Colección Pensamiento Político Venezolano del Siglo XIX, Presidencia de la República.

Pérez Rancel, Juan José. 2002. *Agustín Codazzi: Italia y la construcción del Nuevo Mundo*. Caracas: Petroglifo Producción.

Pino Iturrieta, Elías. 1993. *Las ideas de los primeros venezolanos*. Caracas: Monte Ávila Editores Latinoamericana.

Plaza, Elena. 2011. *Venezuela 1830–1850: La construcción de una nación*. Caracas: Fundación Rómulo Betancourt.

Plaza, Ramón de la. 1883. *Ensayos sobre el arte en Venezuela*. Caracas: Imprenta de La Opinión Nacional.

Pulido, Gonzalo. 2011. "Estudio histórico-militar de la batalla de Carabobo (1821)." Master's thesis, Universidad Católica Andrés Bello, Caracas.

Ríos, Alicia. 2013. *Nacionalismos banales, El culto a Bolívar: Literatura, cine, arte y política en América Latina*. Pittsburgh, PA: Instituto Internacional de Literatura Iberoamericana, University of Pittsburgh.

Salas de Lecuna, Yolanda. 1987. *Bolívar y la historia en la conciencia popular*. Caracas: Universidad Simón Bolívar.

Salvador González, José María. 2001. *Efímeras efemérides: Fiestas cívicas y arte efímero en la Venezuela de los siglos XVIII–XIX*. Caracas: Universidad Católica Andrés Bello.

———. 2009. "Monumentos a Bolívar en Venezuela durante la supremacía de Guzmán Blanco (1870–1888)." *Ensayos Históricos* 21, no. 21 (June 2009).

Straka, Tomás. 2010. "Antimonarquismo y republicanismo bolivariano: Los orígenes del conservadurismo hispanoamericano en el Libertador." *Espacio, Tiempo y Forma* 5, no. 22:151–68.

Torres, Ana Teresa. 2009. *La herencia de la tribu: Del mito de la independencia a la Revolución Bolivariana*. Caracas: Editorial Alfa.

Urueña Cervera, Jaime. 2006. *Bolívar republicano. Fundamentos ideológicos e históricos de su pensamiento político*. Bogotá: Ediciones Aurora.

Villavicencio, Rafael. 1900/1966. "La evolución social y política de Venezuela." Speech. Reprint, *Discursos de incorporación*, vol. 1. Caracas: Academia Nacional de la Historia.

Part II

Disruptions and Unhingings in the Twentieth Century

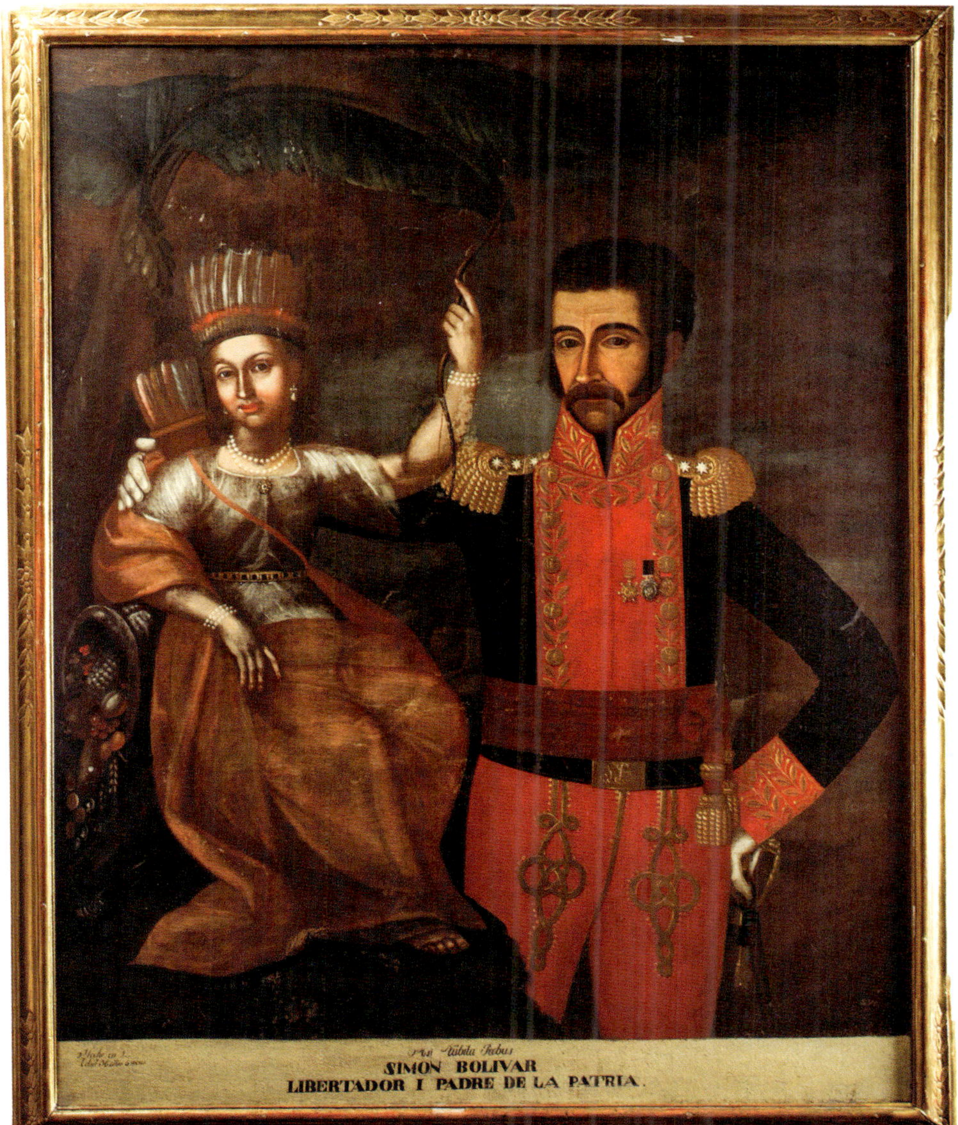

PLATE 1. Pedro José Figueroa. *Simón Bolívar, Libertador y Padre de la Patria*. 1819. Oil on panel. 49.21" × 38.58" (136 × 108.5cm). Permission of the Museo de la Independencia Casa del Florero and Casa Museo Quinta de Bolívar del Ministerio de Cultura de Colombia, Bogotá.

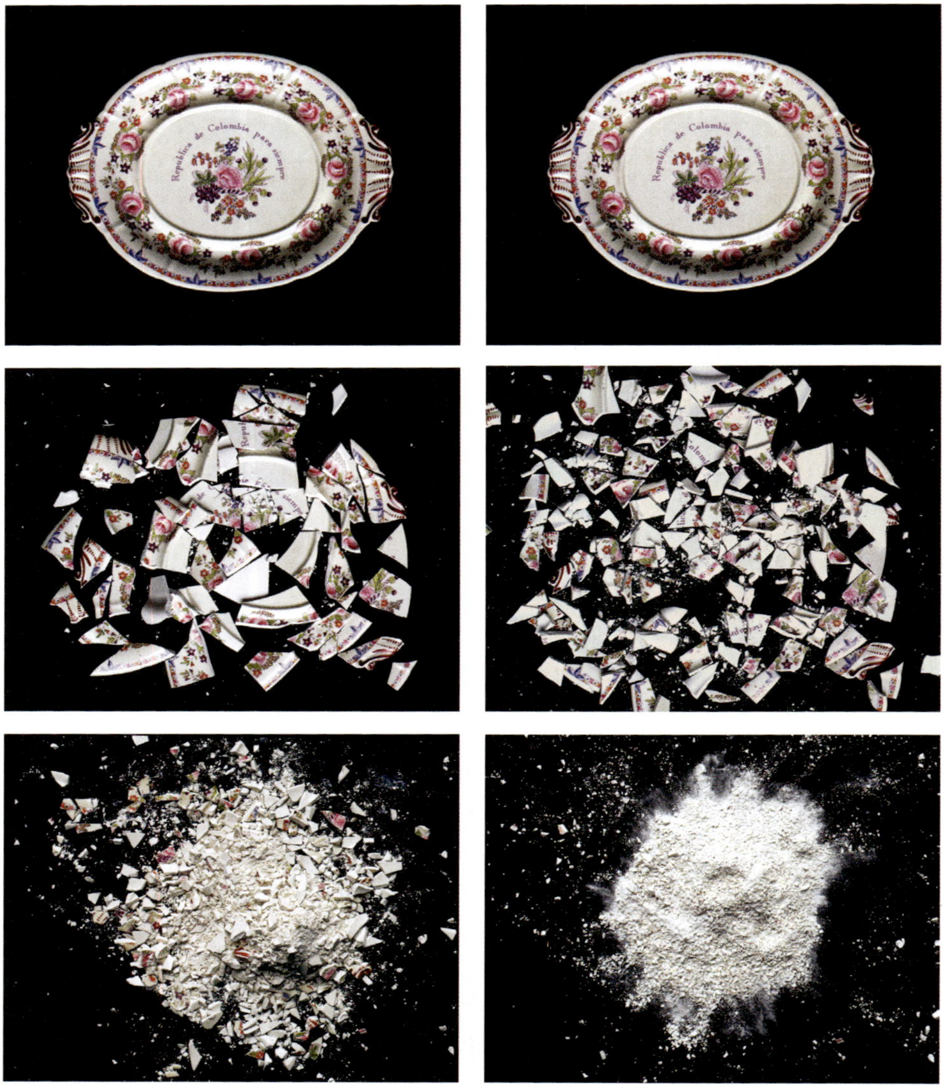

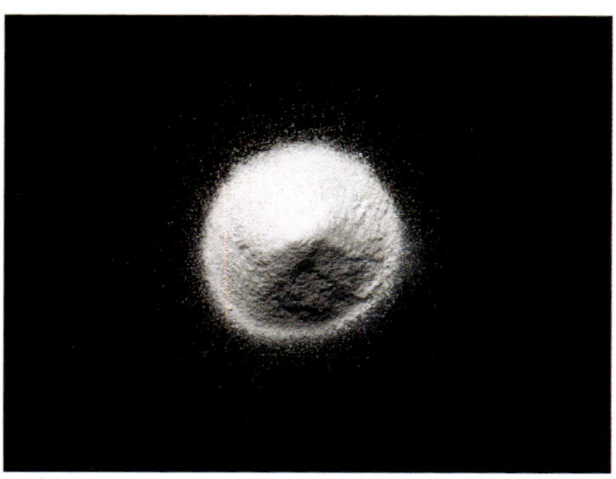

PLATE 2. Juan Manuel Echavarría. ***La bandeja de Bolívar***. 1999. Stills of video installation. Courtesy of the artist.

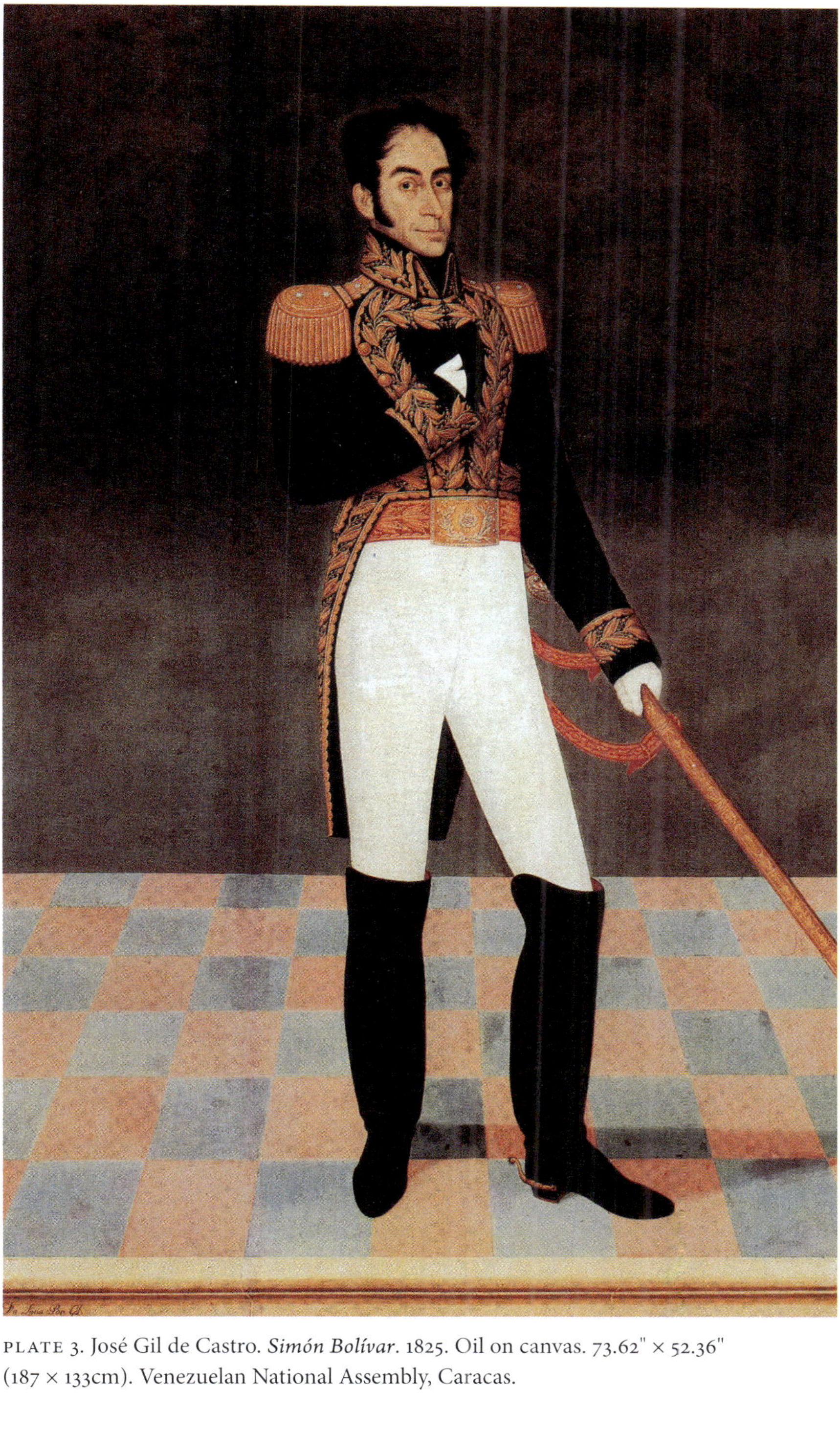

PLATE 3. José Gil de Castro. *Simón Bolívar*. 1825. Oil on canvas. 73.62" × 52.36" (187 × 133cm). Venezuelan National Assembly, Caracas.

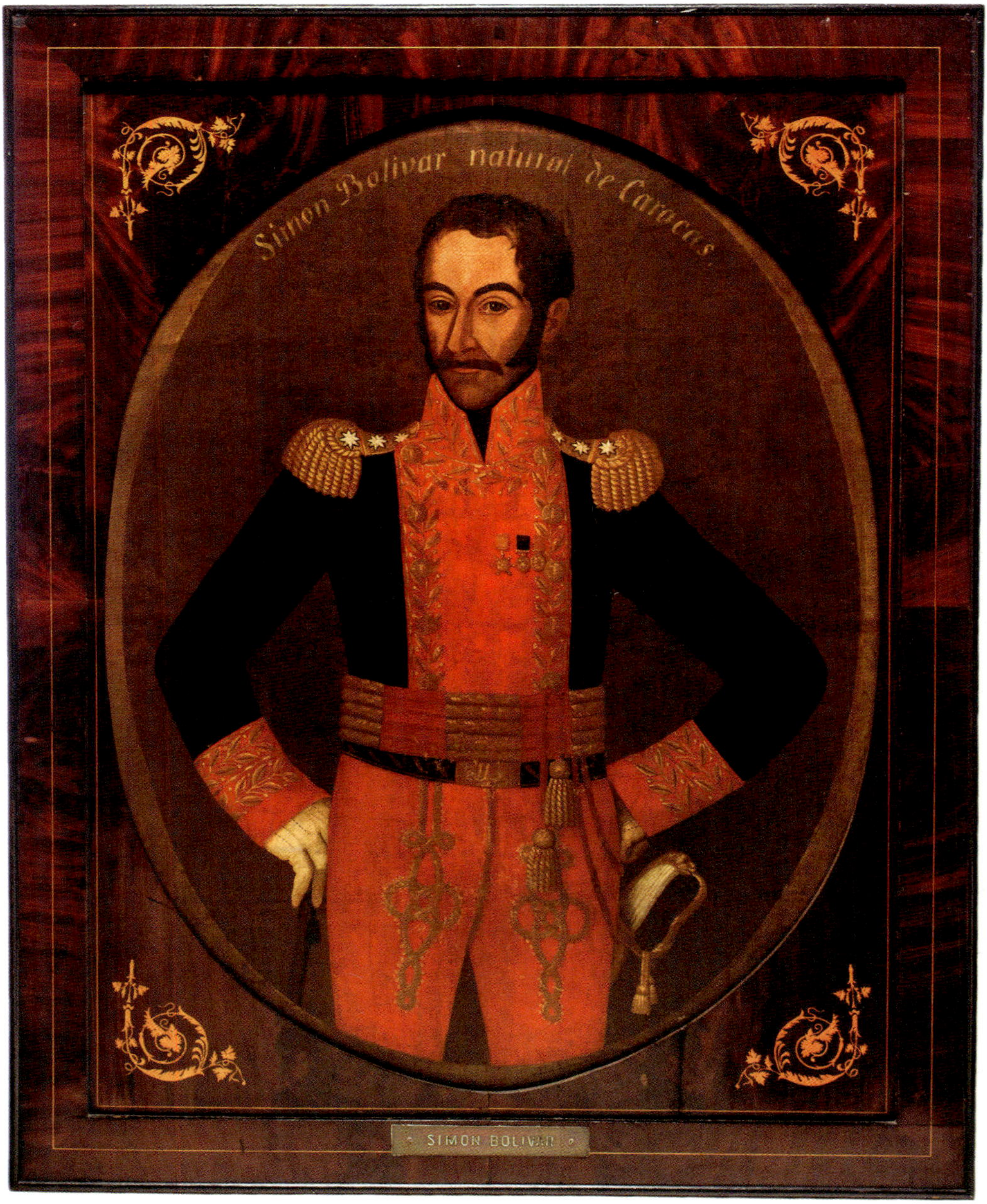

PLATE 4. Pedro José Figueroa. *Simón Bolívar natural de Caracas*. 1820. Oil on canvas. 38.19" × 32.67" (97 × 83cm). Permission of the Museo de la Independencia Casa del Florero and Casa Museo Quinta de Bolívar del Ministerio de Cultura de Colombia, Bogotá.

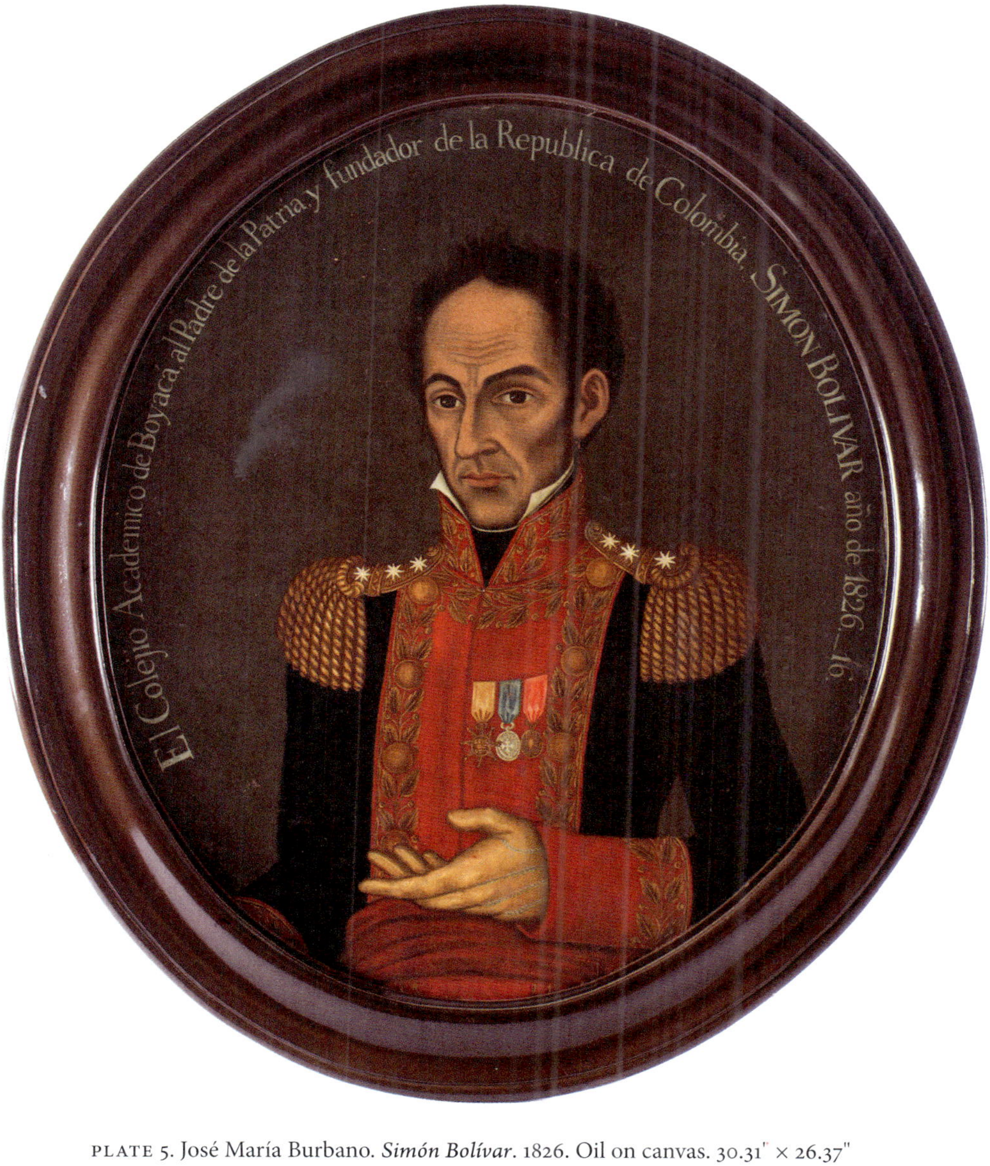

PLATE 5. José María Burbano. *Simón Bolívar*. 1826. Oil on canvas. 30.31" × 26.37" (77 × 67cm). Permission of the Museo de la Independencia Casa del Florero and Casa Museo Quinta de Bolívar del Ministerio de Cultura de Colombia, Bogotá.

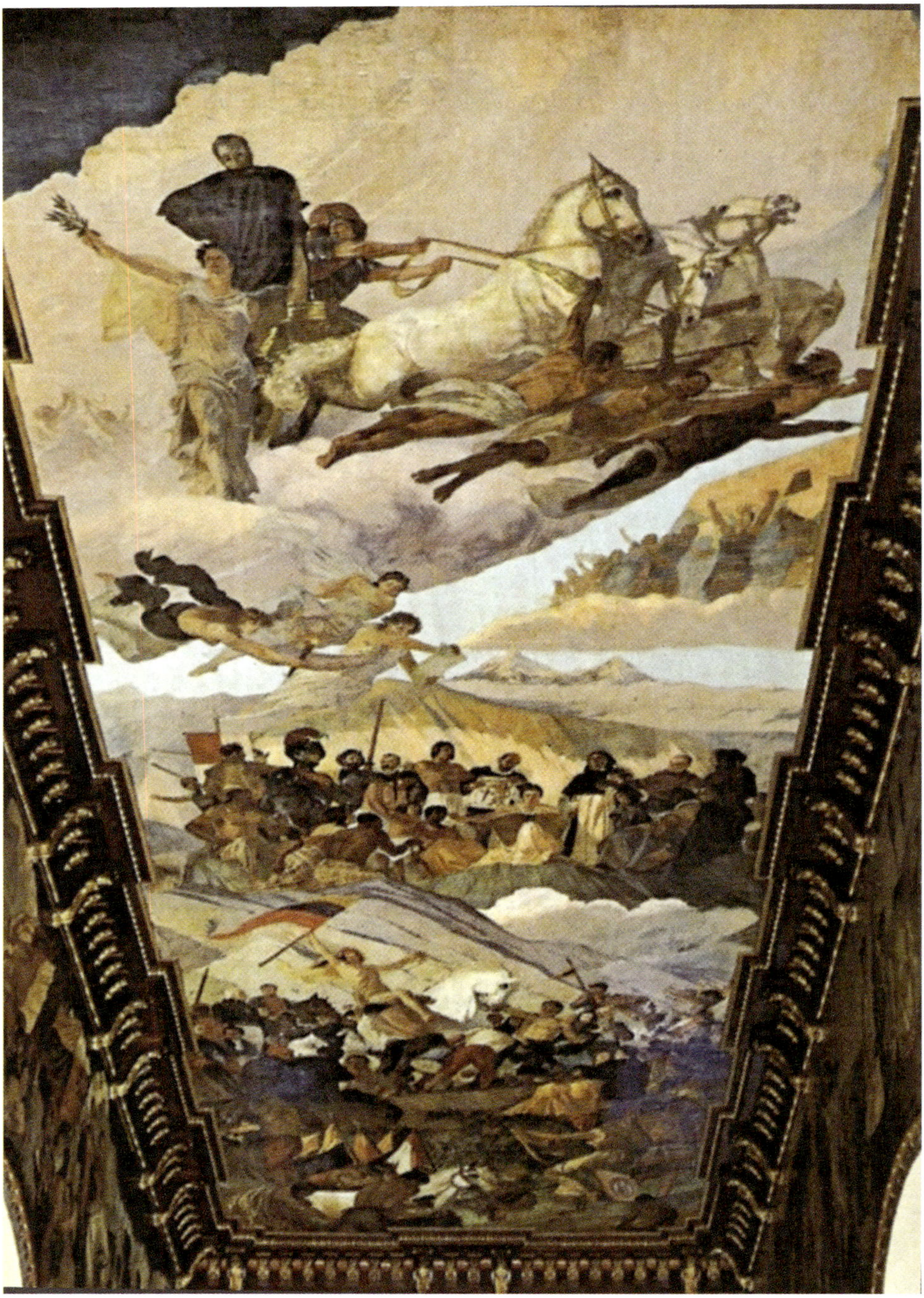

PLATE 6. Tito Salas. *Apoteosis de Bolívar*. Finished by 1942. Mural, ceiling of the Panteón Nacional de Venezuela, Caracas. In the public domain.

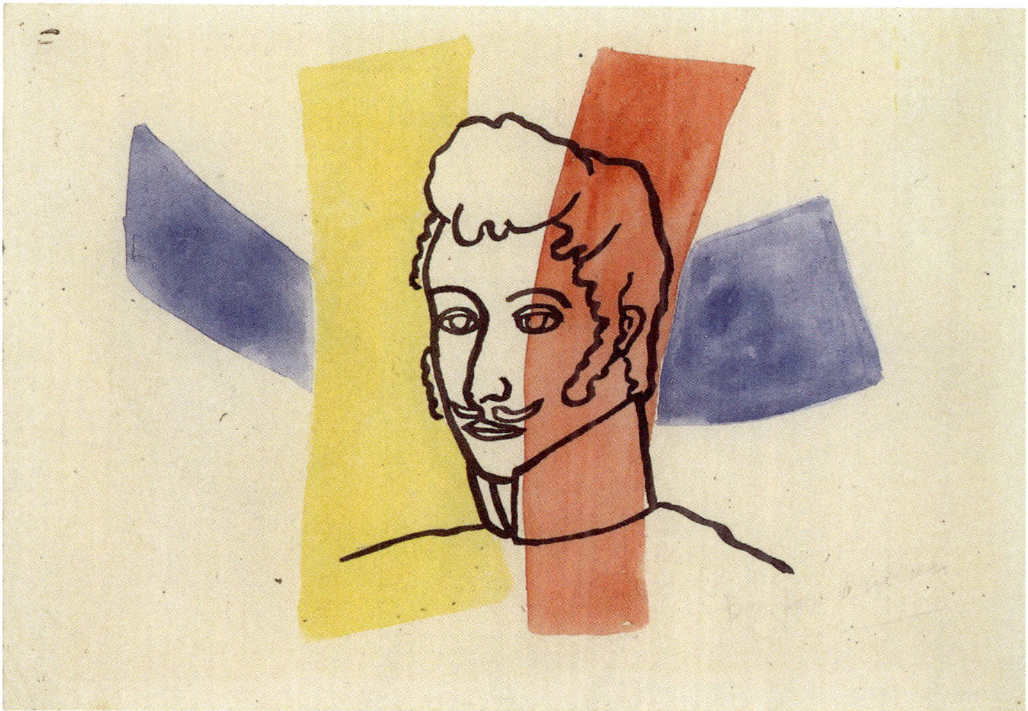

PLATE 7. Fernand Léger. *Bolívar*. Opera curtain design. 1950. Gouache. 7.25" × 9" (18.4 × 22.86cm). Bibliothèque Nationale de France, Paris. © 2014 Artists Rights Society (ARS), New York; ADAGP, Paris.

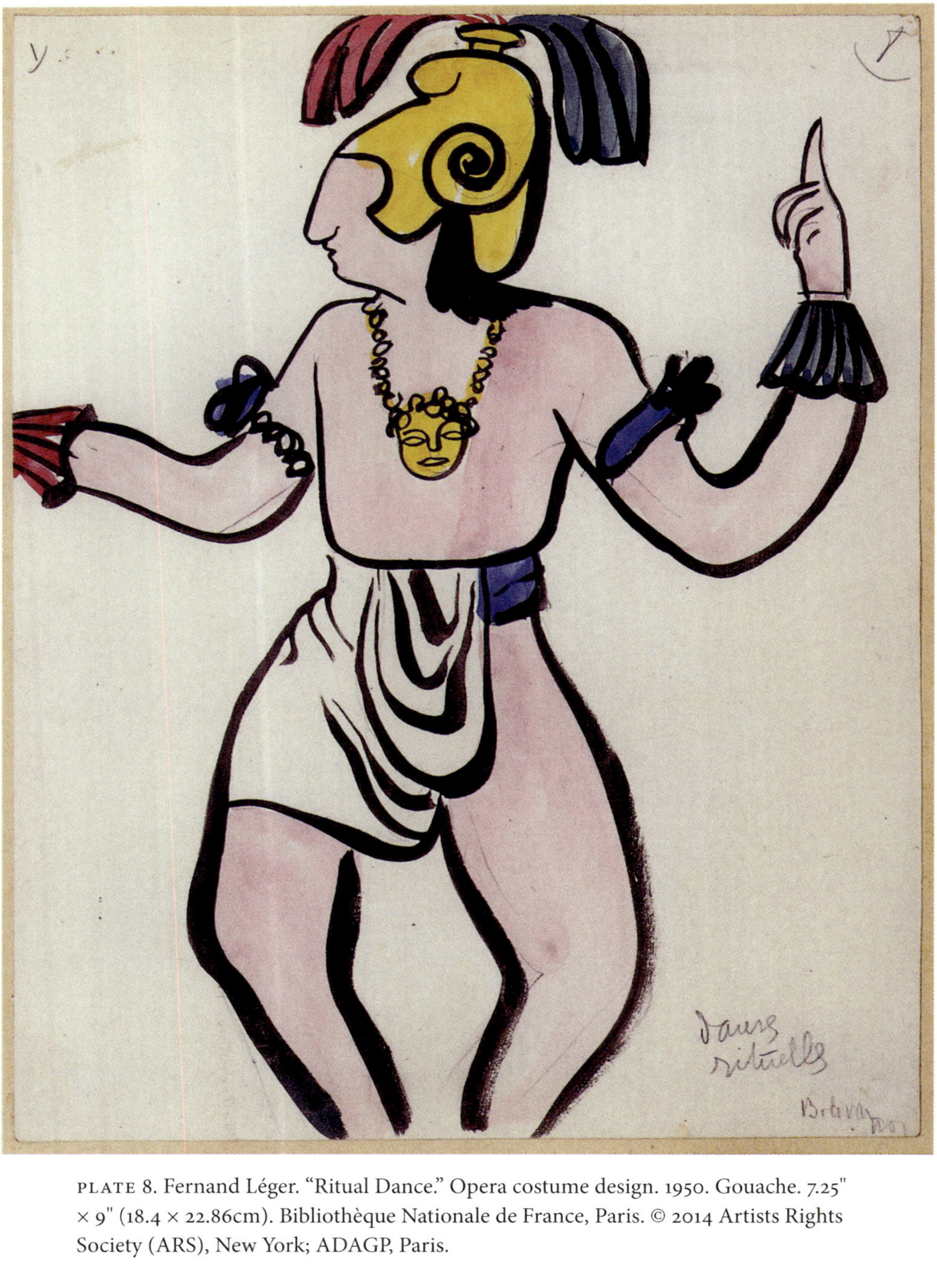

PLATE 8. Fernand Léger. "Ritual Dance." Opera costume design. 1950. Gouache. 7.25" × 9" (18.4 × 22.86cm). Bibliothèque Nationale de France, Paris. © 2014 Artists Rights Society (ARS), New York; ADAGP, Paris.

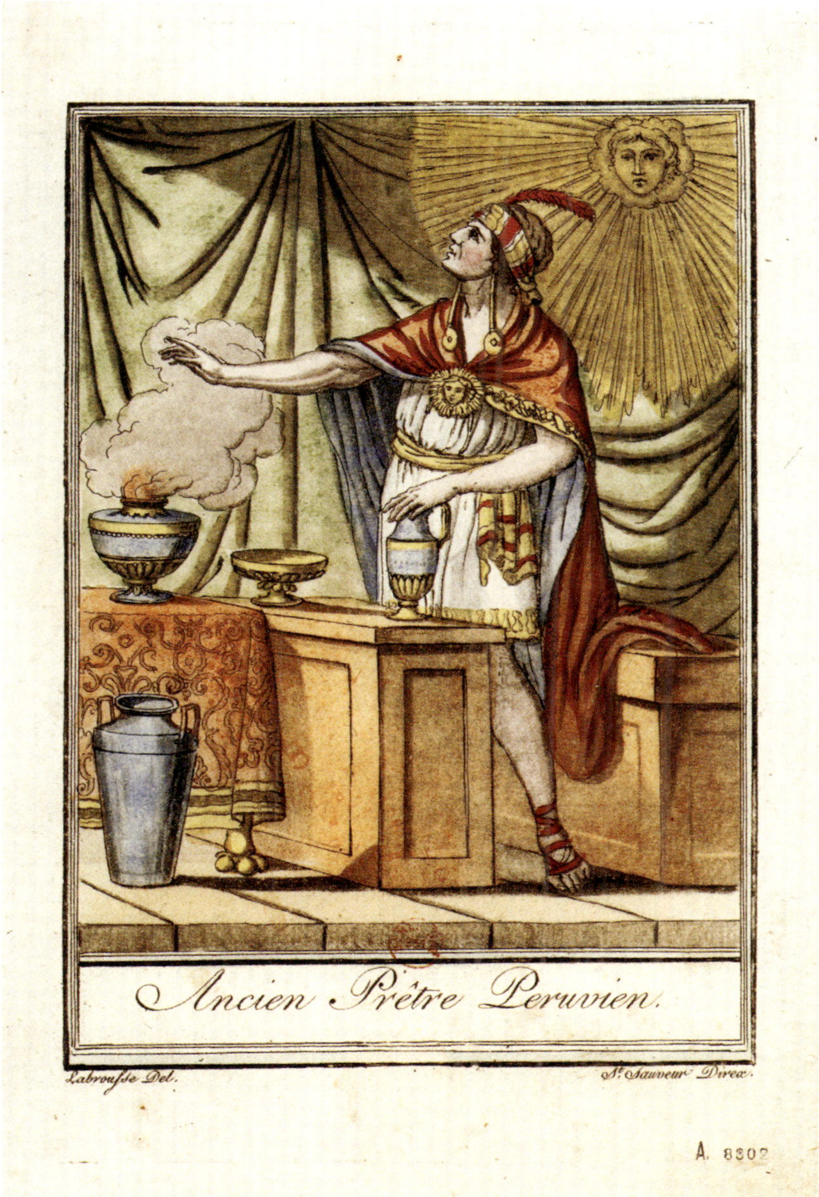

PLATE 9. Jacques Grasset de Saint-Sauveur (designer) and Labrousse (engraver). "Ancient Peruvian priest." Late eighteenth century. Hand-colored engraving. 5.5" × 8" (13.97 × 20.32cm). *Histoire d'Amérique Latine et les Antilles*, vol. 2. Bibliothèque National de France, Paris.

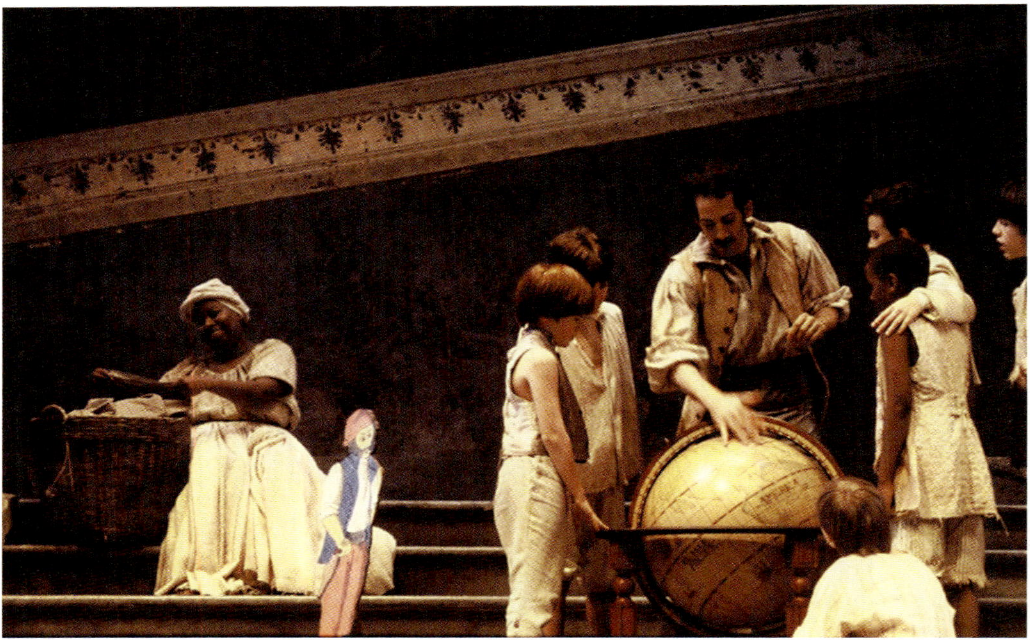

PLATE 10. Production shot of act 1, scene 1, of Thea Musgrave's opera *Simón Bolívar*. 1995. Virginia Opera, Norfolk. Hipólita (Patricia Nixon) sings the Afro-Venezuelan melody "El quirimare." Photograph by Kathy Keeney, courtesy of Virginia Opera.

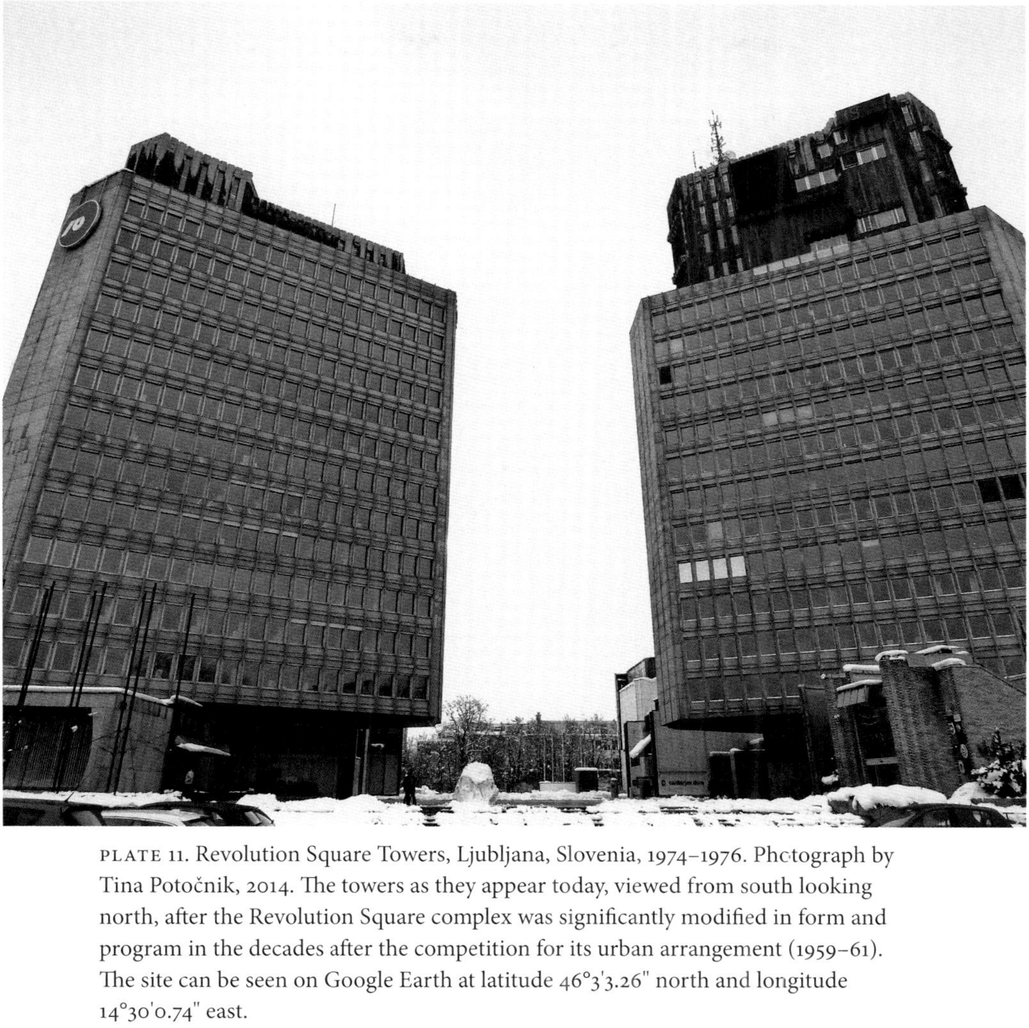

PLATE 11. Revolution Square Towers, Ljubljana, Slovenia, 1974–1976. Photograph by Tina Potočnik, 2014. The towers as they appear today, viewed from south looking north, after the Revolution Square complex was significantly modified in form and program in the decades after the competition for its urban arrangement (1959–61). The site can be seen on Google Earth at latitude 46°3'3.26" north and longitude 14°30'0.74" east.

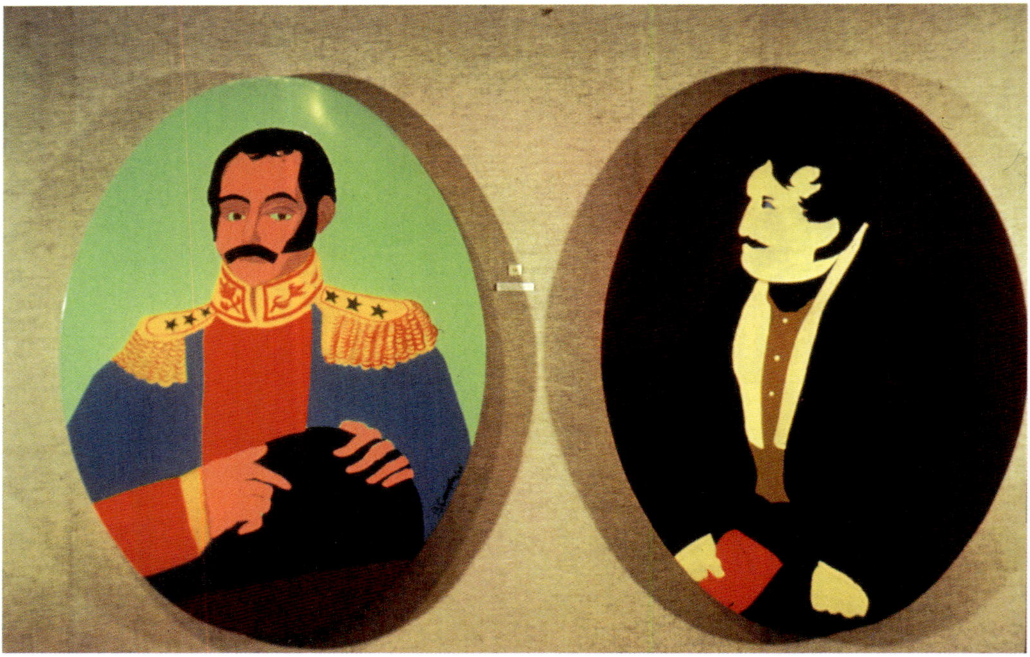

PLATE 12. Beatriz González. Front view. *Apuntes para la historia extensa, Tomos I* (Bolívar, left) and *II* (Santander, right). 1967. Enamel on tin plate. 39.37" × 31.5" (100 × 80 cm) each. Courtesy of the artist.

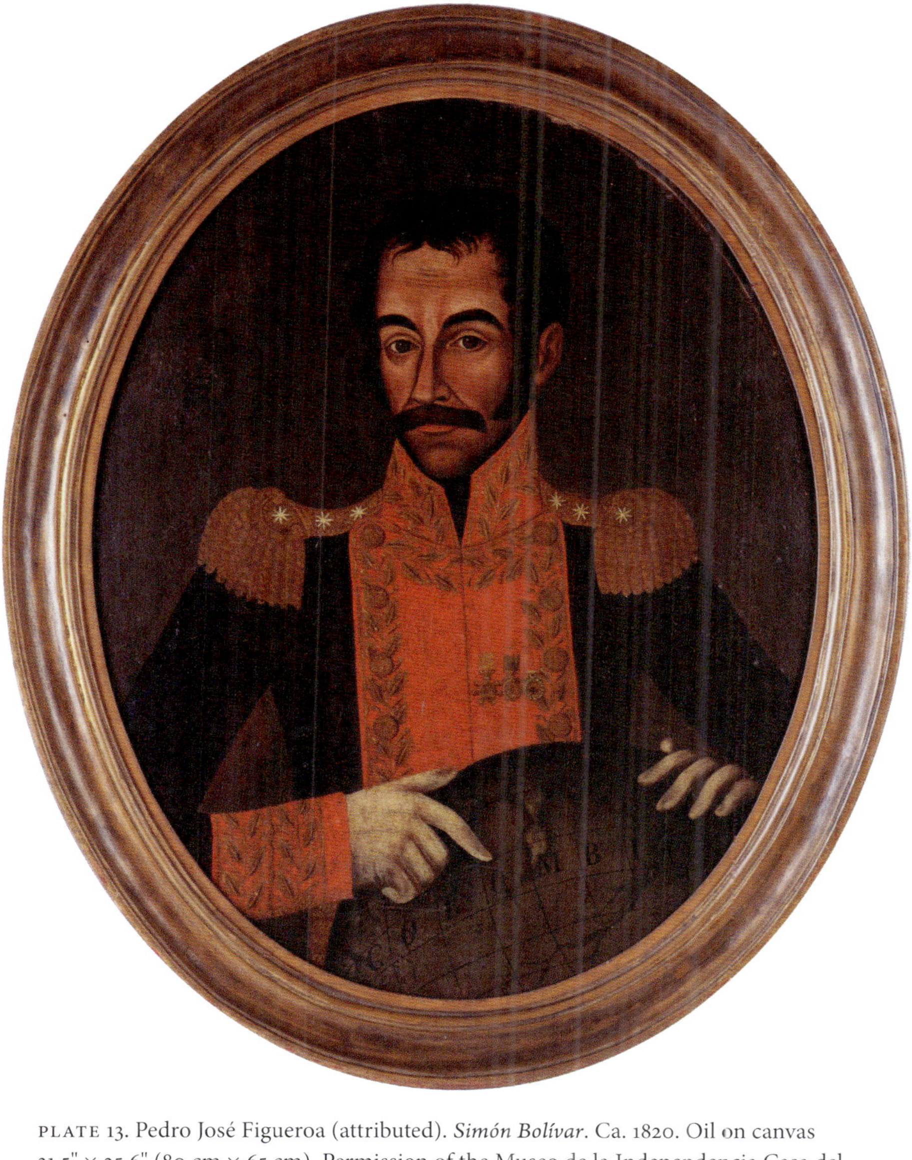

PLATE 13. Pedro José Figueroa (attributed). *Simón Bolívar*. Ca. 1820. Oil on canvas 31.5" × 25.6" (80 cm × 65 cm). Permission of the Museo de la Independencia Casa del Florero, del Ministerio de Cultura de Colombia, Bogotá.

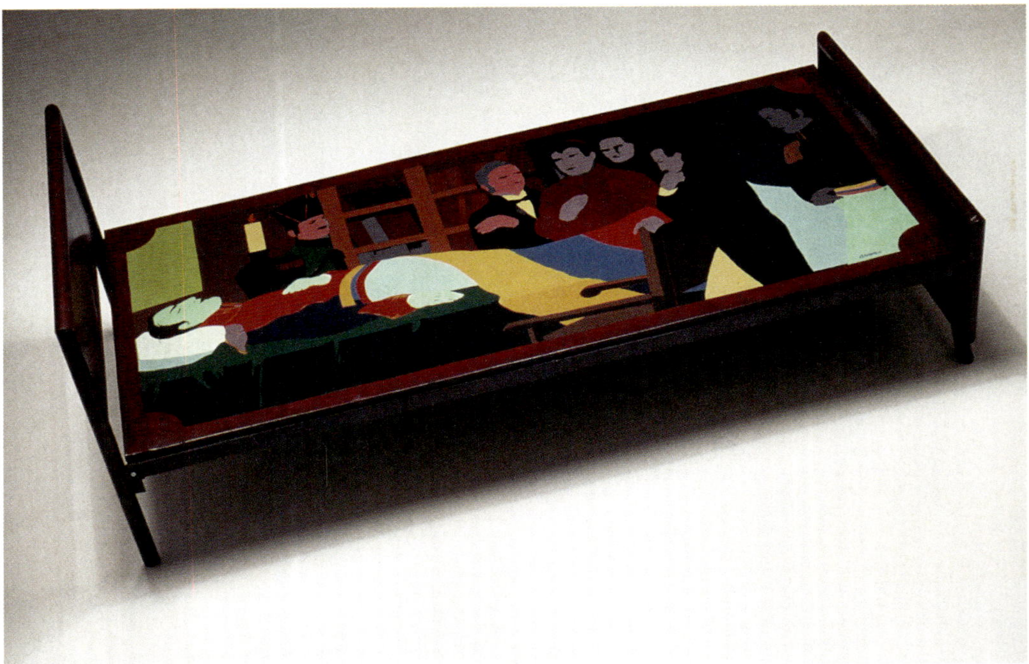

PLATE 14. Beatriz González. *Mutis por el foro*. 1973. Enamel and metal sheet joint on metal furniture. 47.24" × 89.71" × 35.43" (120 × 205 × 90 cm). The Museum of Fine Arts, Houston, museum purchase funded by the Caroline Wiess Law Accessions Endowment Fund, Leslie and Brad Bucher, Karol Kreymer and Robert Card, M.D., Anne and John C. Moriniere, and the Latin Maecenas. Courtesy of the artist.

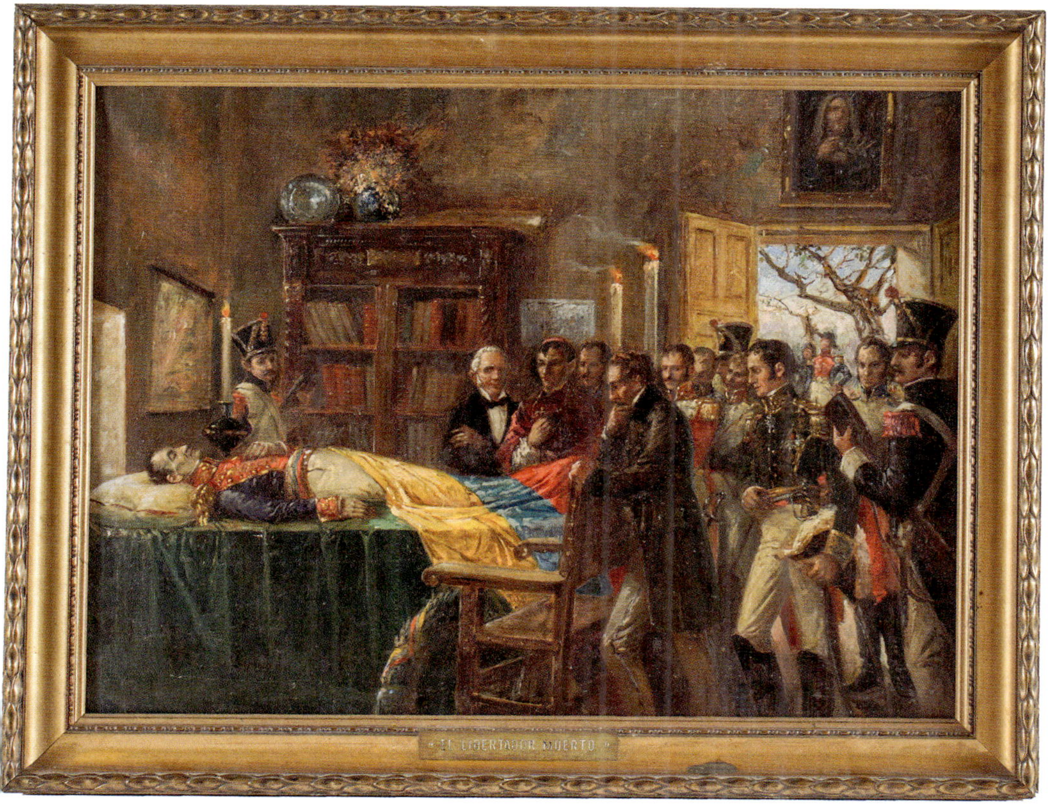

PLATE 15. Pedro Alcántara Quijano Moreno. *El Libertador muerto*. Ca. 1930. Oil on canvas. 40.95" × 32.68" (104 × 83 cm). Permission of the Museo de la Independencia Casa del Florero and Casa Museo Quinta de Bolívar del Ministerio de Cultura de Colombia, Bogotá.

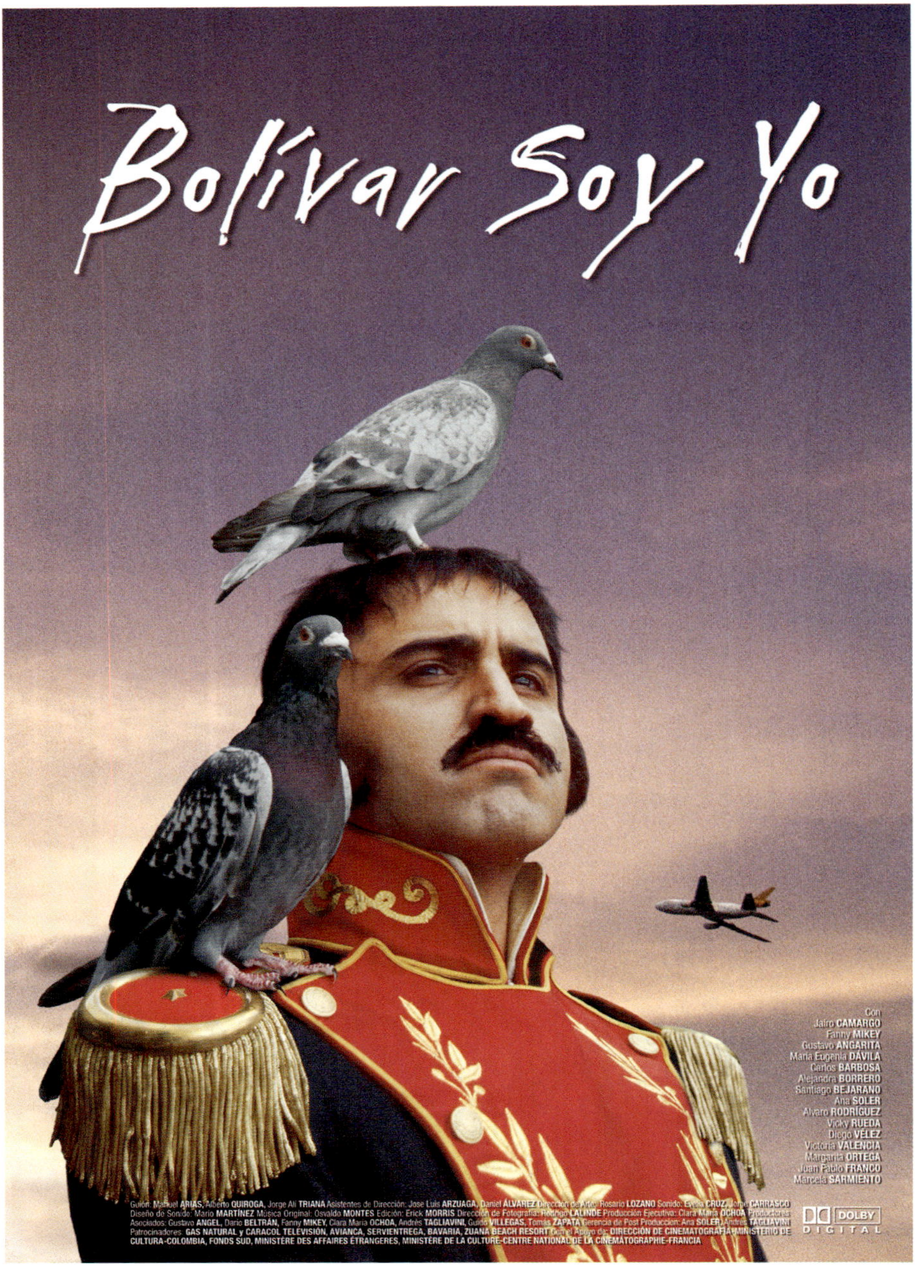

PLATE 16. Carlos Duque, designer and photographer. Film poster for *Bolívar soy yo* (Jorge Alí Triana, 2002). Courtesy of Dramax.

6

Bolívar on the Operatic Stage

Enlightenment Hero and Tyrannical Failure

MAUREEN G. SHANAHAN

El Libertador Simón Bolívar is one of the mythic heroes of the revolutionary era, whose epic military and romantic campaigns have made him the subject of at least three tragic operas, a genre that lends itself to a critique of the "great man" once imagined to be a catalyst of history. Some of Bolívar's most fabled achievements—his perilous crossing of the Andes mountains, his freeing of slaves, his vision of a Gran Colombia—have placed him in the ranks of military strategists from Hannibal to Napoleon and Enlightenment leaders from Washington to Lafayette. On the operatic stage, Bolívar, his allies, his competing and treasonous generals, his cross-dressing lover Manuela Sáenz, and "loyal servants" (slaves) become condensations of history as spectacle. Opera as a synthesis of the arts invokes grand narratives of tragic heroes, deploys the musical rhetoric of profound emotions (grief, love), and the staging of historic lives and events, making it particularly suited to the baroque pageantry of the cult of Bolívar in the countries that formerly comprised the Gran Colombia.

Yet in this operatic history, Bolívar emerges not so much a deified cult figure as a contested sign of the Enlightenment ideals of liberty and citizenship, particularly in the contexts of two modern empires with slave-holding histories: France and the United States. Andrés Delgado Pardo (1870–1940) created what is probably the first Bolívar opera (ca. 1931), but it has never been staged (Martínez Benedicto 1999a, 1999b; Sánchez 2010).[1] The first fully staged Bolívar opera was composed in 1943 by Darius Milhaud, a member of the French modernist composers group Les Six. First performed in

Paris in 1950, Milhaud's opera is the only version that has been performed in Caracas (in 1983 and 2012).

Almost a half century later, in 1995, Scottish American composer Thea Musgrave created a two-act Bolívar opera with a Spanish libretto that premiered in the United States. In turning to the Bolívar narrative as a subject of grand operas produced in proximity to the imperial capitals of Paris and Washington, D.C., Milhaud and Musgrave created framing contexts that invited spectators to see Bolívar in terms of French and U.S. heroes, histories, and politics: their revolutions, their politics on slavery and liberation, their ongoing racial hierarchies, and their twentieth-century colonial empires. The historical moment of production, each within ongoing national debates about colonialism and neocolonialism, thus inflected these productions with multiple significations to liberation and servitude. In these contexts, the Bolívar operas theatricalize societal investments in heroic or deified masculinities as well as material representations of "freedom."

Milhaud's *Bolívar* as Enlightenment Hero

Milhaud, a prolific composer who generated more than four hundred works including eighteen operas, created *Bolívar* as part of a trilogy about Euro-American figures, along with *Christophe Colombe* (1928) and *Maximilian* (1930) (Collaer 1988, 226–29; Drake 1989, 291–305; D. Milhaud 1974/1995, 216, 223; M. Milhaud 2008, 13, 68, 78). Milhaud's *Bolívar,* thus situated among other great men of history who were all disgraced or forgotten at their deaths, figures as a tale of grand imperial visions gone awry. Yet Milhaud wanted the opera to be masculine and muscular: "the subject of Bolívar suited me admirably because I wanted a libretto crammed full of action, with a masculine hero" (D. Milhaud 1974/1995, 216). Milhaud's desire for action and a masculine hero arose from a contradictory position of impotent safety as a distant observer of events in Nazi-occupied and Vichy France. He created the composition during World War II while he was in exile teaching at Mills College in California.

Fernand Léger, Milhaud's longtime friend and collaborator also teaching at Mills, created the set and costume designs, including the heroic masculine protagonist that Milhaud wanted. Léger's curtain design (plate 7) depicts Bolívar in the three-quarter profile bust of portraiture and the heavy black outlining of stained glass or French *image d'Epinal* prints, overlaid by the broad bands of unmodulated red, blue, and yellow that sweep across the pictorial field. Léger's simplified use of line, with its modernist rejection of one-point linear perspective and verisimilitude, nevertheless draws upon earlier portraiture. Many of Léger's set designs borrow from a collection of nineteenth-century prints and photographs grouped together in an album entitled *Histoire d'Amerique Latine*. The album, held in the French national library where Léger worked on his costume ideas (Léger 1950), includes a black and white British print by M. N. Bate (discussed more fully in Emily Engel's essay in this collection). Léger's design inverts Bate's three-quarter profile and transforms Bolívar's undulating curls into a kind of calligraphic outline bespeaking the dynamism of an energetic personality.

Like Andy Warhol or Roy Lichtenstein, who later appropriated the imprecise printing processes of cartoons, advertising, and mass reproductions, Léger borrows from block color printing of the folkloric *image d'Epinal*. Léger's designs reinforce the image of a man of action and a man of the people through the incorporation of moving sets and allusions to film (Francia 1983, 191–94; Musée National Fernand Léger 1995, 166–85; Shanahan 2005, 199–207). The bands of color, which Léger also used in his painting series *Les Plongeurs* (The Divers, 1941–45), were inspired by powerful searchlights used early in the century by dancer Loïe Fuller, then in Times Square and at film openings. For the 1937 International Exhibition in Paris, Léger had even proposed colorful searchlights sweeping over the monochrome Parisian architecture (Léger 1973). The curtain thus plays on notions of light and modernity as well as the French word for Enlightenment figures, Lumières. Léger's Bolívar becomes a projection, a site of investment and fantasy for an imagined collective social body.

When it was first performed in 1950, the opera functioned as a major state-sponsored celebration of France's liberation from Nazi occupation. It was the first new opera performed in seven years and a grandiose state-financed production commissioned by the director of the Paris Opera costing between twenty and sixty million francs (Antoine 1950; Hermant 1950). The four-hour opera has twenty-five singing roles and spans twenty-four years, beginning with Bolívar's marriage in 1802 to the young Spanish aristocrat María Teresa del Toro y Alayza (1781–1803) and ending with his death in 1830. Bolívar's first act of leadership is to free his slaves at the time of María Teresa's death in 1803 (act 1, scene 2). The choir of freed slaves sings, "A bas la marque! A bas la traite des esclaves! Ah! Citoyen! Liberté! Libertas!" (Down with the brand! Down with the slave trade! Citizenship! Liberty! Libertas!) (M. Milhaud [1950]) In the following scenes Milhaud makes further allusions to the Enlightenment. Shortly after the liberation scene, Bolívar receives a visit from a Spanish *visitador extraordinario*, a royal emissary with oversight over all judges and public officials (Castro 2007, 77). The Spaniard accuses Bolívar of being "poisoned by the writings of Jean Jacques Rousseau and the Encylopedists," alluding to Rousseau's lessons on citizenship and the social contract. Milhaud's Bolívar is also aligned with Enlightenment critiques of religion and absolutism when, like Voltaire, who rejected the notion that the Lisbon earthquake of 1755 was God's will, Bolívar challenges a monk who claims that the Caracas earthquake of 1812 was God's punishment (act 1, scene 3).

In presenting Bolívar as an Enlightenment figure, however, the opera envisions liberation in broad strokes that obscure historical complexity. At the time of the opera's premiere Milhaud stated, "I wrote *Bolívar* during my exile dreaming of our liberation" (D. Milhaud 1950). But his statement begs the question of whose liberation, whose exile, and whose nation this dream envisions. Léger's costume designs reference the misery of slavery by incorporating neck yokes and manacles at the wrists and ankles. (In their 2012 Caracas production of the opera, the producers and set designers Atahualpa Lichy and Diana Lichy projected eighteenth and nineteenth-century prints of slaves such as William Blake's engravings for J. G. Stedman's *Narrative* from 1796.) However, the scene is not only historically anachronistic; it also functions to disavow ongoing racial hierarchies. "Liberation" and citizenship were not co-equal nor a single defining moment but rather a contested and long-term struggle. At best the scene is a condensation of Bolívar's pronouncements around slavery, of emancipation tied to conscription, without an interrogation into the racial hierarchies that Enlightenment thinkers left intact (Chasteen 2006, 27). The Gran Colombia nations ended the slave trade and enacted free-womb laws during the independence era. However, the laws only granted freedom to those born after 1821, thus deferring an end to slavery and full citizenship rights until later in the century (Andrews 2004, 57, 64–65).

In act 2 of the opera, Bolívar shifts from being an Enlightenment thinker to becoming a heroic general who resorts to dictatorial powers only in order to save the union. In the crossing of the Andes scene (act 2, scene 2),

Bolívar's remarkable military feat recalls similar exploits by two legendary French generals: Napoleon, whose famous passage over the Alps is celebrated in Jacques-Louis David's painting, and Charles de Gaulle, who mounted his reclamation of the French hexagon through colonial North Africa. Bolívar's army is an international, multiethnic, colonial military force supported by the revolutionary-minded French: "American Indians, Black Africans, who came as slaves and are no longer so, and sons of Spaniards, French, and English, from all countries." But in the Andes scene, Milhaud gestures to the colonialist civilizing mission with its coercion and conscription. In an exchange between Bolívar and Manuela about how the Indians of the army are responding to the difficult crossing, Manuela reports that she told the Indians that Bolívar is "their destiny incarnate" and that they must follow him. In response, she says, "they stared at me for a long time, then lowered their eyes to separate their thoughts from mine, and I left them in profound silence." How this moment was performed is unclear since there are only audio recordings of the French performances, and the Venezuelan versions cut certain scenes, including this one. But the turn of the gaze and the refusal to share Manuela's vision, as indicated in the libretto, convey a kind of silent dissent.

The crossing of the Andes leads directly to Bolívar's ascension to absolute power in 1826, celebrated as a divine event by an Inkan astronomer and a Catholic bishop (act 3, scene 1). In the libretto, the Indians promise unstinting loyalty to "our Cacique Bolívar," and the astronomer proclaims, "Your glory rises so high that a new star is unveiled. We will give it your name, Liberator." The bishop of Lima and mayor enter, "carrying the keys to the city and a miniature cathedral," and the delegate from Upper Peru announces a province named Bolivia. Bolívar proclaims his vision of a Gran Colombia from the Orinoco River to Rio de la Plata in which each country will retain its independence: "I would create with Washington a spiritual and moral union in the American sense." But when the Colombian delegate offers him a crown, Bolívar rejects it, declaring, "Colombia is not France; I am not Napoleon" (act 3, scene 1). In the next scene, two years later Bolívar has already assumed dictatorial powers. In a neocolonialist move, Bolívar's authoritarianism is validated by the subjugated. Bolívar's slaves Nicanor and Précipitation defend his actions: "If he doesn't take absolute power, it is the end of the country," Nicanor contends, and Précipitation adds in support, "Anarchy is everywhere" (act 3, scene 2). And in crafting his final testament,

Bolívar calls for unification to avoid chaos: "people must obey their current government to be free from anarchy" (act 3, scene 3).

Where the libretto presents Bolívar as a reluctant dictator who assumes total power to prevent anarchy, Léger's designs for the Inkan astronomer tell the viewer to read Bolívar's assumption of absolute power as an inevitable, auspicious, and desirable ascent to a deified status. One of Léger's designs depicts an Indian wearing a loincloth and doing a "ritual dance" while pointing to the heavens (plate 8). At the same time, the Indian is encoded with an antique nobility expressed by his profile, gold solar medallion, and feathered version of a Praetorian guard's helmet. Léger's design borrows heavily from a print of an "ancient Peruvian priest" in the *Histoire d'Amérique Latine* album (plate 9), which seems the most likely design intended for the Inkan astronomer of the libretto.

Like a degraded version of the images in Jean de Léry's *Histoire d'un voyage faict en la terre du Brésil* (1578) that inspired Montaigne's *Des cannibales* (1580) and Levi-Strauss's *Tristes tropiques* (1955), the *Histoire d'Amérique Latine* print is part ethnographic study and part imperial spectacle of antiquity. It depicts a priest on a wooden platform before a draped wall gazing (in profile) upward as he performs an offering with incense and ablutions from various amphorae; he wears a feathered Orientalist headdress, the red cape of a Praetorian guard, a Greek tunic and sandals, and a gold medallion that is a miniature of the Cathedra Petri–like sun behind him. Both Léger's version and the nineteenth-century print invoke a populist and theatricalized version of Rousseau's noble savage as well as a kitschified idea of the antique whose referent is the primitive and Orientalist other of colonial exhibition performances. Whether or not the Inkan astronomer ever appeared in any performance of the opera, the libretto and costume design show that he functioned as an exoticizing backdrop naturalizing Bolivar's imperial ambitions.

Contemporary communist reviewers, however, interpreted the opera as a critique of colonialism. While many of the first reviews complained about Milhaud's populist music and Léger's noisy moving sets, within days of the opening night on May 13, 1950, French critic Claude Roy of Louis Aragon's Communist Party paper, *Les Lettres françaises,* rose to the opera's defense. Roy charged the disparaging reviewers with being "politically motivated": "Imagine then a liberator who begins by liberating slaves," a narrative promoting a "national war of independence," and a story in which "one hears a black man cry out from the opera stage of a government that imprisons the black leaders of the RDA" (Roy [1950], 18, 50). The RDA, or Rassemblement démocratique africain, formed in October 1946, was a coalition of French West African parties initially allied with the French Communist Party, the only party in France that "supported the colonial demand for full citizenship" (Manning 1988, 142). The RDA sponsored legislation that brought an end to forced labor in Africa (in 1946) and achieved pay equity in government service, but it lost a constitutional initiative that would have made all colonial inhabitants citizens of France (Manning 1988, 118, 142–44).

Other critics saw "oppressed Indians" (Brillant 1950a) in the Andes crossing or read Spanish cruelty as a reference to the "atrocities in Vietnam" (Bloch 1950). At least two critics compared Bolívar's scaling the Andes not to Napoleon's surmounting the Alps but to the two most famous communist marches of the era: Mao Tse Tung's Long March in 1934–35, when some 80,000 soldiers marched 12,500 kilometers in just over a year; and in Brazil in the 1920s, Luis Carlos Prestes's column, which covered some 25,000 kilometers over twenty-seven months (Roy 1950; Parmelin 1950).

While the communists may have found it useful to interpret the opera as a call for revolution and a protest against colonial oppression, the opera nevertheless depicts the slaves' happy servitude and unstinting loyalty to Bolívar, thus failing to trouble an ongoing racial hierarchy. In this sense, Milhaud and Léger, who both had supported the left-identified Popular Front government in the 1930s, represent what Tony Chafer and Amanda Sackur characterize as the front's "left-wing colonialism," a reform-minded approach extending socialist ideas while retaining the notion of *la plus grande France* (1999, 17). Further, the blackface performances of the slave couple Précipitation and her husband, Nicanor (figure 6.1), both in the original staging in 1950 and subsequent productions in Venezuela in 1983 and 2012, point to typologies embedded visually and musically in the opera genre.

As critical literature on blackface performance reveals, song, dance, and comedy minstrel shows were often on the same stage as opera. The minstrel show typically presented blackness as buffoonery, drunkenness, deceitfulness, and ignorance, playing an important role in shaping and perpetuating demeaning stereotypes (André, Bryan, and Saylor 2012, 1). In Jules Supervielle's play first performed in Paris in 1936, Nicanor is a comic minstrel figure or circus entertainer, a type that Léger carried over into his costume designs—a polka-dotted shirt and striped pants—that borrows

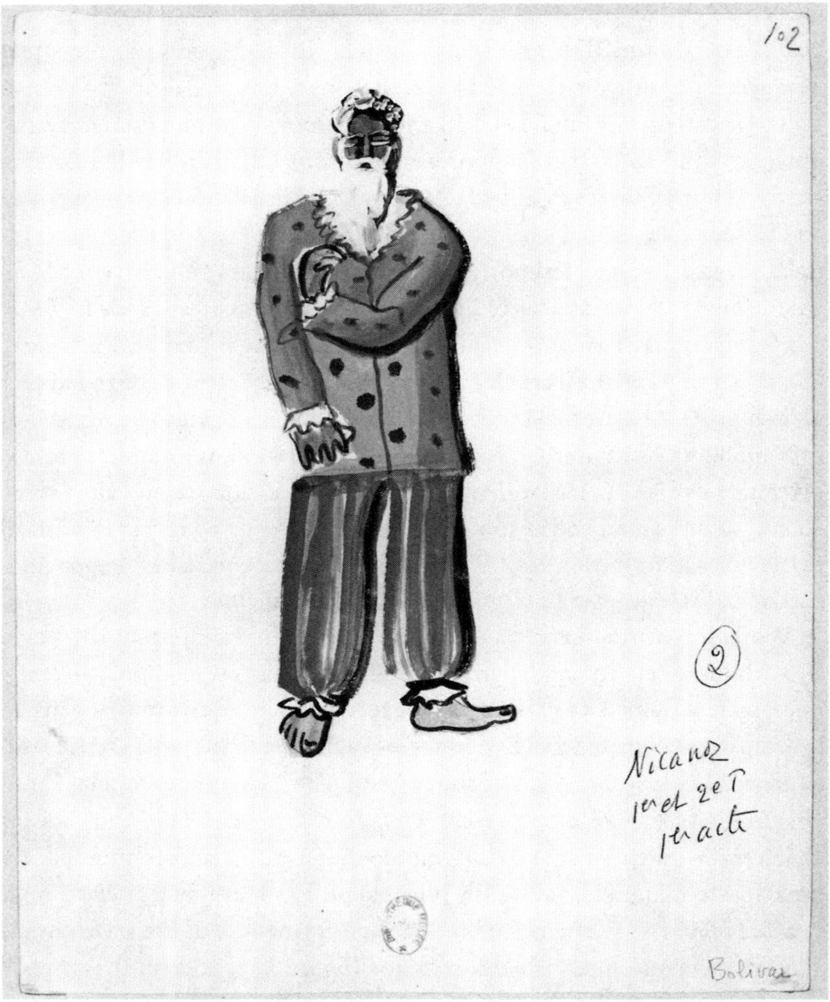

FIGURE 6.1. Fernand Léger. Costume design for Nicanor, Bolívar's "loyal servant." 1950. Gouache. 7.25" × 9" (18.4 × 22.86cm). Bibliothèque Nationale de France, Paris. © 2014 Artists Rights Society (ARS), New York; ADAGP, Paris.

from the circus clown. One reviewer described Nicanor as "excellent and smiling," thus recognizing him as a blackface type (Brillant 1950b). As Harlem Renaissance writer James Weldon Johnson observed about Ernest Krenek's opera *Jonny spielt auf* (1927), blackface functioned not only as a perpetuation of stereotypes but also as a refusal to fill roles with black singers (in Wipplinger 2012, 256n55). In Milhaud's opera, Nicanor as the comic lowbrow counterpart to Bolívar's tragic high-culture hero reveals a class and race-based divide between the two subjects, one highly circumscribed and another with a wide range of emotions and experiences.

Musgrave's *Bolívar* (1995)

Thea Musgrave's opera, generated fifty years after Milhaud's, envisions Bolívar less as an Enlightenment figure than as a military man who justifies tyranny to achieve unification but fails at that project and only foments anarchy. Compared to Milhaud's original production, Musgrave's is a more modest opera, crafted as a two-hour, two-act work requiring only five major characters, responding to a more limited budget. Musgrave's opera was originally commissioned by the Los Angeles Music Center Opera Association and the Scottish Opera, but Plácido Domingo, then artistic advisor to the Los Angeles Opera, backed off from the opera, and the Scottish Opera funding diminished due to financial crises (Kerner 1995; Milnes 1995). The opera was eventually staged, with a Spanish libretto, in 1995 in Norfolk and Richmond by the Virginia Opera Association, which Peter Mark, Musgrave's husband, founded and directed from 1975 to 2010. Although the opera company performs around the state, it is headquartered in Norfolk, the site of the United States'—and the world's—largest naval base as well as Norfolk State University, a historically black college that offers degrees in military history. In March 1994, Virginia Opera had just become the official opera company of the Commonwealth of Virginia, with politicians from both major parties as honorary members of its board. Patrons and audiences, therefore, came from the dominant state and national institutions, and the staging and libretto respond to these hegemonic powers.

Because of Musgrave's interest in female subjectivity and the slave narrative, one might have expected her to invent a Bolívar narrative envisioning greater agency for women and for female slaves. After studying with Nadia Boulanger, a French conductor and composer contemporary to Darius Milhaud, Musgrave became one of the few internationally recognized women composers in the male-dominated opera field. She has composed a significant body of orchestral works, including at least ten operas, two of which are about famous women: *Mary, Queen of Scots* (1977) and *Harriet Tubman, the Woman Called Moses* (1984). Like her *Bolívar,* Musgrave's *Harriet Tubman* had its premiere at the Virginia Opera, presents a narrative of liberation, demonstrates historical research by quoting from primary sources, and aims for musical authenticity such as the use of vernacular song. But while *Harriet Tubman* makes the slave hero central to the opera genre, Musgrave's *Bolívar* returns the subjectivity of the slave or freedman to the periphery even as the narrative content casts more doubt on the possibilities of liberty and unity than did Milhaud's version. One might expect that in the postcolonial and post–civil rights era of the late twentieth century, an opera about a revolutionary era would gesture to those incomplete revolutions from colonialism and slavery. This proves not to be the case, a point I will return to. Instead, the shift in focus from Harriet the slave hero to Bolívar the founding father hews more closely to the sensibilities of new patrons, particularly those in Richmond.

Although the opera opens with a gesture toward the Enlightenment ideals of liberty, equality, and fraternity, it soon turns into a military history as though anticipating a particular Norfolk audience. In the opening scene, the adult Bolívar pauses in battle to recall his childhood self and his lessons from his tutor Simón Rodríguez, who appears with a group of boys telling them to resist inequality as divisive: "Always a people divided, those who have and those who have not" (act 1, scene 1). But the libretto shifts from a disputation on values and republican ideals to a series of battles, skipping over the Admirable Campaign of 1813 and starting with the military campaigns of 1819, then focusing on the period between the crossing of the Andes and Bolívar's assumption of absolute power. The narrative emphasizes Bolívar's debates over unification with his generals—José Antonio Páez, Antonio José Sucre, Francisco de Paula Santander, and Daniel O'Leary—who appear only briefly as "officers 1, 2, and 3" in Milhaud's opera. Interludes envision the Battle of Boyacá, which liberated Colombia in 1819, and the Battle of Ayacucho, which liberated Peru in 1824. The music furthers the emphasis on a military narrative.

In his review, Carl Dolmetsch (1995) characterizes the opera as a "flawed masterpiece" that focuses "too little on his [Bolívar's] personal life"; it opens with "a taped crescendo of exploding shells and gunfire," and "much of the music has a martial quality." Themes that might have resonated with the histories of slavery and immigration in the United States—struggles for equality, enfranchisement, or even military service as a path to citizenship—are not developed. In an allusion to the manumission awarded to soldier-slaves, Bolívar promises his soldiers freedom after the battle: "The time will come

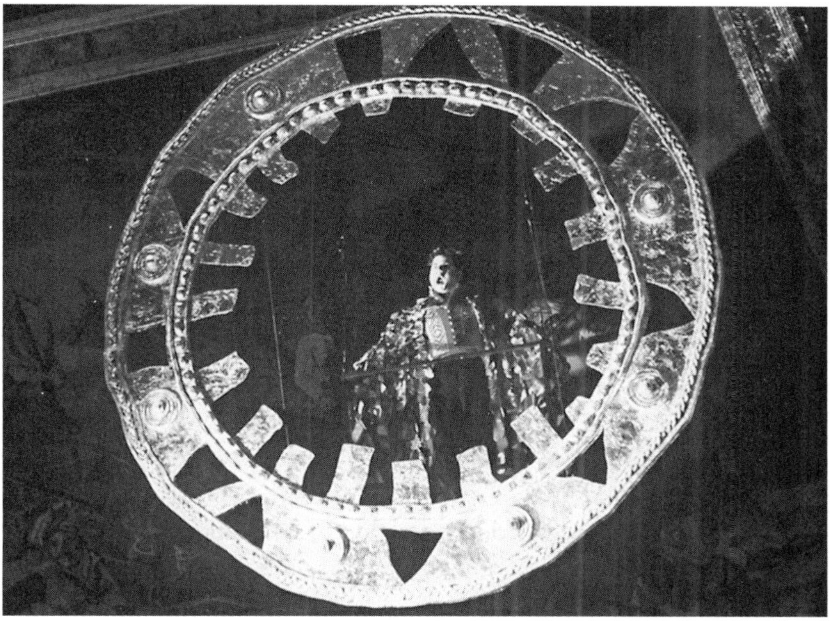

FIGURE 6.2. Production shot of act 2, scene 7, of Thea Musgrave's opera *Simón Bolívar*. 1995. Virginia Opera, Norfolk. Bolívar (Steven Guggenheim) celebrating his victory at Ayacucho. Photograph by Kathy Keeney, courtesy of Virginia Opera.

when those who have fought for their freedom will at last be free" (act 1, scene 2). Yet this theme never returns. Instead, the tensions between unification and tyranny, a statesman or general's concern, come to the fore.

Act 2 turns to the formation of Gran Colombia and Bolívar's dictatorial turn as a kind of deification. At the victory celebration, Inkan maidens sing a hymn to Inti the sun god in Quechua as they don Bolívar with a cloak whose hundreds of red and gold flaps cause Bolívar to resemble a tropical feathered bird. In John Conklin's dramatic staging, Bolívar ascends in a chariot framed by a monumental golden halo whose design borrows from Inkan arts and whose iconography conflates Christian hagiography and imperial investiture into a secular deification (figure 6.2). Musgrave's musical composition is historically informed by Spanish and Venezuelan music and dance, including Afro-Venezuelan and Andean Quechua song. The libretto and program notes for the opening performance indicate numerous sources: the galerón, a corrida, trinitaria, "La Vencedora" (composed for Bolívar's entry into Bogotá), an original pavanne dance (from Musgrave's

Mary, Queen of Scots), a tirana dance, and an ancient hymn to the sun sung in Quechuan. Musgrave's libretto identifies Ramón y Rivera's *La música afrovenezolana* (Caracas, 1971) as the textual source for the song "El quirimare" and Raoul d'Harcourt's *La Musique des Incas et ses survivances* (Paris, 1925) for the Inkan hymn to the sun. The aims of authenticity suggested by Conklin's designs and Musgrave's music do not, however, extend to an interrogation of racial and social hierarchies and their significations at the time of production.

Within the terms of the opera, liberty has more to do with the cessation of conflict and improved material conditions that are presumably possible with unification rather than with liberties of speech, debate, citizenship, and equality. Immediately following the victory celebration, Bolívar returns to Caracas, where the people complain that Bogotá has betrayed them: "we have known no freedom, no justice, only hunger, fighting, and sacrifice" (act 2, scene 7). Tyranny is the imposition of taxation and conscription; anarchy, disunity, hunger, and misery are the absence of liberty. Bolívar's decision to take absolute power (act 2, scene 10) results in an assassination attempt by Santander and others who chant, "death to the tyrant . . . death to the dictator." Páez declares, "He promised you equality and freedom, he gave you civil war," and the people respond, "We are slaves" (act 2, scene 11). In this rare reference to slavery, the historical conditions of the African slave trade have been elided in favor of casting all people under the yoke of war as impoverished slaves.

In the closing lines of the opera, Bolívar's words encode a tension between liberty and tyranny as he calls for "freedom: the fierce unending battle against tyranny, against anarchy" (act 2, coda). This version of freedom, from war or anarchy, remains silent on the question of racial hierarchies. Unlike Milhaud's opera, there is no scene celebrating the liberation of slaves and only a displaced mention of slavery. The silence about African slavery also means that the slave is transformed into a loyal servant and protector: Hipólita warns of the arrival of police (act 1 and coda); Palacios is Bolívar's "lifelong valet," who defends him during the assassination attempt (act 2, scene 11); and Manuela's slave Jonatás wields a knife in defense of her mistress (act 1, scene 6; act 2, scene 11).

The opera's ambivalence on the nature of freedom is compounded in the coda set in the twentieth century in "a square in a Latin American capital." Under the shadow of an enormous equestrian Bolívar, Hipólita cries out a warning, "Police," as troops enter to suppress a disaffected populace. The spirit of young Bolívar, uncorrupted by power, appears and returns to close the opera with a song of freedom against tyranny and anarchy. The coda thus references the repressive Latin American regimes of the 1980s, some of which had been supported by the U.S. government. Acknowledging this allusion, a *New York Times* reviewer accused Musgrave of "shaking her finger while driving home lessons about oppression and exploitation" (Rothstein 1995). By 1995, however, these regimes had largely been removed, culminating in 1990 with the end of General Augusto Pinochet's presidency in Chile. Most reviewers declined to consider political contexts, instead praising Musgrave's composition or calling for more prominent venues for her work (Hammer 1995; Kerner 1995; McLellan 1995; Milnes 1995).

In commenting on the contemporary political relevance of the opera, Peter Mark (1995) avoids mention of U.S. history, preferring instead to invoke other global politics, citing nation-states that failed due to ethnic or racial divisions: "*Simón Bolívar*—which was committed to before the fall of the Berlin wall, the dissolution of the Soviet Union, and the fratricidal disintegration of Yugoslavia, Somalia, Rwanda and now Haiti—deals directly with the ideals and difficulties of not just freedom from colonial oppression but larger federation and union; how much people are willing to give up for the common good." Mark's call to set aside ethnic divisions ("fratricidal disintegration") in favor of national unity ("the common good") aligns with a position of silence about slavery and civil rights in Virginia, the former capital of the Confederacy.

That Musgrave's *Bolívar* libretto never engages directly with the question of slavery or racial hierarchy accords with the new politics of the era, particularly in Virginia. At the time of the opera's production, Douglas Wilder had just stepped down as the first African American governor of Virginia (1990–94); he was also the first African American governor of any state since Reconstruction. George Allen, a welfare-reform-oriented Republican, had assumed the governorship in January 1995. Marks's statement and the opera's historical amnesia both function to disavow political and historical divisions in the United States and in Virginia. Many of the African American singers and actors came from the region, which had been an important site of slave importation (Walsh 1999), or from elsewhere in Virginia, which had been home to many of the nation's slaveholding founding fathers (Washington, Jefferson, Madison). The opera narrative, with its obvious parallels to the U.S. revolution to overthrow British colonial rule and Washington as Bolívar's counterpart, both invites and deflects questions about African servitude in the formation of the nation as well as ongoing inequality.

Although it is not clear that state partisanship directly influenced Musgrave's libretto, the ambivalent politics of race in the opera appear in the figure of Pablo, a fictional black soldier. While the secondary roles include several slave figures (Hipólita, Jonatás, Palacios), Pablo is significant because he is the only one who challenges rather than serves authority. His challenge to Bolívar's leadership resonates with the historical figure of José Prudencio Padilla, the Afro-Venezuelan general executed in 1828 for his participation in an assassination attempt, or possibly with the *pardo* general Manuel Piar discussed more fully in Alicia Ríos's contribution to this collection. Musgrave's opera even briefly mentions Padilla (act 1, scene 5). However, Pablo's direct resistance to Bolívar's tyranny is not depicted as a heroic act or justified resistance to the reinscription of Creole racial hierarchies. Pablo is a soldier who first appears as a *llanero,* the kind of Venezuelan plainsman who was instrumental in Bolívar's early victories. He is skeptical of the value of years of battle and later joins Santander in the assassination attempt, striking Manuela in the process (act 1, scene 2; act 2 scene 11). Because Manuela is depicted as a sympathetic and heroic figure with more stage time, the narrative organizes our identification with her. Pablo neither acts on behalf of a larger constituency nor embodies an ideal such as democracy, effectively muting any challenges to the racial order. In contrast, Musgrave's earlier opera, *Harriet Tubman,* as well as predecessors like Frederick Delius's *Koanga* (1899) and Scott Joplin's *Treemonisha* (1910, 1972) make slaves or freedwomen central to their narratives. Similarly, more recent opera narratives endow slaves with greater complexity, notably David Blake's *Toussaint* (1977), Anthony Davis's *Amistad* (1997), Glenn Paxton and Leroy Aaron's *Monticello* (2000), and Richard Danielpour and Toni Morrison's *Margaret Garner* (2005).

Nevertheless, Musgrave's *Bolívar* uses the historical figure of Hipólita to frame the narrative, conveying her maternal role in birthing revolution even while her agency remains circumscribed. Hipólita appears briefly in only a handful of scenes—act 1, scene 1; act 2, scene 8; act 2, scene 12; and act 2, scene 13—and in the coda. In the opening scene, the adult Bolívar recalls his youth, and the young Bolívar enters the stage with his tutor. Hipólita labors industriously (plate 10), attentive yet at an appropriate distance from her charge, who joins a multiracial group of boys described in the libretto as "mestizo, Indian, white." A cardboard French revolutionary complete with his red Phrygian cap signals the subject of the lesson as the youths gather around a globe to listen to their teacher. Hipólita sings the traditional Afro-Venezuelan melody "El quirimare," a mournful song about slaves under the threat of beatings "crying . . . singing . . . praying." Her song prefaces Simón Rodríguez's lessons on inequality when he points to Bolívar's shoes and the bare feet of Palacios, Hipólita's son who is the same age as the young Bolívar. She warns of the arrival of police coming to arrest Rodríguez, and again in the coda Hipólita cries out a warning. Hipólita's voice functions, then, as the metaphor for the cyclical return of enslavement, mourning, tyranny and resistance, and struggle, even as the opera's narrative and scenography occlude slavery's brutality, liberation into peonage rather than full citizenship, permitting historical amnesia about slavery in the Americas.

Conclusion

The multiple patrons, sites of production, and social-historical contexts of these Bolívar performances have generated a range of associations with other oppressions, liberations, and revolutions beyond Spanish colonialism. In 1950, Milhaud's opera resonated with French liberation from Nazi occupation but also with ongoing French colonialism. Fifty years later, the Virginia context of Musgrave's opera begs for comparisons not simply to the U.S. revolution but also to slavery, civil rights, social inequality, and U.S. militarism. In all contexts, ongoing racial and social hierarchies and the question of freedom persist. Questions of enslavement and servitude haunt the conventional associations of liberty with resistance to colonialism and so are tied to postmodern interrogations of not only whose liberty but whose history.

The historical Hipólita offers a postmodern response to the centrality of the great man and to marginalized histories. Bolívar famously described Hipólita as the woman "whose milk sustained my life" and "the only father I have ever known" (in Arana 2013, 22). If, as Nicholas Roberts and Luis Duno-Gottberg have argued in their contributions to this collection, Hugo Chávez transformed Bolívar from a floating signifier to a material (re)incarnation, perhaps a new symbolic order has emerged that could be populated by the marginalized. During Chávez's regime, Hipólita was one of many neglected historical African-diaspora and indigenous figures that were recuperated into the national symbolic. A Venezuelan news website quotes a letter written by Bolívar to his sister requesting that "our mother Hipólita" be cared for by the Bolívar family as a populist explanation for establishing a government health care program named after her (Reardon 2011). Hipólita's role as a sign of both national maternal care and the disenfranchised foregrounds the new discourse of revolution, one that has shifted from voting rights and free speech to health care, education, and the material conditions of well-being. In this sense, Hipólita might serve as a counterpart to Bolívar and the multiple forms of tyranny disguised as unification that he has represented: the great man of history, old colonial orders, deference to patriarchal orders, and emerging global capitalism.

Note

1. A special thanks to Juan Francisco Sans for sharing his expertise on Andrés Delgado Pardo and to the Lichys for sharing their research, especially Madeline Milhaud's libretto for her husband's opera.

References

André, Naomi Adele, Karen M. Bryan, and Eric Saylor. 2012. "Introduction: Representing Blackness on the Operatic Stage." In *Blackness in Opera*, edited by Naomi Adele André, Karen M. Bryan, and Eric Saylor, 1–10. Urbana: University of Illinois Press.

Andrews, George Reid. 2004. *Afro-Latin America, 1800–2000*. Oxford: Oxford University Press, 2004.

Antoine, Jean. 1950. "Bolívar à l'opéra." *Paris Presse,* May 14.

Arana, Marie. 2013. *Bolivar: American Liberator.* New York: Simon and Schuster.

Baignères, Claude. 1950. "La création de Bolívar." *Le Figaro Littéraire,* May 18.

Bloch, Gilbert. 1950. "Bolívar à l'opéra." *L'Humanité-Dimanche,* May 21.

Briggs, Ronald. 2010. *Tropes of Enlightenment in the Age of Bolívar: Simón Rodríguez and the American Essay at Revolution*. Nashville, TN: Vanderbilt University Press.

Brillant, Maurice. 1950a. "A l'opéra." *L'Aube,* May 15.

———. 1950b. "Bolívar." *L'Aube,* May 17.

Castro, Daniel. 2007. *Another Face of Empire: Bartolomé de las Casas, Indigenous Rights, and Ecclesiastical Imperialism*. Durham, NC: Duke University Press.

Chafer, Tony, and Amanda Sackur. 1999. Introduction to *French Colonial Empire and the Popular Front: Hope and Disillusion*, edited by Tony Chafer and Amanda Sackur, 1–32. New York: St. Martin's Press.

Chasteen, John. 2006. "Simón Bolivar: Man and Myth." In *Heroes and Hero Cults in Latin America*, edited by Samuel Brunk and Ben Fallaw, 21–39. Austin: University of Texas Press.

Collaer, Paul. 1998. *Darius Milhaud*. Translated and edited by Jane Hohfield Galante. San Francisco: San Francisco Press.

Derrick, Jonathan. 2002. "The Dissenters: Anti-Colonialism in France, c. 1900–40." In *Promoting the Colonial Idea: Propaganda and Visions of Empire in France*, edited by Tony Chafer and Amanda Sackur, 53–68. New York: Palgrave.

D'Harcourt, Raoul. 1925. *La Musique des Incas et ses survivances*. Paris: P. Geuthner.

Dolmetsch, Carl. 1995. Review of Thea Musgrave's *Bolívar*. *American Record Guide*, May–June, 44–46.

Drake, Jeremy. 1989. *The Operas of Darius Milhaud*. New York: Garland.

Dumesnil, René. 1950. "Bolívar à l'opéra." *Le Monde*, May 14–15.

Francia, Peter de. 1983. *Fernand Léger*. New Haven, NJ: Yale University Press.

Hammer, Janice. 1995. "Liberator." *Opera News*, January 7.

Hermant, Denis. 1950. "Un Tremblement de terre." *France-Soir*, May 13.

Kerner, Leighton. 1995. "South of the Border." *Village Voice*, February 14.

Léger, Fernand. 1950. "Notes de Fernand Léger sur Bolívar." *Arts*, April 28.

———. 1973. *Functions of Painting*. Translated by Alexandra Anderson. New York: Viking Press.

Manning, Patrick. 1998. *Francophone Sub-Saharan Africa, 1880–1985*. Cambridge: Cambridge University Press.

Mark, Peter. 1995. "From the Directors." Program, world premiere of Musgrave's *Simón Bolívar*. January. Archives of the Virginia Opera, Norfolk.

———. 2013. "About Peter Mark." *Peter Mark Opera*. http:\\www.petermarkopera.com.

Martínez Benedicto, Margarita. 1999a. "Andrés Delgado Pardo (1870–1940)." *Revista Musical de Venezuela* 39:81–135.

———. 1999b. "Andrés Delgado Pardo: Un precursor del nacionalismo musical." *Revista Musical de Venezuela* 40:95–125.

McLellan, Joseph. 1995. "In Norfolk, an Epic 'Bolivar.'" *Washington Post*, January 23.

Milhaud, Darius. 1950. Interview. *Le Monde*, May 13.

———. 1974/1995. *My Happy Life*. New York: M. Boyars.

Milhaud, Madeline. [1950]. *Bolivar*. Libretto. Livret francais. Collection of Atahualpa and Diana Lichy.

———. 2008. *My Twentieth Century*. Cleveland, OH: Darius Milhaud Society.

Milnes, Rodney. 1995. "In Harmony with History." *Times of London*, February 1.

Musée-National Fernand Léger. 1995. *Léger et le spectacle*. Exhibition catalogue. Paris: Réunion des Musées Nationaux.

Parmelin, Hélène. 1950. "La Liberté traverse les Andes à l'opéra." *Action* (Paris), June 19.

Ramón y Rivera, Luis Felipe. 1971. *La música afrovenezolana*. Caracas: Imprenta Universitaria.

Reardon, Juan. 2011. "Venezuela Marks Five Years of 'Mission Negra Hipólita.'" *Venezuelanalysis*, January 14. http://venezuelanalysis.com/news/5936.

Rothstein, Edward. 1995. "Heroes Make Good Opera; Icons Don't." *New York Times*, February 12.

Roy, Claude. [1950]. "Supervielle, Milhaud, Léger: Bolívar entre à l'opéra." *Lettres françaises* [May 13].

Sánchez, Juan Manuel. 2010. "Edición crítica de la música para piano de Andrés Delgado Pardo." *Revista Musical de Venezuela* 47:126–47.

Shanahan, Maureen G. 2005. "The Franco-Venezuelan Migrations and Metamorphoses of Simón Bolívar: 1950/2004." In *Democracy and Culture in the Transatlantic World*, edited by Charlotte Wallin and Daniel Silander, 199–207. Växjo, Sweden: Växjo University Press.

Virginia Opera. 1995. Synopsis. Program, world premiere of Musgrave's *Simón Bolívar*. January. Archives of the Virginia Opera, Norfolk.

Walsh, Lorena S. 1999. "New Findings about the Virginia Slave Trade." *Colonial Williamsburg Interpreter* 20:2.

Wipplinger, Jonathan O. 2012. "Performing Race in Ernst Krenek's *Jonny spielt auf*." In *Blackness in Opera*, edited by Naomi Adele André, Karen M. Bryan, and Eric Saylor, 236–59. Urbana: University of Illinois Press.

7

Centro Simón Bolívar

A Symbol of Liberation for Revolution Square in Ljubljana, Slovenia

TINA POTOČNIK

The primary concept for the Revolution Square complex in Ljubljana (1960, renamed Republic Square in 1991) by Slovenia's most important architect of the postwar period, Edvard Ravnikar, answered the mandate to architecturally conceptualize notions of revolution, independence, and anti-imperialism. While Ravnikar's inspiration has eluded scholars, in this study I connect his designs to the Yugoslav delegation sent to Latin America in 1959 on the occasion of its 150th anniversary of independence from Spain and more specifically to the Centro Simón Bolívar architectural complex erected in 1955 in Caracas.

Many studies, research projects, and popular media published since the mid-1990s deal with the work of Edvard Ravnikar, a former student of the architects Jože Plečnik, who designed numerous important buildings in Vienna, Prague, and Ljubljana, and of Le Corbusier, the pioneer of modernism and the international style (Ivanšek 1995; Krečič, Mušič, and Zupan 1995; Vodopivec and Žnidaršič 2010). In 1960, Ravnikar won the design competition for the urban arrangement of the Revolution Square complex in Ljubljana, one of the most important architectural complexes in Slovenia and in the former Yugoslavia. The first design for this complex along with its formal and symbolic dimensions were, I argue, informed by Caracas's architectural complex Centro Simón Bolívar. The erection of the Revolution Square complex and its formal aspects have been considered in many studies to date, but existing literature fails to address some crucial questions, notably the inspiration for the initial design as submitted to the competition.

The winning design entry depicts a monumental architectural composition with twin towers overlooking a wide platform. There are no studies that consider this design within architectural history or account for any connection between the Revolution Square complex's formal properties and the symbolic meaning attached to "revolution" in that era. By assessing the political context we gain a better understanding of the idea of revolution for this project and its primary design. Recent studies have unveiled the presence of strong transnational connections and influences among many Eastern European countries after World War II (for example, Stanek 2012, 361–86), while in the case of Yugoslavia, the most important transnational relations were with the non-aligned nations (Kulić and Mrduljaš 2012; Sekulić 2012). In 1961, the first Conference of Non-Aligned Heads of State or Government, representing twenty-five countries, took place in Belgrade, largely through the initiative of Yugoslavian president Josip Broz Tito. The non-aligned movement, which represented a counterbalance between the Soviet-aligned bloc and the NATO-aligned bloc and led to political, economic, and professional benefits for the participating countries and their leaders, arose at about the same time that Ravnikar developed his initial idea for the Revolution Square complex.

My research relies on these contextualizing events and contributes to the studies about them by revealing the ties between the initial concept for the Revolution Square complex in Ljubljana and the Centro Simón Bolívar in Caracas. I base my argument on new archival findings, architectural analyses (on both formal and symbolic levels), and, most importantly, primary documents regarding the transnational influences and the era's politics. With this historical approach, I find a link between Bolivarian symbolism and the idea of revolution in Yugoslavia. The transmission of architectural forms and concepts between Venezuela and Yugoslavia occurred at a key moment when Latin America celebrated its 150th anniversary of independence from Spain, and the Cold War raised new concerns about imperialism worldwide. The architectural complex in Caracas named after Simón Bolívar was, as interpreted by Slovenian leaders during the Cold War, a synonym for independence and anti-imperialism and provided a symbolic and formal model for the architectural complex in Ljubljana.

Yugoslavia, Latin America, and Revolution(s)

In the late 1950s, Yugoslavia, then a federal, socialist state of two autonomous provinces and six republics (one of which was Slovenia) under the leadership of President Tito, strengthened its political as well as economic contacts with Latin America. The latter was perceived on one hand as a promising new market for the export of Yugoslav goods and on the other hand as a source for raw material Yugoslavia needed (*Delo* 1959b). Although Yugoslav-Venezuelan economic exchange was still relatively low, good political relations were formed and perceived as the best basis for further economic development. Thus, in 1959, a Yugoslav delegation known as the Misija dobre volje, or Goodwill Mission, arrived in the post–coup d'état Venezuela after the dictatorship of Marcos Pérez Jimenéz was overthrown in 1958. The delegation also visited Cuba, Colombia, Peru, Ecuador, and Bolivia, all with the mission of a "political journey for the expansion and strengthening of the cooperation between Yugoslavia and Latin America" (*Delo* 1959d).

In 1959, when the Cuban Revolution "installed the Marxist regime led by Fidel Castro" and "prefigured Latin America's political and economic climate for the rest of the Cold War" (Almandoz 2006), Yugoslavia initiated a new politics outside the two blocs while simultaneously condemning colonialism and stressing the necessity of peaceful coexistence (Pirjevec 1995; Rajak 2005). Several anticolonial conferences were organized in Belgrade at that time; this kind of international politics reached its peak around 1960. In September 1961 Yugoslavia hosted the first conference of the non-aligned countries, to which—in order to express its interest in cooperation with Latin America—Cuba was also invited (Pirjevec 1995, 265).

In the same year as the Cuban Revolution, more precisely in July 1959, the Executive Council of the People's Assembly of the People's Republic of Slovenia adopted a decree to erect a monument to the Slovenian revolution of 1941 in Ljubljana, the capital of Slovenia. At the same time, the council appointed a committee to manage the process of its erection and entrusted the committee with the responsibility of creating a "coordinated urban arrangement of the area around the monument" (OPSR IZITR 1963). The committee's decision was to position the monument on the future Revolution Square on a nearby religious site, the Ursuline nuns' garden behind

Holy Trinity Church and the convent of the Ursulines, which was opposite the recently constructed People's Assembly building. This area, on the edge of Ljubljana's old town center, was projected to be the location for the new town center (Mihelič 1983, 38–43). In the same year, 1959, there was a separate competition for the urban development of this area; it required a plan for a new governmental, administrative, and cultural center of the socialist country that would at the same time be a plan for a place to commemorate the anniversary of the "insurrection of the Slovenian people and their victory" (Šlajmer 1960, 54). The deadline for the completion of the square with all the main buildings and the monument to the revolution was set for May 9, 1965, the twentieth anniversary of the country's liberation from fascism (ZAL 1960a).

In early June 1960, the competition committee finished evaluating the entries (*Delo* 1960). The winning concept by Ravnikar included only a few clearly defined structures and is published here for the first time (figure 7.1). The main idea of his design was a vast platform intended for public manifestations and two thick towers, each more than twenty stories tall with a triangular ground plan. The towers were meant to house the central state administrative offices of the People's Republic of Slovenia, the republic's Executive Council, and the secretariats or main offices of the Communist Party. There were some other small-scale buildings in the design as well on the edges of the platform, such as a hexagonal pantheon as a monument dedicated to Slovenians of great significance (ZAL 1960b). The red lines of the plan demarcate three zones, as noted on the document: the "zone of intensive daily life" on the left; the "zone of national reverence" on the right; and the "zone of the Executive Council and the Central Committee of the Communist Party" in the middle and at the top. The middle zone is depicted as a platform framed by the two towers with triangular ground plans. Revolution Square extends between the towers and north of them in the rectangular space linking all three zones. The Ursuline church and convent are located in the southern part of the zone of intensive daily life, while a hexagonal pantheon (never constructed) is located in the southern end of the zone of the Executive Council.

In addition to the monument to the revolution, a statue of President Tito was planned for the square, as indicated by Ravnikar's notes, although it was never made. Furthermore, a statue of Boris Kidrič, the leading Slovenian

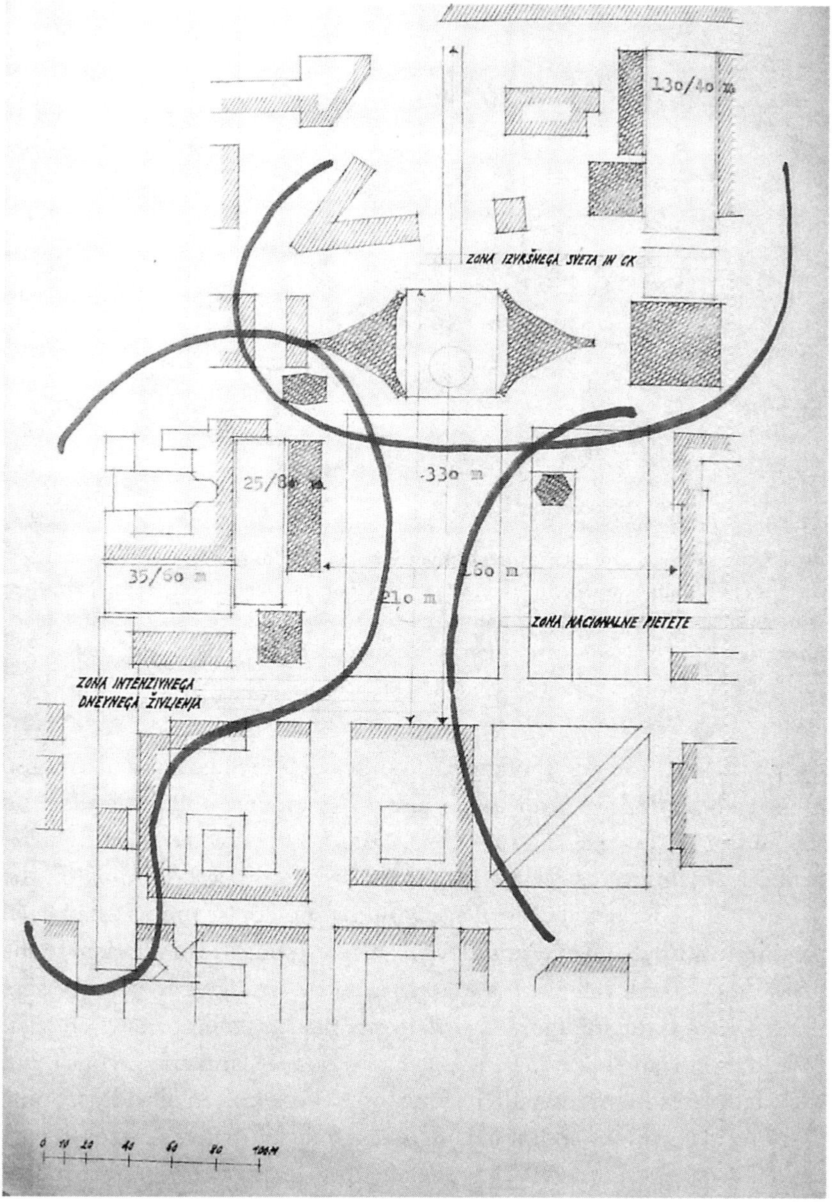

FIGURE 7.1. Edvard Ravnikar's competition entry for Revolution Square in Ljubljana, Slovenia, 1960. This diagram is oriented on a south–north axis, with south at the top of the photo. Courtesy of the Historical Archives Ljubljana (ZAL).

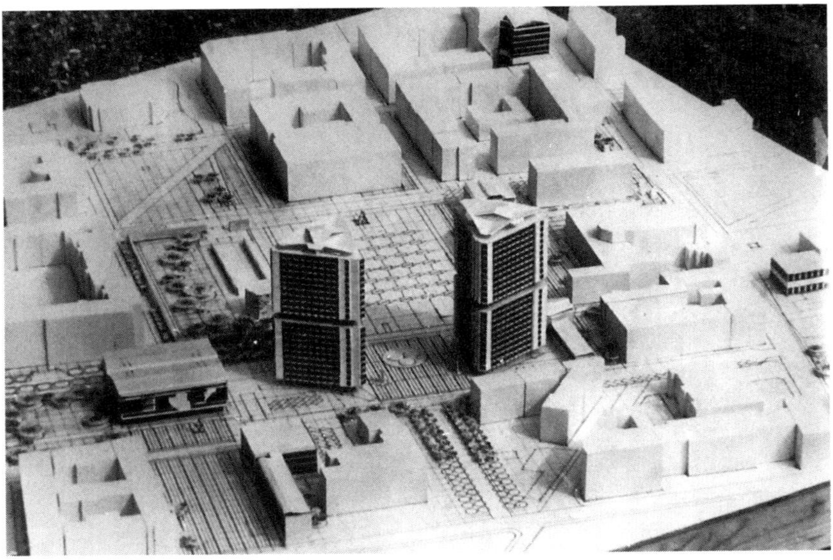

FIGURE 7.2. Edvard Ravnikar's three-dimensional model for the Revolution Square complex in Ljubljana, 1960. The model is oriented on a roughly north–south axis, with south at the bottom of the photo. Edvard Ravnikar Collection, fasc. II/51, folder Kompleks Trga revolucije. Permission of the Museum of Architecture and Design, Ljubljana.

Communist and organizer of the partisan struggle in Slovenia, and a monument dedicated to Edvard Kardelj, also a Communist political leader and the author of the first Yugoslav constitution, were erected on the square in the following years. By the early 1980s, when the last building on the square was constructed, Ravnikar's winning project (figure 7.2) had been significantly modified in terms of form and program. The monument to the revolution was relocated to the western edge of the square; the towers were moved toward the middle of the platform, turned around (now joined at their corners), and lowered (but not equally, so the symmetry is gone), and their façades were modified (to stone instead of glass on all sides). Some single- and two-story additional buildings were constructed on the square as well. It nevertheless managed to retain the primary architectural concept of two towers dominating a vast platform (plate 11).

Venice or Venezuela

Despite the lack of research on the concept of the Revolution Square complex, its architectural composition, or Ravnikar's winning competition entry, scholars have nevertheless made an attempt to link this complex to Venice, or to be more exact, to the Piazza San Marco. Marjan Ocvirk, Ravnikar's student and later coworker, makes this linkage in Amir Muratović's documentary film on Ravnikar (Muratović 2002–2003). Similarly, architect Rok Žnidaršič (2004, 20) and art historian Gojko Zupan (2001, 102) compare the Revolution Square complex to Piazza San Marco. Other interpretations cast Revolution Square's twin towers as a symbol of the so-called Ljubljana Gate, a geographic passage in the Ljubljana basin that has been a path for human migration since antiquity and within which the square is geographically located. Still others see the twin towers as a dialogue with Ljubljana's many paired church bell towers; close to the square are the cathedral, the Franciscan Church of the Annunciation, St. Peter's Church, and the Church of St. John the Baptist. Yet other architects and historians compare the square's twin towers to twin towers beyond Slovenia's borders, such as Toronto's City Hall, Lake Shore Drive Towers in Chicago, a doubled version of the Seagram Building in New York, and twin towers in Stockholm and Minsk, probably Kungstornen and Minsk's City Gates (Košir 1972, 20; Krečič, Mušič, and Zupan 1995, 33, 66; Lajovic 1972, 21). In this context, the architect Vladimir Braco Mušič, another former Ravnikar student and later his co-worker, has pointed to Venezuela and Caracas. However, Mušič does not mention any specific architectural complex (in Muratović 2002–2003).

In a survey of architecture in Caracas, the Centro Simón Bolívar (figure 7.3), one of the most important architectural complexes in Latin America, stands out. Designed by the Venezuelan architect Cipriano J. Domínguez and constructed by 1955, it was for years one of the most important centers of the Venezuelan government's administrative activities. The complex of offices and shops it contains was part of a major—though never completed—urban redevelopment of Caracas initiated in 1939 by the French urban planner Maurice Rotival. Instead of planning the city around the Plaza Bolívar, an area too small for the anticipated growth of the city, the Plan Rotival proposed a new urban center around the new Avenida Bolívar. In developing his urban design Rotival envisioned in 1946 a Foro Bolívar commercial center, and Domínguez was then commissioned to orchestrate

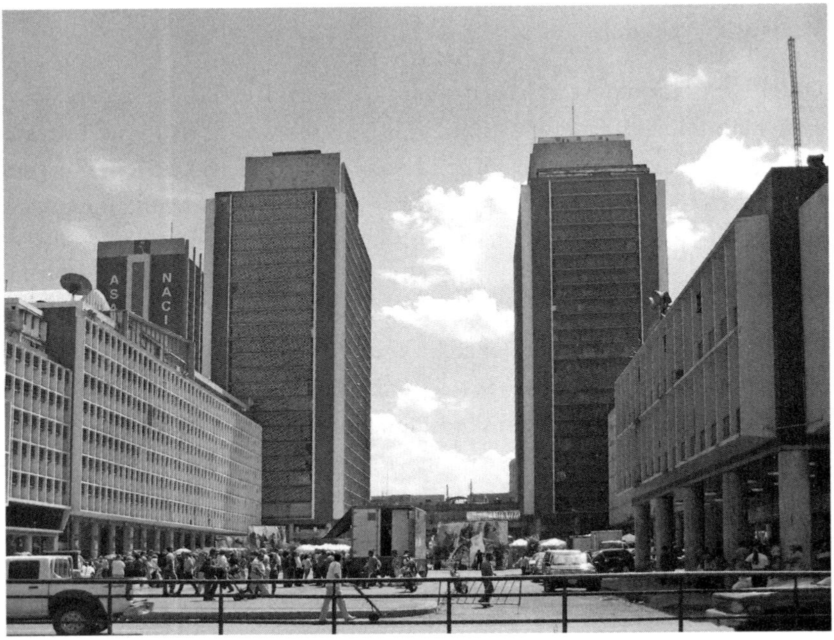

FIGURE 7.3. Centro Simón Bolívar in Caracas, 1954. Photograph by Tina Potočnik, 2013.

the architectural project (Gasparini and Gómez 2010). The architectural complex consists of two parallel building blocks adjoined by thirty-story high twin towers, each of which has a rectangular ground floor; together the twin towers dominate the Plaza Mayor. The complex includes a system of underground and ground-level walkways, porches, and passages, while the Avenida Bolívar passes under the architectural complex through a tunnel so that the road then leads to El Silencio housing complex designed in 1942 by Venezuela's premier modernist architect, Carlos Raúl Villanueva, and completed in 1945.

At first glance a comparative analysis of Ljubljana's Revolution Square complex and the Centro Simón Bolívar complex reveals some obvious differences in their urban arrangements as well as their architectural compositions. One of the differences concerns scale, which is understandable since Caracas was—and is—a much bigger city than Ljubljana. The composition of Ljubljana's square does not consist of two parallel, low blocks bordering the square to the west and east, as is found in Caracas. Nevertheless, there are compositional similarities. In Ljubljana an existing building, notably an apartment block built in the beginning of the 1940s, forms a western edge, while on the eastern edge Ravnikar foresaw a new building of a similar height (built in the beginning of the 1970s and used as a department store). An additional important difference is the triangular ground floor of the towers in Ljubljana. As Ravnikar wrote in his competition entry for Revolution Square, he used the triangular plan because "the analysis of different shapes of ground plans for tall administrative buildings has shown that the triangular form is the most rational" (ZAL 1960b). However, in his competition entry Ravnikar presented several possibilities for ground floors, including a rectangular plan.

Despite the differences in the architectural compositions in Caracas and Ljubljana, the key aspects of transmission are, I propose, in the connections between Bolivarian symbolism and the idea of revolution in Yugoslavia that then became infused within the design of the Revolution Square complex. But how to account for the transmission of the concept of revolution represented by the Centro Simón Bolívar to Ljubljana's Revolution Square? My research shows that the general guidelines for the architectural composition were suggested to Ravnikar by Boris Kraigher, one of the most powerful politicians in Yugoslavia and president of the Executive Council of the People's Assembly, the original investor in the Revolution Square complex. Until now there have only been oral statements regarding Kraigher's role in the square's plan. Krečič, Mušič, and Zupan (1995, 66) state that the art historian Nace Šumi had made this claim on several occasions. In Muratović's 2002–2003 documentary on Ravnikar as well, Mušič reports that Ravnikar himself mentioned Kraigher's influence.

Now documentary evidence corroborates these reports. Archival records show two important historical facts: the deadline for completion of the square was set in Kraigher's office (ZAL 1960a), and he knew of the complex in Caracas. At the end of May 1960—when the competition for Revolution Square was being held—Kraigher visited Caracas and other places in Latin America, including Argentina, Brazil, Chile, and Bolivia. According to several documents and Kraigher's unpublished travel diary, Kraigher was president of the Yugoslav delegation that traveled to Latin America to celebrate the 150th anniversary of Latin America's independence from Spain (Kraigher 1960b; ARS 1960).

In addition, before the 1959–60 competition, Ravnikar had made several earlier projects and studies for the Revolution Square site, but none of these contemplated twin towers, as has already been pointed out by some of the scholars, among them Lajovic (1972, 21) and Jelka Pirkovič (1986, 156–57). These earlier projects, in which Ravnikar sought to preserve the historical town, include the competition entry for the broader area of Congress Square (1939–40); studies for the building of the Presidium of the People's Assembly (1947; several variants); and the variant development proposition for the surrounding area of the People's Assembly (1958) (cf. *Arhitekt* 1960, 49–58; Košir 1972, 18–19; Mihelič 1983, 38; Mušič 1958, 11; Mušič and Ivanšek 1948, 104–5; Ravnikar 1993, 15–17). The 1960 competition for Revolution Square was based on Ravnikar's 1958 design for the People's Assembly (Investicijski 1985). Ravnikar then came up with his Revolution Square design that boasted twenty-story twin towers. All this speaks to the creation of Revolution Square as part of a political and ideological agenda with a strong symbolic function.

Parallels in Liberator Cults and Architectural Complexes

Architecture and urban planning became ideological tools in many developing states after World War II. In some of Latin America's metropolises, architectural modernism was put into the service of the progressive goals of both democracies and dictatorships (Almandoz 2006, 97). In both realms, architecture functioned as a showcase for displaying the rapid modernization pursued for postwar economic development (Fraser 2000, 15–18). Such development projects were a common part of the agenda in Latin America and were influenced by U.S. efforts against communism (Williamson 1992, 338–39). University cities, housing projects, and administrative buildings in Venezuela, characterized by the "alliance between modernizing governments and modernist architects," were among the best exponents of the modern architecture movement in the world (Fraser 2000, 15–18). The architectural complex of the Centro Simón Bolívar served for many years as the symbol of the city's progress and development (Gasparini and Gómez 2010; Goldberg 1980, 27). Ravnikar was surely familiar with the Centro Simón Bolívar, as it was published in the world-famous *L'Architecture d'Aujourd'hui* in 1956 (116–17) and again in 1960 (72–79).

Venezuela's independence from both Moscow and Washington, D.C., was crucial in aligning it with Tito's new non-aligned coalition. In 1960

Venezuela secretly signed an agreement with OPEC with the aim of promoting independence from British and U.S. corporations dominating the global oil industry. I argue that Yugoslavia's anticolonial international politics and fear of new imperialism represented by both U.S. and Soviet power in the Cold War caused Slovenian revolutionary authorities to look for an ideological alignment and architectural composition from outside of the two world blocs. The Centro Simón Bolívar represented not only modernism, progress, and development but also liberation from colonialism and imperialism. After the Cuban Revolution, a shifting political and economic climate saw the rise of opposition to U.S. policies in Latin America. The notion of unity and revolution, characterized as liberation from dictatorship and imperialism in the Bolivarian iconography articulated in the Centro Simón Bolívar, could have represented a key ideological affinity for the transmission of the architectural composition to Ljubljana. In 1939, Rotival had invoked a Bolivarian discourse in the expansion and modernization of Caracas: "the great guideline for Caracas, the new Mecca of a civilization based on education of the new principles of the state, . . . uses the concept of the ingenuity of Bolívar, who gave a great part of Latin American civilization a certain unity" (Vallmitjana 1991, 106). Furthermore, Rotival even states that the "fundamental objective . . . is to revitalize the center of Caracas, returning its true character to the heart of the city, in which the multiplicity of activities culminates in the monumental complex dedicated to the Bolivarian cult" (Vallmitjana 1991, 102).

In 1959, shortly before Kraigher's visit to Caracas and the competition for the Revolution Square complex, Bolívar received increasing historical attention in Yugoslavia. Bolívar's biography and notes from his diary had been translated to Slovenian (Edschmid 1959). This publication was followed by numerous articles on Bolívar, Venezuela, and Latin America in the leading Slovenian newspapers. One of the articles alludes to Bolívar's reputation in Slovenia as the liberator of Latin America: "Latin American countries have two . . . qualities: they have been independent for 150 years, and it does not occur to anyone to contradict the independence of their states" (*Delo* 1959a). This also indicates that the Latin American example could have served as an affirmation of the autonomy of Yugoslavia. Thus, the complex named after Bolívar would have been an appropriate model for an architectural complex that was essentially interlaced with the "insurrection of the

Slovenian people in 1941 for national liberation . . . in the frame of the uprising of all Yugoslav nations," as Kraigher put it (in *Delo* 1959c). He argued for the need to commemorate ideas of revolution and autonomy:

> Therefore, it is the right of our people to devote their attention to reviving memories of the most important as well as the most heroic period of our nation, and to place stress also on public spaces. Everything that we build today, we create on the foundation of those victories; therefore, it is right to give it a suitable expression. . . . The republican monument to the revolution should be built in Ljubljana, in the very center, as Ljubljana was the central point and the main organizer of the people's revolution in Slovenia . . . also under Tito's leadership. (In *Delo* 1959c)

Kraigher explicitly sought to create a connection between Venezuelan and Slovenian conceptions of liberation. In June 1960 Kraigher gave an interview to the Caracas newspaper *El Nacional* in which he (partially inaccurately) claimed, "Similar to other Yugoslavian countries, Slovenia has been in its past subjected to the rule of Bulgarians, Hungarians, Turks, Austrians, Germans etc. . . . After the liberation at the end of World War II, the constituent assembly abolished the monarchy and founded a Federal Republic, at the head of which was Josip Broz (Tito), a national hero and a chief of the Yugoslav communist Party" (Kraigher 1960a). Kraigher's statement reveals what he saw as the parallel between two liberator cults—of Tito in Yugoslavia on one hand and Bolívar in Latin America on the other, both created by somewhat similar historical circumstances, above all the liberation from imperialism.

* * *

Venezuela's cult of Bolívar reached the Slovenian state in the western part of the Balkans through the beliefs held by certain political figures—especially Kraigher—who played a crucial role in the creation of the architectural complex in Ljubljana. This impetus relied on the perception of parallel histories of the liberation of the respective nations of Slovenia and Venezuela as well as the justification for those revolutions. This perception was generated within the context of and enabled by the historic events of the years 1959–1961. In 1959 the Cuban Revolution culminated in January, the Yugoslav goodwill mission including Kraigher went to Venezuela and Latin

America in May, and the Slovenian Executive Council formed a planning committee for Revolution Square starting in July. In 1960 the design competition for Revolution Square and the 150th anniversary of Latin America's independence took place. And in September 1961 the first conference of non-aligned states occurred. Although in subsequent years the original ideological and symbolical function of the Revolution Square complex has gradually been forgotten, the architectural significance of the complex has only increased in reputation.

References

Almandoz, Arturo. 2006. "Urban Planning and Historiography in Latin America." *Progress in Planning* 2, no. 65 (2006): 81–123. http://www.estudiosurbanos.uc.cl/wp-content/uploads/2011/05/ProgressinPlanningArturoAlmandoz.pdf.

L'Architecture d'Aujourd'hui. 1956. "La arquitectura en Venezuela." No. 67–68 (October): 84–139.

———. 1960. "Caracas. Reprise du plan d'aménagement 1950–1960." No. 88 (February–March): 72–79.

Archives of the Republic of Slovenia (ARS). 1960. Rešenje. April 28. AS 1529, Osebna zbirka Borisa Kraigherja (OZBK), fasc. 18.

Arhitekt. 1960. "Med natečajema za urbanistično ureditev središča Ljubljane." Vol. 10, no. 4:49–58.

Delo. 1959a. "Latinska Amerika." May 1, p. 15.

———. 1959b. "Naši izdelki v Južni Ameriki." May 13, p. 5.

———. 1959c. "Ljudska vstaja je prvič v naši zgodovini združila vse napredne, borbene sile slovenskega naroda (Govor Borisa Kraigherja)." July 22, p. 1.

———. 1959d. "Uspešni razgovori." August 20, p. 4.

———. 1960. "Predlogi za izhodiščni program novega Trga revolucije v Ljubljani." June 11, p. 2.

Edschmid, Kasimir. 1959. *Simon Bolivar*. Ljubljana: Državna založba Slovenije.

Fraser, Valerie. 2000. *Building the New World. Studies in Modern Architecture of Latin America 1930–1960*. London: Verso.

Gasparini, Graziano, and Hannia Gómez. 2010. "The Partaking of Modern Architecture with the City of the Past: the Case of the Centro Simón Bolívar." Lecture, Venezuelan Working Party, 11th International Docomomo Conference, "Living in the Urban Modernity," Mexico City, August 26. Docomomo Venezuela, October 2. http://docomomovenezuela.blogspot.com/2010/10/partaking-of-modern-architecture-with.html.

Goldberg, Mariano. 1980. *Guía de edificaciones contemporáneas en Venezuela. Parte*

1. Caracas: Facultad de Arquitectura y Urbanismo, Universidad Central de Venezuela.

Historical Archives Ljubljana (ZAL). 1960a. LJU 30, Okrajni ljudski odbor Ljubljana (OLO LJ) 128/1320. May 18. Povzetek sklepov v zvezi z nadaljnjimi deli za ureditev Trga revolucije in gradnjo novega objekta izvršnega sveta ter upravnih organov.

———. 1960b. Competition entry no. 26534. Investicijski zavod za izgradnjo Trga revolucije (IZITR), fasc. 37.01.

Investicijski zavod za izgradnjo Trga revolucije Ljubljana, 1960–1985. 1985. Graditev Trga revolucije: Zaključno poročilo in pregled 25 let dela Investicijskega zavoda za izgradnjo Trga revolucije v Ljubljani. Ljubljana, Slovenia: IZITR.

Ivanšek, France, ed. 1995. *Hommage à Edvard Ravnikar: 1907–1993*. Ljubljana, Slovenia: France Ivanšek and Marta Ivanšek.

Koselj, Nataša. 1995. *Arhitektura 60-ih let v Sloveniji: kontinuiteta ideje*. Ljubljana: AB.

———. 2003. "Tradicija napredka." PhD diss., Faculty of Architecture, University of Ljubljana.

Košir, Fedja. 1972. "Odzivi." *AB*, no. 6–7:18–21.

Kraigher, Boris. 1960a. Interview. "Yugoslavia escogió su propio camino hacia el socialismo." *El Nacional* (Caracas), June 4. ARS.

———. 1960b. Travel diary. [May]. ARS.

Krečič, Peter, Marko Mušič, and Gojko Zupan. 1995. *Edvard Ravnikar: Arhitekt, urbanist, oblikovalec teoretik, univerzitetni učitelj, publicist: Umetnostnozgodovinski oris*. Ljubljana, Slovenia: Arhitekturni muzej.

Kulić, Vladimir, and Maroje Mrduljaš. 2012. *Modernism In-Between: The Mediatory Architectures of Socialist Yugoslavia*. Berlin: Jovis Verlag.

Lajovic, Janez. 1972. "Odzivi." *AB*, no. 6–7:21.

Mihelič, Breda. 1983. *Urbanistični razvoj Ljubljane*. Ljubljana: Partizanska knjiga.

Muratović, Amir. 2002–2003. *Iskanje popolnega mesta. Portret Edvarda Ravnikarja*. Film. Ljubljana, Slovenia: Radiotelevizija Slovenija.

Mušič, Marjan, and France Ivanšek, eds. 1948. *Zbornik oddelka za arhitekturo na Univerzi v Ljubljani 1946–1947*. Ljubljana: Državna založba Slovenije.

Mušič, Vladimir Braco. 1958. "Smrtna obsodba plemenite hiše." *Arhitekt* 8, no. 23:7–12.

Odbor za postavitev spomenika revolucije, Investicijski zavod za izgradnjo Trga Revolucije (OPSR IZITR). 1963. *Spomenik revolucije na novem Trgu revolucije v Ljubljani*. Archives of the National Museum of Contemporary History, Ljubljana (MNZ).

Pirjevec, Jože. 1995. *Jugoslavija (1918–1992): Nastanek, razvoj ter razpad Karadjordjevićeve in Titove Jugoslavije*. Koper: Lipa.

Pirkovič, Jelka. 1986. "Danes, nekoč in Trg revolucije." *Sinteza,* no. 65–68:156–57.

Rajak, Svetozar. 2005. "In Search of a Life outside the Two Blocs: Yugoslavia's Road to Non-Alignment." In *Great Powers and Small Countries in Cold War, 1945–1955,* edited by Ljubodrag Dimić. Belgrade: Faculty of Philosophy, Department of Yugoslav History, University of Belgrade.

Ravnikar, Edvard. 1953. "Za pravilno obravnavo centra Ljubljane." *Arhitekt* 3, no. 10:13.

———. 1993. "Razmišljanja o Ljubljani leta 1946." *Urbani izziv,* no. 23–25:15–17.

Sekulić, Dubravka, 2012. "Constructing a Non-Aligned Modernity: The Case of Energoprojekt." In *Unfinished Modernisations between Utopia and Pragmatism. Architecture and Urban Planning in the Former Yugoslavia and the Successor States,* edited by Maroje Mrduljaš and Vladimir Kulić, 122–33. Zagreb, Croatia: Croation Architects Association.

Stanek, Łukasz. 2012. "Miastoprojekt Goes Abroad: The Transfer of Architectural Labour from Socialist Poland to Iraq (1958–1989)." In "Cold War Transfer: Architecture and Planning from Socialist Countries in the 'Third World.'" Special issue, *Journal of Architecture* 17, no. 3:361–86.

Šlajmer, Marko. 1960. "Natečaj za ureditev novega Trga revolucije v Ljubljani." *Arhitekt* 10, no. 4:54–58.

Vallmitjana A., Marta. 1991. *El Plan Rotival: La Caracas que no fue: 1939–1989, un plan urbano para Caracas.* Caracas: Ediciones Instituto de Urbanismo, Facultad de Arquitectura y Urbanismo, Universidad Central de Venezuela.

Vodopivec, Aleš, and Rok Žnidaršič, eds. 2010. *Edvard Ravnikar: Architect and Teacher.* New York: Springer.

Williamson, Edwin. 1992. *The Penguin History of Latin America.* London: Penguin.

ZAL. *See* Historical Archives Ljubljana.

Žnidaršič, Rok. 2004. "Metoda projektiranja arhitekta Edvarda Ravnikarja." *AB* 34, no. 165–66:8–33.

Zupan, Gojko. 2001. "Trg revolucije." In *20. stoletje: Arhitektura od moderne do sodobne: Vodnik po arhitekturi,* edited by Damjana Prešeren, 101–5. Ljubljana: Zavod za varstvo kulturne dediščine Slovenije.

8

In Bed with Dead Bolívar

Beatriz González's Case for Critical History Painting

ANA MARÍA REYES

In a 2011 documentary film, painter Beatriz González remarks, "Colombia is a country of violence and laurels" ("violencia y condecoraciones") (in García Moreno 2011). This phrase, in González's typically dry and biting humor, captures the deep rift between experiences lived by different sectors of Colombian society. Perhaps no other historical figure in Spanish America has received more laurels than Simón Bolívar. Yet his legacy remains deeply controversial and even polarizing, from canonized Liberator, the selfless genius preordained by God to liberate his people, to condemned tyrant, a narcissistic, womanizing, and glory-hungry caudillo, as well as all the permutations in between. Official narratives tend to simplify and abridge history in order to forge cohesive national identities. Simón Bolívar is unequivocally such an icon enlisted time and again to legitimize political programs or to unite socially fragmented communities. Honored across class lines, Bolívar has proven to be a malleable icon appropriated in the name of myriad causes—like a vampire who is unable to capture a "true" reflection in the mirror but whose body resurfaces again and again.[1] In two works by Beatriz González the artist repurposed well-known representations of Bolívar: *Apuntes para la historia extensa* (1967) (plate 12) and *Mutis por el foro* (1973) (plate 14). These works revitalized contemporary history painting, being neither the falsified and decorous official versions nor the complete disavowal of the genre through abstraction—which has served as evidence of Latin American modernity in the international art circuit—but rather a critical re-vision.

Beatriz González's pictorial interventions were produced during the period of transition in Colombia when the iconic Bolívar became unhinged from the Conservative Party, then drifted temporarily as an ambivalent signifier before being anchored onto a revolutionary socialist program. Since the nineteenth century Colombian politicians and historians have habitually accredited Bolívar with planting the ideological seeds of the Conservative Party and his first vice president, turned political foe, Francisco de Paula Santander, with the Liberal Party (Safford and Palacios 2002; 118). Even though scholars have convincingly dispelled this neatly convenient foundational myth, it served as a poignant political mobilizer during times of partisan civil war, such as the War of a Thousand Days (1899–1902) and La Violencia (1946–66). In fact, ultraconservative Laureano Gómez, founder of the Bogotá newspaper *El Siglo* and president of the proclaimed Bolivarian Nation (1950–53) during the most vicious years of La Violencia, fueled the ire of partisan retaliation by enlisting Bolívar as anti-Liberal and anticommunist protector of Catholicism, patrimony, and national order (Melo 2010, 119).

When the bloodshed in rural areas of Colombia spiraled out of control, the elites supported a short-lived military dictatorship (1953–57) by General Gustavo Rojas Pinilla. Rojas Pinilla's own form of militaristic Bolivarianism took a populist direction, at which point the political elites understood that their survival depended on the cordial coexistence, or *convivencia*, of the leaders of both parties. Out of this general anxiety emerged a power-sharing concordat known as the National Front (1958–74), which ensured a mathematical division of political offices between the two parties and alternation of the presidency. This *convivencia* put an end to the escalating partisan violence but in effect canceled out all political alternatives and thus restricted the parameters of democracy.

On January 17, 1974, the Marxist guerrilla movement M-19, Movimiento 19 de Abril,[2] stormed Bolívar's estate in Bogotá, the Quinta de Bolívar, and took his sword that was on display (as Alejandro E. Gómez Pernia describes in this volume). From that moment the Colombian Left claimed to continue Bolívar's unfinished struggles for liberation. This new Bolívar, recast as revolutionary *guerrillero*, took hold and inspired both the Colombian Communist Party, which proclaimed itself Bolivarian in 1980, and the guerrilla insurgencies' umbrella alliance Coordinadora Guerrillera Simón Bolívar. Beatriz González painted and displayed her Bolivarian works at a volatile time for the Liberator's signification in Colombia—his legacy, from conservative to revolutionary, was contested terrain. This is not to say that González's Bolivarian iconography should be read as either a prelude to socialist or revolutionary Bolivarianism or as a pivot on which the symbol turns but rather as an active player in this interstitial juncture when cultural representations of history and patrimony played an important role in disrupting discourses of political legitimacy.

* * *

In 1967 González submitted to the Salon of National Artists in Bogotá a double portrait—of Simón Bolívar in *Apuntes para la historia extensa, Tomo I,* and of Francisco de Paula Santander in *Tomo II* (plate 12). For an international audience, *Apuntes para la historia extensa* may appear to be a pop art rendition of historical figures—Bolívar as Sergeant Pepper or, in Traba's term (1984, 174), a "pop drummer." For a Colombian audience, the images represented an irreverent and critical rendition of the national founding fathers. A detailed look at the local referents as well as the anxious or condescending responses they evoked demonstrates that González tapped into a crisis of confidence in Bolivarian or patrimonial signification while deliberately assaulting the very mechanism of social exclusion of the National Front government, the traditional two-party system, and the social hierarchy in Colombia.

In August 1967 González found two low-grade reproductions in the newspaper *El Tiempo,* one of Simón Bolívar attributed to Pedro José Figueroa (plate 13) and a miniature of Francisco de Paula Santander by Francisco Evangelista González (figure 8.1).[3] These rarely displayed paintings diverge greatly in size, the Bolívar approximating life size and the Santander a miniature.

Thus, *El Tiempo,* in its rescaled printed reproduction of the works on August 6, 1967, created a juxtaposition of uniform medallions impossible to achieve with the nineteenth-century paintings. By doing so, the newspaper and González's medallions based on them evoked the one-peso bank note that positions oval medallion representations of Bolívar and Santander on the same side of the bill and that circulated from 1959 to 1977 as symbolic of two-party *convivencia* (figure 8.2). In her appropriation, González emulated the effects of the newspaper's mechanical reproduction; she further impoverished the images by simplifying the contours, reducing the color

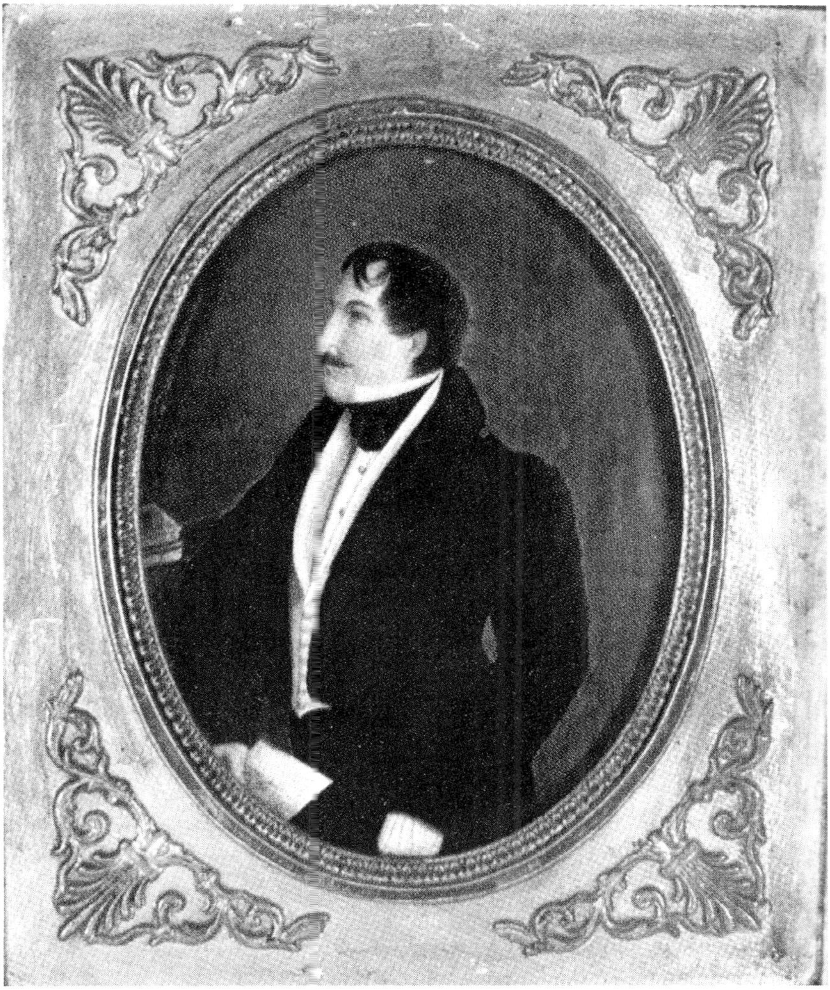

FIGURE 8.1. Fernando Evangelista González. *Francisco de Paula Santander*. May 12, 1831. Watercolor on ivory. 5.3" × _" (13.5 cm × 10 cm). Permission of the Museo de la Independencia Casa del Florero, del Ministerio de Cultura de Colombia, Bogotá.

palette, and flattening the figures with commercial enamel paint on metal plates. *Apuntes para la historia extensa* points to the mutation that occurs as the images passed from one socially codified space to another (museum to treasury to newspaper), from manual production to mechanical reproduction and back to manual production, from a skilled to an unskilled hand, from a cultivated to an uncultivated artist and back again.

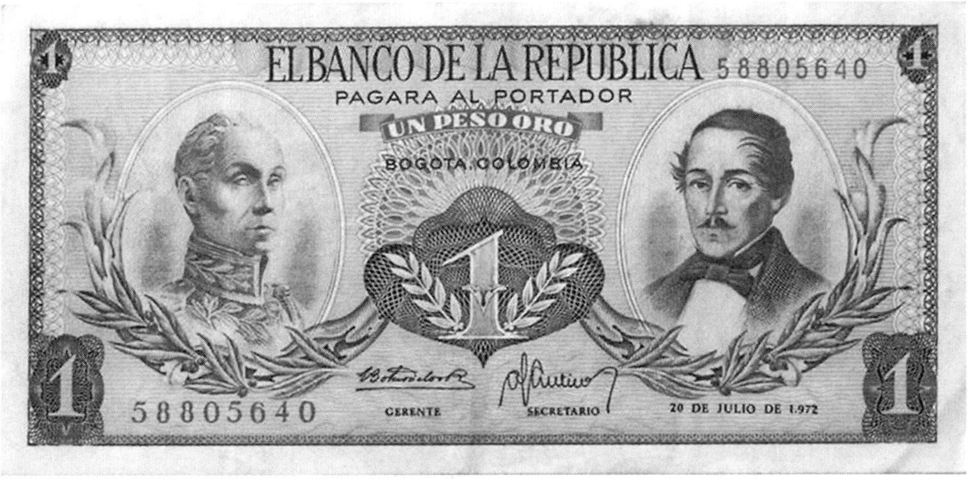

FIGURE 8.2. One-peso bank note. Banco de la República, Colombia, 1959. Public domain.

González's "representation of a representation," to use her phrase, calls attention to the process by which legitimate official culture is approached from the periphery (Calderón 1988). González's initial idea for the medallions came from an oval tin parking lot sign across the street from her Bogotá apartment, Parqueadero el Libertador, or the Liberator parking lot. Inspired by the image, González commissioned two tin ovals from the same manufacturer (González Aranda 2005). The lot owner was playing with national Bolivarian iconography in order to liberate his clients from the burden of driving around an overly congested city looking for a parking spot. Her *Apuntes* draws on this historical and semiotic joke in order to connect to informal commerce both conceptually and materially. Moreover, by painting yellow, blue, and red bands along the sides of the circumference of the medallions—evocative of marching-band drums used in popular festivals and sold at informal markets—González transports the Figueroa painting and the Santander miniature away from museums into the street pageantry of popular civic festivities (figure 8.3). These associations among private, commercial, and popular interests with patriotic iconography generated indignant responses in the press. In a letter published by Cali's *El País* (1967), the author, Aurita de Cali, explains her outrage at the irreverent representations of Santander and Bolívar. She mockingly suggests an alternative title for the double portrait: "Before and After Taking Scott's [cod liver oil] Emulsion."

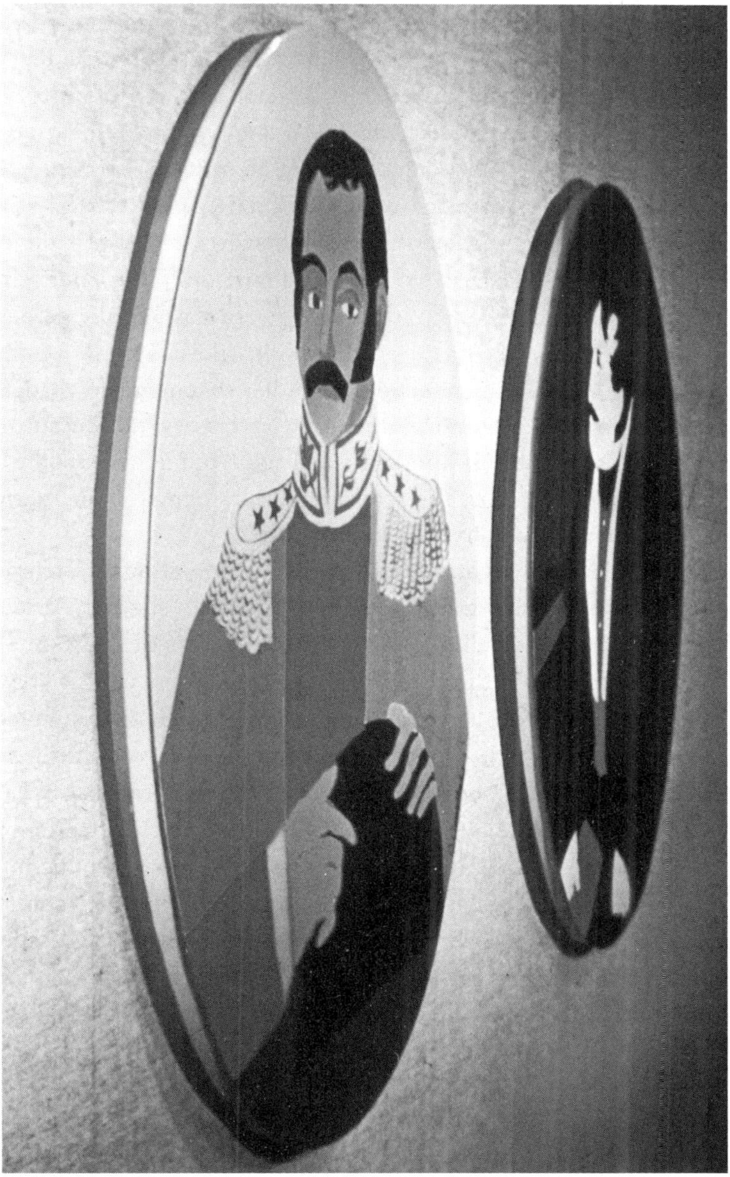

FIGURE 8.3. Beatriz González. Side view. *Apuntes para la historia extensa, Tomos I* (Bolívar, left) and *II* (Santander, right). 1967. Enamel on tin plate. 39.37" × 31.5" (100 × 80 cm) each. Courtesy of the artist.

Aurita's outrage was directed at the affront on official culture by the artist's debased representations and by the National Salon's legitimizing prize.

González went further in her critique of official culture by wielding these images as a protest gesture toward the National Academy of History. The very year that González painted *Apuntes para la historia extensa*, 1967, the National Academy of History launched the third printing of its encyclopedia titled *La historia extensa de Colombia*. González deliberately ridiculed the academy's claim to provide a comprehensive survey of Colombian history: "I conceived of these works, not as museum pieces, but as rebelliousness. . . . [F]or me the important thing was to assault the heroes and above all the academy . . . who purportedly holds 'the last word'" (González Aranda 2005). This sentiment echoes an earlier statement she made: "My position is of irreverence and aggression with history, not because I am against history or traditions—both fascinate me—but rather with the tenor of solemnity adjudicated by the academy in this country. I am anti-tenor, anti-academy, anti-solemnity" (in Tafur 1974).

The title discloses this connection; instead of suggesting the preliminary stages of a painting using the word *boceto*, or sketch, she chose the word *apuntes*, or notes, which alludes to the unedited state of a text. She conjured up the sections of the academy's "extensive history" that had been edited out and not her simplified pictorial interpretations of the nineteenth-century paintings. Indeed, the twenty-four encyclopedic volumes excluded women and *el pueblo*.[4] In 1967 the Colombian Academy of History defined culture as high art made by men. Colombian women—authors, subjects, and gender issues—were omitted altogether.[5] In the arts, the omission was all the more glaring given that the Colombian cultural scene was dominated by women like Marta Traba in art criticism, Gloria Valencia de Castaño in radio and television, Sonia Osorio in dance, and Fanny Mickey in theater.

Colombian visual artists like González herself, Judith Márquez, Lucy Tejada, Olga Amaral, and Feliza Bursztyn, among others, were leading figures in the art world. And popular culture was barely detectable in the edition aside from a brief mention of musical traditions.[6] The Academy of History was founded in the spirit of restoring *convivencia* in 1902 after the bitter partisan War of a Thousand Days. Its pages, historian Jorge Orlando Melo notes (2010, 116), course through with artificial bipartisan politeness and skirt the bitter and bloody ideological conflicts that plagued the nation since Bolívar and Santander's rift in the early nineteenth century. Thus, the academy demonstrated that it was completely out of touch with heated historical debates as well as with everyday Colombian life and in particular with a dynamic youth, women, and pueblo. The purportedly comprehensive study of Colombian history served to emphasize the exclusionary process of national construction. González's *Apuntes* interrogates the validity of the National Academy of History's metanarrative as based on the power struggles between the Liberal and Conservative Parties that obscured class, race, and gender struggles.[7]

Her *Apuntes* generated radically polarized reactions in the reviews of the 1967 salon; the defense called them biting and daring, while the prosecution called them ugly, frightening, and offensively plagiaristic. These strong reactions disclose the implied limits of representing patrimonial culture and by extension anxieties concerning the challenge to the power-sharing agreement of the political elites during the National Front period. Although this renewed form of *convivencia* was publically characterized as a solution to end partisan violence, it served more effectively as a defensive maneuver by the political elites against alternative threats. By placing Bolívar and Santander side by side, the two national heroes conventionally accredited with laying the ideological groundwork for the two-party system in Colombia, González's medallions fueled the fire of discontent with the National Front regime. The diptych functioned as a pictorial challenge to the elite notions of legitimacy by injecting patriotic hagiography with references to popular and uncultivated forms of visual culture. González herself admitted, "I do everything possible to shock . . . to attack *los próceres*" (in Tafur 1974).

On Thursday, November 9, 1967, the famous journalist and director of Laureano Gómez's Conservative newspaper *El Siglo* Arturo Abella published an article accusing González of plagiarism, an article he signed by hand to provide a more emphatic endorsement. Abella argued that González illicitly copied the work of the nineteenth-century painter Pedro José Figueroa:

> This is why I dare pose the question to the art experts, so that they may clarify if Figueroa, dead in 1838, plagiarized Beatriz González or Beatriz González plagiarized Figueroa? . . . The artist [González] did not leave a thing out, not even the *mapamundi* that the Liberator holds in his hands.

There are many equivocations here worth mentioning. Abella, in his haste to judge a misdeed, overlooked that González deliberately substituted the *mapamundi*, which prominently displays the word "Colombia" in front, with a blackened tunnel, thus erasing the map's signifying function. Secondly, the caption published in *El Tiempo* did not definitively attribute the painting to Figueroa. It could also have been a copy. Copying images was a frequent and unproblematic practice in the colonial and early republican periods (as Emily A. Engel discusses in this volume). In fact, the more loyal the copy, the more it would be considered to carry over the original's power. In her appropriation, González tapped into the repetitive cycle of reproductions, not only the practice of repainting images for distribution but also the reproduction of these images in newspapers, currency, popular culture, and parking lot signage.

Abella, however, did hit the mark when he wrote, "Figueroa would be even more avant-garde than artists today—since they need to be 'inspired' by his style. . . . Figueroa's figures are as plump as those that appear on Botero's paintings and other followers." Abella's assertion that Figueroa would be considered a vanguard artist in modern terms was more fitting than his indictment of plagiarism. During the early nineteenth century and the military campaign of independence from Spain, around the time Figueroa was painting, the resolve was in uniting elite *criollos* with the lower classes. Therefore, independence-era leaders commissioned guild artists working in nonacademic styles to paint their portraits or to represent key historical moments and symbols, as José Gil de Castro and Pedro José Figueroa more famously did. Finding affinities between Figueroa, González, and Fernando Botero, Abella unwittingly endorses an art that was strategically enlisting popular forms of expression.

The anxiety latent in Abella's accusation of plagiarism was deeply steeped in broader concerns about the changing social order manifest in the historiographic dispute over Bolivarian legacy. What was at stake for Abella was the concept of legitimacy and not originality. He focused on González's citation of Bolívar and not of Santander, suggesting that what stung was his perceived offense against the Conservative icon. Simón Bolívar, in the eyes of Conservatives, was not only founder of their party but also its ideological justification for authoritarianism, general distrust of anarchic masses, and defense of a traditional patriarchic structure. In the years leading up to and during La Violencia, Laureano Gómez broke with the general *convivencia* agreement that the nation had been formed jointly from the military stewardship of the Liberator and the administrative and legislative talents of Santander, "the Man of Laws." Rather, Gómez cast the founding fathers in polarized terms: Santander as assassin and traitor, Bolívar as inspiration for a Catholic, authoritarian, and anti-anarchic "Bolivarian Nation" (Melo 2010, 118–19). Gómez renamed the publication of the Ministry of Education from *Revista de las Américas* to *Bolívar,* a magazine in part dedicated to discussing the Liberator's political ideas (Lleras 2005, 34–35). His successor, General Rojas Pinilla, pledged to continue to lead a nation inspired by Bolívar. However, his so-named Estado Cristiano y Bolivariano interpreted the Bolivarian legacy as a military-pueblo coalition against the oligarchy (Melo 2010, 119). Rojas openly challenged the legitimacy of the traditional ruling elites and positioned himself as a social liberator. He also brought his daughter, María Eugenia Rojas, into the public arena as a key player and finally ratified women's suffrage in 1954. The Rojas Pinilla regime thus included a strong feminist component (Galvis and Donadío 1988).

Meanwhile, the Colombian left had been challenging the Conservative hold on Bolívar's legacy since the 1930s and emphasized instead the Liberator's anti-imperialist, anticolonial, and revolutionary ideas. Bolívar's unfulfilled wishes of uniting Spanish America against imperial aggression, his multiracial "democratic" army, and the emancipation of his slaves lent themselves to a revalorization of his revolutionary role now recast in Liberal and even Marxist terms (García Nossa 1952; Liévano Aguirre 1983; Melo 2010; Pividal 1977; Schelchkov 2002; Torres Giraldo 1978). Picking up this reevaluation begun by the Cuban independence hero José Martí and after the Cuban Revolution of 1959, Soviet scholars, especially in Moscow and Leningrad, became interested in exploring the revolutionary legacy of the Latin American wars of independence. Several Soviet historians associated with the Latin American Institute founded in Moscow in 1961 and the magazine *Latinskaia Amerika* interpreted the wars of independence from Spain as a populist liberation movement and characterized Bolívar's political ideas as a form of utopian socialism (Schelchkov 2002, 208).

In 1958 the Colombian Communist Party magazine *Documentos Políticos* republished a text by Soviet historians Andrei Schelchkov, Anatoli Shulkovski, and I. R. Lavretsky that characterized Bolívar's struggle as one of popular mobilization, emancipation of slaves, and redistribution of indigenous lands (Melo 2010, 128). These authors who emphasized Bolívar's revolutionary character interpreted his exclusion of the United States on the occasion of the Panama Congress as a clairvoyant warning against a neo-imperialism emanating from the northern neighbor. Bolívar's authoritarianism was reinterpreted as realism, a necessarily strong position to challenge the oligarchic privilege concealed behind formalist legalism. These revisionist texts became the basis for the radicalization of the Bolivarian icon within the Communist Party and the guerrilla movements of the 1970s and 1980s (see Shanahan and Potočnik essays in this volume for French and Yugoslavian reformulations of the Bolívar narrative in post–World War II Europe).

A populist and revolutionary Bolívar would be antithetical to the Conservative icon. At the heart of Laureano Gómez's and the Conservative Party's endorsement of a central and authoritarian power inspired by Bolívar was the perception of the pueblo to be an unruly mob. Nothing could have confirmed the elite's worst fears about the threatening masses than the riots known as the Bogotazo on April 9, 1948, following the assassination of Liberal leader Jorge Eliécer Gaitán. Historian Herbert Braun (1985) has demonstrated that the pueblo directed its destructive rage at institutions and establishments that were perceived to have complicity in Gaitán's demise, or that barred the masses from participation. The mobs burned to the ground *El Siglo*'s building, where Arturo Abella served as general editor. The only building left standing on the Calle Real leading to the Plaza Bolívar was the small Museo de la Independencia, which commemorates the site of the "grito de independencia" and houses the nineteenth-century Santander miniature. The Bogotá elites looked down upon the "nueve-abrileños," as the rioters of the Bogotazo are still known, as vulgar opportunists rather than as agents of political and social change who charged the institutions that physically and symbolically barred them from participation. After the Bogotazo, the historic center of Bogotá was abandoned by the elites, who considered themselves legitimate citizens, to be inhabited subsequently by illegal squatters. The ensuing informal economy, with tin signage very much like the Parqueadero el Libertador forever changed Bogotá's center.

In this context, González's *Apuntes* irritated, if not frightened, and certainly challenged those who claimed a natural distinction between the cultivated leaders of society and the uncultivated who need to be ruled and contained. Underlying Abella's accusation of plagiarism was the belief that only a select few had access to legitimate national symbols. The etymological root for plagiarism is the Latin *plagiārius*, which translates as "kidnapping." For Abella, like many *convivialistas*, the capital city, traditional political parties, and official culture had been held hostage and were again threatened from below. Abella's indignation to a pop or, rather, popular representation of Bolívar demonstrates a crisis of confidence in Bolivarian signification for the Conservative Party.

Apuntes did not function as a clear supporter for any specific Bolivarian interpretation, Left or Right, but as a critique of the official and ossified narrative of history, and thus González tossed her own unstable and multivalent rendition of Bolívar into this symbolic vortex. By using visual and material references that associate national history with informal commerce and popular culture, Beatriz González inserted an alternative history that had been excluded from official narratives. *Apuntes para la historia extensa* thus reproduces at the Salon of National Artists the mechanisms of cultural appropriation by the lower classes that threatened the traditional order.

* * *

Five years after *Apuntes* debuted at the National Salon, González returned to Bolivarian iconography. In 1973 she purchased a metal bed from the Pasaje Rivas informal market in Bogotá. Its modesty brought to her mind Simón Bolívar's death in the Quinta de San Pedro Alejandrino near Santa Marta, where he perished in 1830 while en route to exile in Europe—as a disillusioned outcast, bereft of political and economic power. González pondered, "Dead Bolívar, isn't it best for him to rest on a bed?" (in Traba 1977, 65). She took a postcard depicting Pedro Alcántara Quijano Moreno's *El Libertador muerto* that she had received from the Quinta de Bolívar, adapted the image onto an enamel-on-metal plate, and framed it with the metal bed (González Aranda 2012). In the assemblage *Mutis por el foro* (plate 14), González proposed a democratic and even subversive approach to history painting. As in *Apuntes*, the artist challenged the simplified and patriarchic narratives of state culture and at the same time the illusion of "order and progress" forged within international art exhibitions that privileged so-called technically advanced aesthetic expressions evident in the dominance of geometric abstraction, kinetic, and op art in the biennial circuits and in the Latin American art market in Europe.

Quijano's large canvas was painted in 1930 for the centennial of Bolívar's death (plate 15). Like *Apuntes, Mutis por el foro,* and the postcard, Quijano's painting was also a representation of a representation, a copy of the canvas Quijano himself painted in 1912 and sold to the Venezuelan government in 1913, much to the lament of the Colombian press (Vargas Murcia 2006). Quijano also painted over photographs of his earlier painting, which was then reproduced in *Cromos* magazine in 1930 and on the four-cent stamp of the same year. What is more, Quijano's painting served as a model for the relief sculpture on the frieze of *Altar for the Nation*, a republican chapel at the San Pedro Alejandrino estate gifted by the nation of Colombia to her Liberator for the 1930 centennial of his death. The centennial ceremonies, with all their civic pageantry, including a five-minute silence at the Plaza Bolívar marking the exact moment of his passing, unveiled the hero worship that had largely overshadowed critical discourse in the public sphere. Most centennials involve nostalgia for an idealized time of moral clarity. This one retrospectively corrected the improper send-off that Bolívar received on the part of the Colombian and Venezuelan governments in 1830. Beatriz González, in contrast, chose a more historically accurate title referencing Bolívar's solitary passing. "Mutis por el foro" is a theatrical phrase describing the uneventful, even unperceived, exit of an actor from the stage. The title thus renders visible the sugarcoated version of history reproduced endlessly in patriotic pageantry.

Although created in the grand historical genre, Quijano's painting often resurfaces in popular culture. Remarkably, in 1972, the year before González made her version, the lottery game Extra de la Independencia featured Quijano's painting on the tickets (figure 8.4). Like the Bolívar and Santander medallions, Quijano's painting was also reproduced and circulated in mass culture. While the "original" painting, curiously a Quijano copy of a Quijano, is held in a museum collection, its reproductions lend themselves to myriad popular interpretations and appropriations. Therefore, what may at first seem like a clever aesthetic joke was rather a "meta-picture," to borrow W. J. T. Mitchell's term (1995), a picture about pictures, a picture about picturing, and a critique of representation itself, in this case, both cultural and political.

Mutis por el foro stylistically and iconographically rehearses the way history painting simplifies, sanitizes, and makes patriotic narratives ambivalent. Beatriz González has described this process as "an impoverishment of the scene" (2012), a process of omission, contouring, cropping, and flattening of Quijano's florid and painterly style. While *Mutis por el*

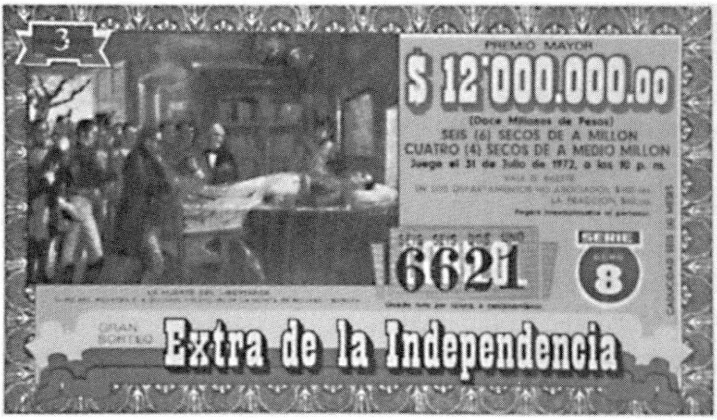

FIGURE 8.4. Lottery ticket, "Extra de la Independencia." 1972. Public domain.

foro evokes the corroding of an image through mechanical reproduction, González did quite a bit of purposeful editing. The absence of lower-ranked soldiers is particularly revealing. Bolívar's prodigious ability to recruit soldiers from the lower castes, including slaves, who would otherwise have perceived him—a slave-owning *mantuano criollo*—with the same distrust as they would Spanish officials, served to aggrandize his myth. Indeed, after Bolívar received support from Alexandre Pétion in Haiti (1815–16), he conflated the rhetoric of independence with that of emancipation, insofar as it augmented military enlistment. In the González version, one guard stands alone for all soldiers. In excluding the *Mater Dolorosa,* hung above the door frame, González removed the only woman in the Quijano painting, also a representation of a representation.[8]

These omissions prompt questions about who is given space in this pictorial narrative. The figures in the Quijano painting represent the influential men who witnessed Bolívar's last days, the bishop of Santa Marta, José María Estéves,[9] his physician, Dr. Alejandro Próspero Révérend, Generals Laurencio Silva and José María Carreño, and the former royalist *hidalgo* Joaquín de Mier, owner of the Quinta de San Pedro Alejandrino (Vargas Murcia 2006, 86). They were, however, not the only ones present at Bolívar's death. Why aren't his slave-butler José Palacios or his beloved cook Fernanda Barriga present in the painting? They were, after all, the most intimately connected to the Liberator. Their exclusion begs us to consider all those who have been generally missing from the national pantheon and the foundational narratives. Where is Benkos Bioho (d. 1619), the runaway slave who founded the Palenque de San Basilio, which a century later, in 1716, became the first independent village in the Americas by royal decree and one of the first actors in a long struggle over independence? Where is Manuela Beltrán along with the other women, indigenous, and artisan leaders who rebelled against the crown during the Comuneros Revolt of 1781?

For this assemblage González chose materials that carry strong class associations—the enamel on tin with which she translated Quijano's history painting and the modest metal cot she bought at the Pasaje Rivas informal market—and by doing so activated the criticality of her iconographic cropping. González has characterized her entire oeuvre as "Pasaje Rivas" on several occasions (Rico and Decaillet 2005). Among elite Bogotá residents the Pasaje Rivas is reputed for its excess and lack of sophistication, identified as an unequivocally popular space with connotations of commercial illegitimacy. This perceived threat is at the heart of González's critique. The chaotic character of the market and perhaps uncontrollable structure deny any type of cultural cohesion. Fascinating for our purposes is the location of Pasaje Rivas adjacent to none other than the Plaza Simón Bolívar, the central square in Bogotá and home to the nation's executive, legislative, and ecclesiastical powers. Pasaje Rivas physically rests on the back walls of Bogotá's city hall. The street vendors' appropriation of the back alleys abruptly contrasts with the heavily militarized official zone of Bolívar Square. The vast open space and the continuous use of ochre-colored limestone emphasize the grandeur of the buildings. Policemen patrol Plaza Bolívar to ensure that no street vendors, solicitors, or even cameras obstruct the site. There is no doubt about the legitimacy of this space. This sociopolitical divide metaphorically highlights the distinction between official models of culture and the diverse, hybrid, and contradictory elements of the cultures that those models exclude, while it also discloses the tense relations between the state and the pueblo.

By referencing informal commerce in both style and material and by calling attention to the exclusive character of official narratives, González challenged the Colombian elite's purchase on political privilege. The justification for an elite monopoly on power in Colombia came from the claim that they alone could serve as public servants precisely because they were unrestricted by private needs. This was also Bolívar's underlying principle for the presidency in his Bolivian constitution, a "disinterest" that he himself cultivated in his reputation (Bushnell and Langley 2008). In *Mutis por el foro*, the bed evokes private, not public or official veneration. By placing a bed, the most private piece of furniture, in a public exhibition space, González conflates the private with the public. She invokes the dictum "The personal is political" and the claim by slain populist leader Jorge Eliécer Gaitán that the public service of the so-called disinterested elite was actually a form of private interest (Braun 1985).

Thus far I have been discussing both *Apuntes* and *Mutis por el foro* as commentaries and challenges to Colombian official culture. However, González's assemblages were not exhibited alongside Quijano's or in *Altar for the Nation*. Rather, they were exhibited at the National Salon, international biennials, Bogotá's Museum of Modern Art, and traveling exhibitions of contemporary Colombian art abroad. González exhibited this assemblage in 1974 at the exhibition "Arte Colombiano de Hoy" in the Fundación Eugenio Mendoza in Caracas, the city that hosted the first Quijano version. Effectively, *Mutis por el foro* replicated the journey made first by Bolívar's remains from Colombia to Venezuela in 1842 and then Quijano's painting in 1913.

Art critic Marta Traba, who relocated to Caracas earlier in 1974 with literary critic Angel Rama, published a review of the exhibition for the local paper *El Nacional* titled "Declaration of Love for Colombia" (1984). She located Colombian artistic virtuosity in its disavowal of international trends by pointing out the powerful currency of figuration and the rejection of an ideologically driven vanguard in favor of a circular or mythical conception of time. In Colombia, Traba explains, "art (ignoring the cries of a global village) continues to be an act of faith in itself, and which will win the game where, more than the triumph of one species, it seeks to warn the artists of this continent against the dangers of cultural dependency that are as sad as they are sterile" (1984, 176). In 1973 Traba had published her most influential treatise on Latin American art, *Dos décadas vulnerables en las artes plásticas latinoamericanas, 1950–1970*, in which the critic condemns Latin American avant-garde artists for blindly following international artistic trends as an act of neocolonial surrender.

Mutis por el foro, Traba wrote elsewhere (1974), left Venezuelan audiences in a stupor. Indeed, the majority of reviewers in the Venezuelan press focused more on the remarkable difference between the artistic productions of the sister countries than on any individual tendency (*El Tiempo* 1974). As art critic for the Caracas *El Universal*, Carmen Teresa Valdez echoed

Traba's endorsement for resistance to international trends. The works in "Arte Colombiano de Hoy" represented for Valdez "a truly committed art vertiginously emerging from its own reality and not from appropriations of a foreign technocism" (cited in *El Tiempo* 1974). This technocism, or as Traba put it, the obsessive desire to be "up to date which operates feverishly in Caracas," conjured up the latest and most advanced expressions of an evolutionary aesthetic rooted in geometric abstraction. Beginning with the construction of the Ciudad Universitaria at the Universidad Central de Venezuela, the lines between nationalism and internationalism had been blurred, and geometric abstraction, kinetic, and op art had become the standard-bearer for Venezuelan modernity. The triumph in the European and American art markets of artists such as Alejandro Otero, Carlos Cruz-Diez, and Jesús Raphael Soto became a forceful entry point into the international art scene that served to legitimate Venezuelan culture abroad.

Artists working in these international constructivist idioms had been cast as leading actors in representing a modernist, industrialist, and international collective identity (contradiction included), especially in Brazil and Venezuela, where Beatriz González exhibited her furniture pieces. These and other forms of expression that were considered technically advanced, such as cyber art, paralleled the modernization aims to update Latin America in global economic and cultural spheres. Indeed, so-called progressive businesses and industries relied heavily on the aesthetics of geometric abstraction to design their corporate logos. The equivalence created between progressive industry and advanced aesthetics was not coincidental. However, Caracas had become a hotbed for intellectuals such as Traba and Rama seeking refuge from military persecution during the not-so-cold dirty wars in Latin America, bringing with them a radicalized and counterhegemonic critical edge that put into question all metanarratives, including Bolivarian and *tecno-desarrollista*.

In this context a historical subject like Bolívar could be seen as excessively provincial, outmoded, and even *cursi*, or tacky. While the sophisticated art critical press failed to connect González's ironic intervention in Caracas, there is no doubt that it must have resonated with a Venezuelan audience, given that *Mutis por el foro* was exhibited only one year after the second edition of Germán Carrera Damas's 1970 *El culto a Bolívar* was published in 1973. González's gesture of exhibiting a modest bed with an impoverished image of Bolívar's death refused to play into the prevalent official narratives that eulogize and reduce history to the actions of a few elite *criollo* men or the scientific futurism that obliterates history altogether in favor of a utopian, industrial, and modernist vision. What was at stake was not so much the image of Bolívar but history itself. In an era where national delegations to international competitions sought to use art as proof of a given nation's ability to compete with ostensibly the most advanced societies, González's use of Bolivarian iconography intervened on behalf of a socially critical and historically dialectical alternative to discourses of the traditional political elites and of the modernization theories backed by the United States and industrializing sector.

Notes

1. I am indebted to W. J. T. Mitchell for pointing out these properties of the vampire.

2. The Movimiento 19 de Abril, or M-19, formed as a response to 1970 elections in which Misael Pastrana Borero was declared president over General Gustavo Rojas Pinilla and which confirmed for them the exclusionary and oligarchic character of the National Front.

3. The entire "Lecturas dominicales" section of *El Tiempo* August 6, 1967, was dedicated to literature, history, and art related to the independence wars; it was published to commemorate the 148th anniversary of the Battle of Boyacá on August 7, 1819, which marked the military triumph over royalist troops in Colombia.

4. All authors except one were male members of the academy. The single female author, Kathleen Romoli, was a North American who specialized in Colombian history during the period of Spanish conquest. She had also published a highly sympathetic narrative of Colombian society to a North American audience in which she made the case for Colombia's strong democratic values in an era of fascist and communist threats. Romoli thus contributed to the export of a sophisticated account of Colombian culture. Nonetheless, *La historia extensa de Colombia* was primarily written by cultivated elite Colombian men about cultivated elite Colombian men.

5. The volume on the arts in Colombia covered only a few subjects: colonial painting and architecture; nineteenth-century painting and architecture; twentieth-century architecture and musical culture. Luis Alberto Acuña's section on twentieth-century sculpture is devoted entirely to two artists: Rómulo Rozo, an indigenist sculptor trained in Mexico and associated with the Bachués in the 1930s and 1940s; and Edgar Negret, standing as the sole artist of the post-Bachue modernist currents.

6. It was not until the 1986 edition that a new volume of *Colombian Culture* would be published that included regional folklore.

7. Only as of the 1991 Constitution did the government officially recognize that Colombia is a multicultural and multiethnic nation.

8. With the *Mater Dolorosa*, a representation of the Virgin Mary's pain and suffering over the death of her son, Quijano makes a pictorial case for Bolívar's martyrdom. He did nonetheless die of a disease, tuberculosis, according to his physician Alejandro Próspero Révérend, and not the firing squad Bolívar so readily used to eliminate his rival General Manuel Piar. See Alicia Ríos's essay in this volume.

9. The bishop was not present at Bolívar's funeral, as has been a matter of historical debate, since there are questions about whether Bolívar confessed. According to those who support the version of Bolívar's protocol Catholic send-off, Esteves was absent due to illness rather than discord with the Liberator. Other officers mentioned to be around Bolívar at the time include Coronels Belford Hinton Wilson and José de la Cruz Paredes, Primer Comandante Juan Glen, and Dr. Manuel Pérez Recuero.

References

Abella Rodríguez, Arturo. 1967. "Aquí Bogotá. ¿Quién plagió a quién?" *El Siglo*, November 9.

———. 1973. *Así fue el 9 de abril*. Bogotá: Ediciones Aquí Bogotá.

Academia Colombiana de Historia. 1967. *La historia extensa de Colombia*. 24 vols. 3rd edition. Bogotá: Ediciones Lerner.

Acevedo Carmona, Darío. 1995. *La mentalidad de las* élites *sobre la violencia en Colombia (1936–1949)*. Bogotá: Instituto de Estudios Políticos y Relaciones Internacionales: El Áncora.

Alape, Arturo. 1983. *El Bogotazo, memorias del olvido*. Bogotá: Editorial Pluma.

Angulo Novoa, Alejandro. 1969. *El movimiento de la población colombiana*. Bogotá: Centro de Investigación y Acción Social.

Ardila, Jaime. 1974. *Beatriz González: Apuntes para la historia extensa*. Bogotá: Ediciones Tercer Mundo.

Aurita de Cali. 1967. "Hepatitis y apoplegía." Letter to the editor. *El País* (Cali, Colombia), November 19.

Bois, Yve Alain, Fogg Art Museum, Harvard University Art Museums, and Colección Patricia Phelps de Cisneros. 2001. *Geometric Abstraction: Latin American Art from the Patricia Phelps De Cisneros Collection*. Cambridge, MA: Harvard University Art Museums.

Bourdieu, Pierre. 1984. *Distinction: A Social Critique of the Judgment of Taste*. Cambridge, MA: Harvard University Press.

Braun, Herbert. 1985. *The Assassination of Gaitán: Public Life and Urban Violence in Colombia*. Madison: University of Wisconsin Press.

Bushnell, David, ed. 1970. *The Liberator Simón Bolívar: Man and Image*. New York: Knopf.

Bushnell, David, and Lester D. Langley, eds. 2008. *Simón Bolívar: Essays on the Life and Legacy of the Liberator*. Lanham, MD: Rowman and Littlefield.

Calderón, Marta. 1988. *Beatriz González: Una pintora de provincia*. Bogotá: C. Valencia.

Calderón Schrader, Camilo. 1990. *50 años, Salón Nacional de Artistas*. Bogotá: Instituto Colombiano de Cultura.

Canal Ramírez, Gonzálo. 1955. *El estado cristiano y bolivariano del 13 de junio*, Bogotá: Antares.

Carrera Damas, Germán. 1973. *El culto a Bolívar: Esbozo para un estudio de la historia de las ideas en Venezuela*. 2nd edition. Caracas: Universidad Central de Venezuela, Ediciones de la Biblioteca.

Cromos. 1930. "La muerte del Libertador, óleo de Pedro A. Quijano." Bogotá. No. 741, December 13.

El Espectador. 1967a. "Adjudicados premios del XIX Salón." November 8.

———. 1967b. "Premios del XIX Salón A Negret, Lugo y Beatriz González." November 8.

Galvis, Silvia, and Alberto Donadío. 1988. *El jefe supremo: Rojas Pinilla en la violencia y en el poder*. Bogotá: Planeta.

García Moreno, Diego, dir. 2011. *¿Por qué llora si ya reí?* DVD. Bogotá: Lamaraca Producciones.

García Nossa, Antonio. 1952. "Bolívar, general revolucionario." *Sábado*, February 16.

González Aranda, Beatriz. 2005. Interview by Ana María Reyes. Bogotá, August 19.

———. 2012. Interview by Ana María Reyes. Bogotá, January 8.

Hurtado de Paz, Amparo. 1967. "La ganadora responde a Abella: En polémica sobre XIX Salón. 'La misma rosca.'" *El Espectador*, November 10.

Lavretsky, Iosif Remuladivich. 1970. *Simón Bolívar*. Moscow, 1960. Reprint, Cochabamba, Bolivia: Editorial Universitaria.

Lleras, Cristina. 2005. *Arte, política y crítica: Politización de la mirada estética Colombia, 1940–1952*. Bogotá: Universidad Nacional de Colombia.

Liévano Aguirre, Indalecio. 1983. *Bolívar*. Madrid: Ediciones Cultura Hispánica del Instituto de Cooperación Iberoamericana.

Martínez, Juan Pablo, and María Isabel Izquierdo. 1972. *ANAPO: Oposición o revolución*. Bogotá: Ediciones CAMILO.

Melo, Jorge Orlando. 2010. "Bolívar en Colombia: Las transformaciones de su imagén." In *Entre el olvido y el recuerdo: Íconos, lugares de memoria y cánones de la historia y la literatura en Colombia,* edited by Carlos Rincón, Sarah de Mojica and Liliana Gómez, 103–38. Bogotá: Universidad Javeriana.

Mitchell, W. J. T. 1995. *Picture Theory: Essays on Verbal and Visual Representation.* Chicago: University of Chicago Press.

Pividal, Francisco. 1977. *Bolívar: Pensamiento precursor del antiimperialismo.* Havana: Ediciones Casa de las Américas.

Rico, Diana, and Richard Decaillet, dirs. 2005. *Plástica: Arte contemporáneo en Colombia.* DVD. Bogotá: Ministerio de Cultura.

Palacios, Marco. 1995. *Entre la legitimidad y la violencia: Colombia 1875–1994.* Bogotá: Grupo Editorial Norma.

Safford, Frank, and Marco Palacios. 2002. *Colombia: Fragmented Land, Divided Society.* New York: Oxford University Press.

Schelchkov, Andrei. 2002. "Los estudios Latinoamericanos en Rusia (y en la URSS)." *Revista European de Estudios Latinoamericanos y del Caribe* 72:205–20.

Schoultz, Lars. 1972. "Urbanization and Changing Voting Patterns: Colombia 1946–1970." *Political Science Quarterly* 87 (March 1972): 22–45.

Shulkovski, Anatoli. 1982. "Bolívar y Bello: Papel en la lucha libertadora de América Latina." *Nuestra América* 5 (May–August 1982).

Tafur, Pilar. 1974. "¡La Oferta del Siglo! Expone Beatriz González." *El Tiempo,* October 10, 1974.

El Tiempo. 1974. "Muestra de arte colombiano causa sensación en Caracas." Bogotá: June 24.

Torres Giraldo, Ignacio. 1978. *Los inconformes.* Vol. 2. Bogotá: Editorial Latina.

Traba, Marta. 1973. *Dos décadas vulnerables en las artes plásticas latinoamericanas, 1950–1970.* Mexico City: Siglo Veintiuno.

———. 1974. "Una clave artística para comprender a Colombia: Beatriz González y la investigación de lo ridículo." *Forum World Features* (Kern House, London), September 7.

———. 1977. *Los muebles de Beatriz González.* Bogotá: Museo de Arte Moderno.

———. 1984. "Declaración de amor a Colombia." *El Nacional,* Caracas, 1967. Reprint, *Marta Traba,* 174–176. Museo de Arte Moderno. Bogotá: Planeta Editorial Colombiana.

Vargas Murcia, Laura Liliana. 2006. *Pedro Quijano: Más allá de la pintura histórica, el hallazgo del color.* Bogotá: Planeta.

9

El Gran Dispensador by Manuel Trujillo

The Weaknesses of the National Hero

ALICIA RÍOS

The 1980s in Venezuela were characterized by the economic collapse of what had been Latin America's most prosperous country. In direct response to the global decline in oil prices and following twenty years of stable exchange with the dollar, the national currency—the bolívar—underwent its first devaluation on February 18, 1983. As a result, the Venezuelan standard of living deteriorated considerably; consumers who had frequently traveled to Miami with an extravagant attitude that can be summed up in the phrase "It's cheap, gimme two"—now spent their vacations on Venezuela's Margarita Island instead; foreign workers who had arrived in the 1970s left for more profitable destinations; and social violence and state repression both exploded, shocking a country that prided itself on the implementation of a successful democracy when its last dictatorship, that of Marcos Pérez Jiménez, ended on January 23, 1958.

In this context, it was natural for intellectual and cultural circles to debate the ideals that had guided the country's course throughout its history. An antecedent to the debates of the 1980s was Germán Carrera Damas's 1970 book *El culto a Bolívar: Esbozo para un estudio de la historia de las ideas en Venezuela.* The book was an early attempt to put the "ascribed and truthful meanings" of the national hero into perspective and examine the mechanisms of ideological and historical construction of the "charismatic hero."

The written histories of Venezuela demonstrate the obsession with Bolívar, the Father of the Nation, that has characterized nearly every exploration of its past. From older studies such as Rafael María Baralt and Ramón

Díaz's *Resumen de la historia de Venezuela desde el año de 1797 hasta el de 1830* (1841), José Gil Fortoul's *Historia constitucional de Venezuela* (1909), and Caracciolo Parra-Pérez's *Historia de la Primera República de Venezuela* (1939) to more recent ones, like Federico Brito Figueroa's *Historia económica y social de Venezuela* (1966), José Luis Salcedo-Bastardo's *Historia fundamental de Venezuela* (1970), and Manuel Vicente Magallanes's *Historia política de Venezuela* (1975), all these histories accord the Liberator Simón Bolívar a place of honor while practically ignoring other key figures of the independence era. Only the three most recent works even consider what happened in Venezuela while Bolívar waged a military campaign to the south; the older studies simply follow his footsteps and leave Venezuela when Bolívar does.

New Fiction in the 1980s

Venezuelan narrative fiction of the 1980s also focused on the independence era, producing no fewer than six novels set in that period.[1] These works dared to depict a number of key figures, not just Bolívar, from the supposedly glorious national past in a less than idealized light. Interestingly, however, the majority of these rereadings did not dismantle or even question the earlier iconic narratives as models. Rather, these texts simply incorporated new figures, acknowledging the continuing failure to recognize the contributions of sectors of society—like slaves, women, and the poor—that did not play an official role but nonetheless made the process possible and without whom many developments in Venezuelan society since the independence era cannot be explained.

Of these six novels, three are by Denzil Romero. *La tragedia del generalísimo* (1983) and *Grand Tour* (1987) both take Francisco de Miranda as their subject; the third, *La esposa del doctor Thorne* (1988), is about Bolívar's lover Manuelita Sáenz. Simón Rodríguez, Bolívar's childhood tutor, is the focus of Arturo Úslar Pietri's *La isla de Robinson* (1987). The fifth novel is Francisco Herrera Luque's *Manuel Piar, caudillo de dos colores* (1987). Finally, Manuel Trujillo's *El Gran Dispensador* (1983),[2] which I explore in detail here, focuses on Bolívar and his relationship with the *pardo* General Piar.[3]

When a novel takes on a historical subject, the historiographical discourse inevitably colors the fictional rereading of that history, especially when the period in question has been studied as intensely as the independence era in Venezuela. It is necessary to unravel the resulting multilayered and intertextual dialogue to understand the vision of the world represented. Although the latter three novels—Uslar Petri's *La isla de Robinson*, Herrera Luque's *Manuel Piar, caudillo de dos colores,* and Trujillo's *El Gran Dispensador*—engage in the most direct and obvious dialogues with historical documents, they take very different approaches in doing so.

The three novels by Denzil Romero construct an imaginative game that focuses on the protagonists' erotic adventures. His two novels about General Francisco de Miranda incorporate an impressive array of cultural references that span a wide variety of sources and historical moments. In both, the figure of Miranda serves as an excuse for a series of clever references and parodic exaggerations whose moments of undisputable lucidity cannot declutter the accumulation of motifs that may or may not be justified by the story. *La esposa del doctor Thorne,* an "erotic biography" of Bolívar's famous lover, Manuelita Sáenz, is somewhat Manichean in its explicit attempt to reveal feminine eroticism, especially in the portrayal of intimate encounters between the protagonist and other women. Within the erotic game, the same mechanism is repeated again and again, except for changes in the masks and disguises that the characters wear. While the novel is both irreverent and accurate in many of its descriptions, its carnivalization of events is ultimately neither innovative nor effective.

In *La isla de Robinson,* Úslar Pietri portrays Simón Rodríguez on his deathbed as he recalls his life's adventures, most notably his long years of pilgrimage through Europe and South America. Through a subtle game of narrative voices, the third-person narrator assumes Rodríguez's perspective, expounding his utopian ideology in a narration that incorporates direct passages from Rodríguez's manuscripts as indicated by quotation marks. The author attempts to extol the Liberator's distinguished teacher on his own merits, especially during the process of post-independence-era nation formation, inviting him out of his famous student's shadow.

Bolívar's Other: Manuel Carlos Piar

There were dark moments and problematic decisions on the way to independence; although they are difficult to interpret or justify, the novels do not overlook them. An example is Bolívar's June 15, 1813, "Decreto de guerra a muerte" (Decree of war to the death), which officially decreed the persecution of Spaniards and Canary Islanders, threatening death to those who remained "indifferent," that is, who failed to support independence. Another is Bolívar's behavior as dictator, particularly in the last two years of his life. The case of General Manuel Carlos Piar has not received the same level of attention, probably because the Liberator's general from Curaçao cannot be researched without also questioning Bolívar himself, who was behind Piar's trial and execution. Such an interrogation would also mean opening the door to the most polemical aspects of the Venezuelan War of Independence: its racial dimensions and its civil character, that is, its not solely being a dispute against the Spanish crown.

Racial tensions marked many crucial episodes of the independence era. The bloodthirsty royalist José Tomás Boves, who hailed from the country's western plains, terrorized whites in the central and eastern regions of the country in 1813 and 1814. Another example is the *pardo* doctor and editor José Domingo Díaz, who published virulent attacks against Bolívar in the *Gaceta de Caracas* newspaper of 1808–21. Although Díaz is hardly mentioned in histories of the period, Simón Bolívar founded the official Republican newspaper *Correo del Orinoco* (1818–22) in Angostura, deep in the Amazon jungle, to have a space to respond to Díaz. A final example is the trial and October 16, 1817, execution of the brilliant patriot leader Manuel Carlos Piar. Other high-ranking officials tried to question Bolívar's authority, notably General Santiago Mariño, responsible for liberating the west of Venezuela, and General José Antonio Páez, who became Venezuela's first president after it split from Gran Colombia; however, only the *pardo* Piar was executed. Interestingly, like these oral traditions around the cult of Bolívar, another in the south of Venezuela questions the real reasons for Piar's execution (Phaf and Röhrig-Assunção 1997; Salas 1995, 2010).

Upon the publication of *El Gran Dispensador*, Manuel Trujillo described his thoughts on historical fiction in the Caracas newspaper *El Nacional*: "The transgression of history through fiction, when it does not contribute to strengthening the historical parameters themselves and giving it its true vital empirical dimension, is nothing more than a poor and mediocre imitation in the style of Walt Disney" (Dabhar 1983, 3). This effort to question historical parameters is reflected in *El Gran Dispensador*'s clear and careful exploration of historical sources. The first of the novel's three parts focuses on the colonial era; Trujillo relies principally on *La historia de la conquista y población de la Provincia de Venezuela* (1723) by José de Oviedo y Baños. Trujillo's novel features many episodes from this first history of Venezuela by establishing an interesting counterpoint between the Spanish picaresque and the Latin American magical realism and then by bringing the two together to represent the violence of the Spanish conquest and colonization.

The two remaining parts of the novel depict events from the Venezuelan War of Independence. They cover the trial against Piar on accusations of inciting race war and failing to follow orders of the Supreme Leader and Piar's subsequent execution. The novel allows Bolívar, in addition to other narrative voices, to speak directly and to edit his own writings. By exploring the thinking behind his actions, the novel does not simply immortalize him like many historical and fictional texts do but rather demythifies him, unmasking his prejudices and motives to begin the complex process of evaluating the historical person and his times.

The other novel to take Piar as its subject, Francisco Herrera Luque's *Manuel Piar, caudillo de dos colores*, constructs a fictionalized account of the life of the general from Curaçao.[4] The author seeks to prove Piar's "Caucasian origin," supposedly clearing up rumors around his birth that has caused him to be labeled *pardo*. In this account, Manuel Carlos Piar was the product of one of three love affairs that a young *mantuana* woman—that is, a member of the Venezuelan *criollo* aristocracy—carried on simultaneously, with a Portuguese prince and two young men of her social class in Caracas—one who would later father Simón Bolívar and the other who would father José Félix Ribas, another famous citizen. What might have been an interesting investigation of the era's socioracial structures and prejudices is instead, according to Trujillo, "a historical novel in the style of Walt Disney" that claims to reveal the truth of a historical figure's racial origin, declaring that he was not a person of color (in Dabhar 1983). This attitude is taken to the extreme in the novel's final appendix, "Fundamentos históricos de Manuel Piar, caudillo de dos colores."

Manuel Trujillo's *El Gran Dispensador* is not a well-constructed narrative; it is uneven and often falls short of its totalizing goal. The first part covers not only the conquest and colonization of Venezuela but also events such as the birth of a baby boy whose father, Joseph, was a carpenter and a drunk and the adventures of a certain Miguel de Saavedra. It does, however, manage different registers of narrative voices in an interesting way that requires the reader to use tangential clues to decode the identity of the narrator and the events described. The novel does not offer any concrete dates, and the leap from colony to independent nation can only be deduced through deep and careful reading. Similarly, the beginning of the second part indicates that a new narrator has taken over, but the reader can deduce that it is Simón Bolívar when she or he reads a letter to another character, Pepita, in his monologue.

The novel's fascinating polyphonic and intertextual display shows the important and delicate demythification of Bolívar and the historical events portrayed. In this sense, the novel revisits the history, suggesting another face of both the War of Independence and its greatest hero. Like Gabriel García Márquez in *El general en su laberinto* (1989), Manuel Trujillo uses historiographical sources, but he uses them to reevaluate Bolívar's role in an episode that has received relatively little attention: the trial and execution of Piar. Gabriel García Márquez allots only two pages of his novel to the entire incident, essentially taking the following allegation at face value: "Piar assembled the blacks, mulattos and sambos, and all the country's destitute, against the white aristocracy of Caracas embodied by the general" (229).

As noted earlier, Simón Bolívar narrates the bulk of the second part of *El Gran Dispensador*. Speaking to his butler Antonio Losada, Bolívar recounts public and private events of his life and reveals his unofficial side as foul-mouthed, ambitious, calculating, and resentful. Bolívar returns to Piar repeatedly in this extensive second-person monologue, trying to make sense of the actions and intrigues of the "troublemaking *pardo*" from his own perspective. The second part begins at the point when Piar has escaped and Bolívar does not know where he is; in the first lines, Bolívar asks where Piar might be and who is protecting him:

> Come onto the balcony, Antonio Losada, and look at the plaza and the remains of the day. Come and talk about the names of these rocks, whether Santo Tomás, or New Angostura, and tell me if you ever saw a river rise and fall so much in one city. . . . The troublemaking *pardo* must be in some corner. He has been recognized not by one pair of eyes, but many, and he may seek protection for his wickedness from the Church. (Trujillo 1983, 118)

In a later passage, Bolívar mocks Piar's aspirations and actions: "Our hero from San Félix, General Piar, claiming to accomplish what is beyond his capabilities . . . I deserve the thanks. Piar was one of the first to demand my return. . . . Invalid claims. Supreme leader Piar! Unending disease, infernal plague" (120).

Bolívar's assertions of Piar's overblown claims and unimpressive capabilities are drawn from historical materials. The Irish aide-de-camp Daniel Florencio O'Leary (1802–54) portrays Piar as an inept commander in his extensive *Memorias* (1879–84), where he also compiles original documents that include many from the Liberator's personal archive. (O'Leary's son, Simón Bolívar O'Leary, published the posthumous *Memorias* in thirty-two volumes.) The elder O'Leary's detailed transcription of the *pardo* general's trial was one of Trujillo's direct sources for his novelistic portrayal of the same event.

In *El Gran Dispensador*, the Bolívar character shares the racial prejudices of his imagined community and, at least in the privacy of his own room, uses Piar's mixed race as a reason to discredit him. He calls Piar "a Republican Boves" (120), playing on the white population's fears of the relentless royalist leader from a few years earlier. Along with the racial violence that began in Haiti in 1791, memories of Boves haunted whites throughout the struggle for independence. The narrative voice insinuates that Piar's goal had been to establish a republic governed by people of color: "What does he seek on behalf of the *pardos*? Equality? They have it. Respect? They enjoy it. Isn't he himself proof of that? His bad blood comes through the bastard skin that tries to cover and hide it" (120–21).

In a portion of an original document that is included in the novel, Bolívar compares Piar and Boves, holding Piar responsible for the deaths of white citizens in Cumaná, a city in the east of the country: "Cumaná was the victim of Piar's passions. Its unfortunate population perished, like the emigration from Caracas to Barcelona, because it obeyed Piar, who made them enclose themselves in the defenseless city. Poor victims trapped there!!!, tell me, who put them under Boves's knife?" (Bolívar 1981, 192–93).

In the novel's first part, the term "El Gran Dispensador" appears to refer to the Christian God of the colonizers, but in the later two, it clearly refers to the patriot leader Bolívar. In any event, this great enforcer is not concerned with ameliorating the racial tensions of the era. *Pardos* enjoyed certain privileges and exemptions; battalions of *pardos* had fought in the army since the seventeenth century and even played an important role in the events of April 19, 1810, that set the process of gaining independence in motion. Nonetheless, they certainly had not been completely integrated within society, as demonstrated by the resentment that their alliances provoked among whites. The novel takes a favorable view of the *pardo* general's behavior, presenting him as a victim, in much the same way that it portrays the indigenous in the first part (Phaf and Röhrig-Assunção 1997, 167).

These first paragraphs develop an interesting exchange between the fictionalized and "real" Bolívars, re-creating places and events from historical documents of the era. Trujillo makes adjustments to these sources to emphasize the narrator's outsized ambition and the racial prejudices that he shares with his social group. The first text featured in the novel is "A los pueblos de Venezuela." Bolívar wrote it from the Guayana general cartel in the south of the country on August 5, 1817, before Piar had been apprehended. Two months later, while in Angostura, Bolívar edited this text in the well-known proclamation "A los soldados del Ejército Libertador con motivo del fusilamiento del General Piar." A comparison of the two historical documents with the novel shows that the fictional Bolívar's aggressive tone is not arbitrary. The tone of the original text is explicitly contemptuous, full of prejudice and resentment toward this man of color and foreign origin: "don't be surprised by this monstrosity coming from a man whose life has been woven from conspiracies, crimes, and violence. Born in a foreign country, of a mother who is not Venezuelan and a father from the Canaries, he received no love upon his birth, and even less in the course of his upbringing" (Bolívar 1981, 190). The Liberator uses Piar's birthplace and upbringing to justify his suffering.

The fictional and historical Bolívars rely on the same instance of supposed military ineffectiveness, namely, Piar's failure to defend the eastern cities of Maturín, Barcelona, Güiria, and Carúpano. This process is repeated in the trial against Piar on allegations of insubordination and abuse of authority. Bolívar describes these charges in his declaration:

> Slandering the government in an attempt to change it from a republic to a tyranny; declaring the beginnings of a race to destroy the equality that has been fundamental from the glorious day of our insurrection to the present moment; inciting anarchy, robbery, and disorder, is in substance what Piar has done since he was granted leave to retire from the army. (195)

The fictional Bolívar recites these same charges to his silent interlocutor, giving them as reasons for the rebel general's fall and condemnation.

Most of this second part of the novel describes the trial itself, held in Angostura in 1817. It is revealing to read the official testimonies—O'Leary's *Memorias* contains detailed versions—for evidence of Bolívar's role in the intrigue. In the fictional text, the situation grows tense when Bolívar orders General Cedeño to capture Piar. Bolívar's inability to contain his happiness upon learning that Piar has been detained betrays at least some of his true motives. The Bolívar character feels he must prevent any action that could damage him, and he will go to any extreme to do so:

> I find myself willing to eradicate so many dirty revolts. I am determined, as in every one of my changeable chimeras, to achieve it. Defeats, exoduses, ostracism, attempts on my life, insults, spoils, abandonment, humiliation, absences, betrayals, even errors and mistakes, have not been able to distract me one iota from my goals. Will a third-rate general like Piar manage to do so? Come on! I am almost grateful for the rebellion. (Trujillo 1983, 138).

J. J. Arocha's *Manuel Piar: El héroe y el genio* (1996) is one of the few historiographical studies to take a cautious and measured approach to the vexed relationship between Bolívar and Piar. He argues that the *pardo* general must have been suffering a "honda depresión moral," a deep moral depression (1966, 98), at the time that he requested leave from the army and the return of his passport. His resentment and rebellion may have grown out of his replacement in the army leadership by his enemy General Bermúdez. The Trujillo novel refers to this episode: "He pretended to retire, a passport, he left, a rest, change of air and temperature" (120); the narrator attributes Piar's behavior to a cold calculus rather than depression.

The novel thus proceeds to construct a counterpoint between historical documents and narrative fiction. In private conversations with his butler, Bolívar reveals the traps he has set to get General Piar out of his way; Bolívar evidently saw Piar as a threat to the consolidation of his power if not necessarily to the country's independence. The narrative voice comments to Losada that he foresaw that the *pardo* "correría en busca del general Mariño" (would run in search of General Mariño) after being replaced by Bermúdez (132). He foresaw too that other officials in addition to Generals Arismendi, Soublette, and Páez would refuse to join Piar's planned uprising: "It is imperative to hunt down the rebel. The trap is laid, and if the venom does not stick, it is because he in his stupidity comes up with some miraculous breach" (137). Bolívar the narrator has carefully laid this trap, assigning Piar to take over the campaign in Los Castillos knowing full well that he would fail and then sending him to the town of Misiones in Venezuela, where he and Father Blanco would get into an intense argument.

In these incidents, the story introduces two letters: the first, whose authenticity I have not been able to verify, is from General Nicolás Briceño to Bolívar; the second, from General Cedeño to Bolívar, is one of many letters contained in O'Leary's *Memorias*. It is noteworthy that Manuel Trujillo chose the letter by Cedeño for this moment in the narration, as opposed to the letters by Sánchez or Bermúdez to which he refers indirectly in the novel's third part.

Briceño's letter comes first, and it highlights the violent and extreme dimensions of the War of Independence, which are connected to the general theme of the novel: the violence that characterizes the entire history of Venezuela—and the Americas. The narrative voice, which characterizes Briceño as "nuestro malandante 'diablo'" (our unfortunate "devil") (Trujillo 1983, 155), joyfully tells his butler and silent witness about Briceño's strategy to determine which prisoners were Spanish and therefore eligible to be executed according to the "Decreto de Guerra a Muerte." Briceño made the prisoners pronounce the words *naranja* (orange) and *corazón* (heart) because the Spanish "could not pronounce the z correctly even if their goddamned mothers birthed them all over again" (157). Cedeño's extensive missive, which is transcribed in the novel, features its author's comments on Piar's letter to Mariño and demonstrates the way the different elements came together in the trial and sentencing of the caudillo from the east.

This second part ends with the triumph of the interests and strategies of the principal narrator, Bolívar:

> In truth, Piar's resentment did not abate; to the contrary, it increased. . . . In conclusion, my friend: General Piar will ruminate on his impotence in a cell as he awaits his trial. Carmona, for his part, can go on enjoying his promotion to Colonel of the Cavalry. We will uncork not one but several bottles. It has been said: heads and bottles tend to share their transparency. (174)

Finally, the novel's third part, which is shorter than the others, focuses on the last days of Piar's trial and his execution by firing squad. The tone of the narration changes dramatically; in contrast to the Great Dispensator's frenetic, ambitious, and foul-mouthed discourse, this voice is measured, striving for distance from the events related, although the force of the actions narrated makes this impossible at times. This narrator, Antonio Losada, has been asked by his employer, Simón Bolívar, for a luxuriously detailed account of the trial, since Bolívar did not participate directly until the end, when he confirmed the sentence and ordered it carried out.

The role of judge in the military trial was filled by General Soublette. A total of nine witnesses testified, including the noteworthy figures Juan Francisco Sánchez, Pedro Hernández, Juan Manuel Olivares, Ramón Machado, Navy Captain Antonio Díaz and, finally, the accused. The novel describes events that happened parallel to the trial, events outside of the military process that nonetheless contributed to the general atmosphere in which it took place. Losada talks with Bolívar about the latter's frustration with the "distortions" in the international press and the resulting need to found a newspaper for official republican news: "¿qué le parece algo así como 'El Correo del Orinoco'?" (what do you think of something like "The Orinoco Mail"?) (205). They also comment on the disappointing performance by Bermúdez, the general assigned to replace Piar.

Each witness testifies about some treasonous or suspect action by the *pardo* general. The final verdict—to convict—is rendered notwithstanding a magisterial performance by defense attorney Coronel Galindo, who rapidly and effectively points out the partiality of the witnesses:[5]

> Did you not, Colonel Sánchez, serve in General Piar's troops? The witness meets Piar's eyes as he replies in the affirmative. Galindo reminds him of his expulsion from Piar's army. Sánchez dislikes the term used, it was nothing more than a tactical discrepancy that caused him to separate from those troops. Galindo paints a portrait of the episode: you wanted to abandon the campaign for Guayana and the return to the East . . . [but] if General Piar had not proceeded as he did, perhaps neither you, nor I, nor any of the witnesses would be here, and Guayana would not belong to the patriots. (181)

When it is the defendant's turn to speak, he denies the charges against him—"accused of the crimes of insubordination to the supreme authority, conspiracy against public order and tranquility, and lastly of desertion" (O'Leary 1952, 351)—although he admits that he spoke inappropriately on a few occasions: "I deny those charges, I have dedicated my entire life to the defense of my country, my military service is proof of it and all the rest is the product of the blackest intrigue. I do not deny my complaints, but they were the natural venting of a highly offended man" (Trujillo 1983, 219). Notwithstanding Galindo's brilliant defense, the War Council unanimously condemned Piar, basing its decision on the testimony of "respectable and unimpeachable witnesses, among them . . . generals, leaders, soldiers and countrymen" (O'Leary 1981, 195). O'Leary, like nearly every historian to study the trial, defended the impartiality of the process.

The historiographical discourse is rife with speculation about Piar's reaction to his sentence, asking whether he received the news with cowardice or honor. In Trujillo's novel, the accused reacts with a moment of weakness and is promptly reprimanded for it; he explains that he responded out of shock, as he had never imagined that his punishment would be so severe.

The entire novel, including the last part's narration in the voice of the Great Dispensator's butler, plays with the two levels of reality and fiction. The last paragraph combines them, blending Bolívar's process of editing his October 17, 1817, proclamation with the sounds of Piar's execution:

> [Bolívar], pacing from one side to the other, orders me to get paper and pen and begins to dictate a proclamation to the army: "Soldiers, yesterday was a day of pain for my heart. . . . General Piar was executed for crimes that damaged the country, conspiracy and desertion . . . (orders from bugles are heard) . . . a just and legal tribunal . . . has pronounced a sentence against that disgraced citizen . . . (drum beats announce the defendant's presence, and S. E. [Bolívar] takes a few steps toward the balcony, hesitates, comes back, and returns to his dictation) . . . disgraced citizen who, drunk on the favors of fortune and in satisfaction of his ambition . . . sought to bury his country under ruins . . . (the murmurs die down, the wind can almost be heard, almost the sound of the river, soon shots will be heard) . . . and General Piar, in truth, has rendered important services to the Republic. (226)

In the novel, in the privacy of his room, the Bolívar character describes himself as a man whose military and intellectual attributes make him superior to all others. In his view, it was his cleverness above all that allowed him to get people and events right where he wanted them. This Great Dispensator is ruthless, a man who delights in recalling the most terrible episodes of the war. He justifies extreme violence by its context. In this way, we finally meet the other Bolívar that García Márquez promised us: a Liberator we did not expect, completely immersed in a total war, directing and responding to that war's dynamic forces.

Notes

This article is taken from the second chapter of my book *Nacionalismos banales, el culto a Bolívar: Literatura, cine, arte y política en América Latina* (Pittsburgh, PA: Instituto Internacional de Literatura Iberoamericana, University of Pittsburgh, 2013). A slightly different version of the first section of this article was published in Spanish in *Hispamérica* 64/65 (1993): 49–54.

1. For an overview of Venezuelan narrative in the 1980s, see Navarro 1989, Méndez Guédez 1999, and Barrera Linares 2006.

2. The novel *El Gran Dispensador* was published in Caracas by Fundación Cadafe, an affiliate of the state-owned electric company. Distribution was poor, and the unsold copies were lost when they were stored in a warehouse that burned down. I am unaware of any other edition. It is probably for this reason that the only critical work on the novel, as far as I know, is Phaf and Röhrig-Assunção 1997.

3. In Venezuela, a *pardo* was a person with African blood in his or her veins, even if inherited from remote ancestors (Lynch 1973, 192–93).

4. Regarding Herrera Luque's novel, see Phaf and Röhrig-Assunção 1997 and Chibán 2004.

5. This same assessment of Galindo's performance can be found in Lecuna's *Crónica razonada de las guerras de Bolívar* (1950).

References

Arocha, J. J. 1966. *Manuel Carlos Piar. El héroe y el genio.* Madrid: Cultura Clásica y Moderna.

Barrera Linares, Luis. 2006. "Llegaron los ochenta: Confluencia y diversidad en la narrativa finisecular." In *Nación y literatura: Itinerarios de la palabra en la cultura venezolana,* edited by Carlos Pacheco, Luis Barrera Linares, and Beatriz González-Stephan. Caracas: Fundación Bigott-Banesco-Equinoccio.

Bencomo Barrios, Héctor. 2006. *Manuel Piar: Estancias de una existencia provechosa.* Caracas: Banco del Caribe.

Bolívar, Simón. 1981. *Discursos, proclamas y epistolario político.* Madrid: Editora Nacional.

Carrera Damas, Germán. 1973. *El culto a Bolívar: Esbozo para un estudio de la historia de las ideas en Venezuela.* 2nd edition. Caracas: Universidad Central de Venezuela.

Chibán, Alicia, ed. 2004. *El archivo de la Independencia y la ficción contemporánea.* Salta, Argentina: Universidad de Salta.

Dabhar, Sergio. 1983. "La escritura y sus culpables. Manuel Trujillo contra la novela histórica a lo Walt Disney." *El Nacional,* June 26.

Herrera Luque, Francisco. 1987. *Manuel Piar, caudillo de dos colores.* Caracas: Pomaire.

Lecuna, Vicente. 1950. *Crónica razonada de las guerras de Bolívar.* 3 vols. New York: New Colonial Press.

Lynch, John. 1986. *The Spanish American Revolutions 1808–1826.* New York: Norton.

Méndez Guédez, Juan Carlos. 1999. "Veinte años no es nada (notas sobre narrativa venezolana del ochenta y noventa)." *Espéculo. Revista de estudios literarios* (Madrid), no. 11. http://www.ucm.es/info/especulo/numero11/li_venez.html.

Navarro, Armando. 1989. "Narrativa de los '80: Conocidos y por conocer." "Papel Literario" section, *El Nacional* (Caracas), December 31.

O'Leary, Daniel Florencio. 1881/1981. *Memorias del General O'Leary.* Vol. 15. Caracas: Ministerio de la Defensa.

Phaf, Ineke, and Matthias Röhrig-Assunção. 1997. "History Is Bunk! Recovering the Meaning of Independence in Venezuela, Colombia, and Curaçao: A Cross Cultural Image of Manuel Piar." In *A History of Literature in the Caribbean,* edited by James A. Arnold, 3:161-174. Amsterdam: Benjamins.

Romero, Denzil. 1983. *La tragedia del generalísimo.* Madrid: Argos Vergara.

———. 1987. *Grand Tour.* Madrid: Alfadil.

———. 1988. *La esposa del doctor Thorne.* Madrid: Tusquets.

Salas, Yolanda. 1995. "Piar en las vertientes de la historia colectiva." *Revista Bigott* 33:23–31.

———. 2010. *Manuel Piar. El héroe de múltiples rostros. Una aproximación a la historia desde la perspectiva de la memoria colectiva.* Caracas: Ministerio de Estado para la Cultura.

Trujillo, Manuel. 1983. *El Gran Dispensador.* Caracas: Fundación Cadafe.

Úslar Pietri, Arturo. 1987. *La isla de Robinson.* Barcelona: Seix Barral.

10

Moving Histories

Performing Bolívar in Jorge Alí Triana's Film *Bolívar Soy Yo* (2002)

ARMIDA DE LA GARZA

As a myth and a symbol, Simón Bolívar has ongoing relevance, and indeed his name has become a surface for the inscription of a wide variety of meanings. A number of political parties, guerrillas, cultural policy initiatives, and social movements today all claim to be Bolivarian, that is, inspired by the ideas and dreams of Bolívar, which are taken to be broadly related to various notions of freedom (El Libertador) and struggles for social justice.

This relative open-endedness of Bolívar as a signifier is at the core of the film *Bolívar soy yo,* written and directed in 2002 by the Colombian director Jorge Alí Triana (plate 16). The story revolves around an actor playing Bolívar for a soap opera who becomes so deeply immersed in the part that at times he and others confuse him with Bolívar. A variety of social actors ranging from the Colombian president, the media, and guerrilla insurgents accommodate his delusion for the sake of co-opting, as it were, this incarnation of the symbol to advance their own—not always compatible—agendas, with dire consequences. The film has been read in different ways: as a witty commentary on and criticism of highly relevant contemporary social issues, national foundational narratives, and the society of spectacle. The film has also been praised for its postmodern use of reflexivity and its forms of hybridity that are at once Latin American and global (Kantaris 2007). It has been read as an allegory of a populist "humanization" of the Latin American heroes amid a growing disenchantment with globalization and pessimism toward the future (Tal 2010).

As fantastical as this narrative may seem, its origins are rooted in Jorge Alí Triana's experience directing the television series *Bolívar, el hombre de las dificultades* (1982), written in collaboration with Carlos José Reyes Posada. This ambitious series of forty-three weekly episodes for the program *Revivamos nuestra historia* inaugurated color television in Colombia. The series enlisted the majority of theater and television actors working at that time in Colombia, along with entire towns, to represent the countless characters involved in the forty-seven years of Bolívar's existence. The Colombian armed forces represented the armies gathered throughout Bolívar's epic journey through South America, all the while fighting the various guerrilla groups that soon afterward (in 1987) organized under the umbrella group Coordinadora Guerrillera Simón Bolívar (Melo 2010). The television episodes were filmed in difficult and diverse terrains that served as sets for marches and battles, including entire villages on the Magdalena River banks, the Andean range, the Llanos Orientales bordering Venezuela, and on-site battlefields. Throughout the crew's travels spectators offered gifts and petitioned favors, responding to the character Bolívar and not the protagonist actor, Pedro Montoya (1948–2004). Montoya identified so profoundly with his character that he was unable to take off his uniform after recordings ended, consequently suffering a psychological breakdown (Reyes Posada 2012).

Triana seized upon this identity crisis and transformed it into a metaphor for Colombian and Latin American societies. I focus here on the performative dimension of the film as it revolves around the actor playing the role of Bolívar and reactions to his presence. The epistemological, aesthetic, and ontological dimensions of performance provide a way to turn experience into knowledge, an alternative way of transmitting versions of history and cultural heritage that highlight the role of the body in its construction, as well as communicative display and ways of being in the world. In focusing on specific scenes when the actor performs Bolívar, I ask, in each case: What does it mean to "be" Bolívar? An analysis of the strategies that foreground performativity—costume, acting methods, and music and choreography—foregrounds the various ways in which people may enact their engagement with "Bolívar," including composing songs and staging dances for him. What "Bolívar" means today as depicted in the film and as I argue is above all the birth—or refusal to die—of a consciousness or a growing awareness that the nation-states that followed independence, rather than the subcontinental state, and that continues to be the fundamental problem of the region.

It is this subcontinental state, Gran Colombia, that Jacques (2011) has called a "civilization-state" and that Bolívar and others sought to create. This performance-centered approach to culture attentive to the film's recurring themes and motifs "finds in the unstable aesthetics of repetition an ethics and politics of possibility" (Pollock 2008, 122). Apart from understanding the film as commentary or criticism or as a pessimistic complaint, one can also understand it as an invitation to action and a celebration of action, a coming together to attempt to perform, as it were, a happier ending.

Performing Bolívar

There are several strands of research on the social role and meaning of performance that bridge the humanities and social sciences. These range from John L. Austin's speech-act theories (1962), focused on the way language can sometimes have effects equivalent to action, to Marxist notions of praxis and everyday life—notably Pierre Bourdieu's concept of habitus (1977) and Judith Butler's theories on gender (2006)—to Mikhail Bakhtin's studies of the subversive potential of the carnival (1984). Indeed, the latter strand, on performativity and carnival, goes back to at least Plato, who forcefully condemned theater for the way it could bring the constructed nature of power into sharp relief when the structures that sustain power tend to naturalize it. French philosopher Jacques Rancière writes, "From the Platonic point of view, the stage, which is simultaneously a locus of public activity and the exhibition-space for 'fantasies,' disturbs the clear partition of identities, activities and spaces" (2004, 13). Thus for Plato, theater was dangerous inasmuch as it could bring other times and spaces into the time-space of the performance, suspending, albeit temporarily, the social order of "reality."

Mixing theatrical and cinematic performances, the plot of *Bolívar soy yo* all but confirms Plato's anxieties. A brief plot summary is pertinent here. The film opens with a nineteenth-century firing squad about to shoot a prisoner in military uniform who has been identified as Bolívar. Indeed, as a last wish, the prisoner has just been addressing the audience by reciting a speech by Bolívar to explain the meaning of his actions and how these were all for the good of the people. However, just as the platoon is about to shoot,

"Bolívar" suddenly shouts, "Cut! Bolívar did not die like this. I refuse to kill Bolívar like this or in any other way." At that point "Bolívar" is revealed as an actor named Santiago Miranda (played by Robinson Díaz), co-starring with his girlfriend Alejandra Barberini (played by Amparo Grisales), who in turn plays the role of Manuelita Sáenz in a soap opera entitled *Los amores del Libertador*. Visibly upset, Miranda leaves the set and returns to Bogotá. In this way, the film employs the "film within the film" device—or rather, the soap opera within the film—to turn the whole of Colombia into a stage where a set of reflections on the history and the hopes for the future of Latin America, loosely termed "Bolívar," come back from the grave or, in the words of Miranda, try to fulfill the Bolivarian dream of Latin American unification. Producers initiate a search all over Bogotá to bring Miranda back, a search that is as frantic as the Colombian president's efforts to take advantage of Bolívar's presence in the capital by recruiting "Bolívar" to attend military parades and political meetings.

The narrative thus largely revolves around efforts by the media and the government to contain their creation, which has managed to develop a charismatic life of its own. Their strategies for containing the uncooperative Bolívar go as far as pronouncing him mad and attempting to have him confined or simply arrested. The psychiatrist employed to treat Miranda is tasked not so much with curing him but with persuading him to finish the soap opera. Significantly, however, it is Miranda who ends up kidnapping the president, hijacking a boat, and reversing the journey down the Magdalena River that had taken Bolívar to the Quinta de San Pedro Alejandrino, where he died.

In the film voyage, Miranda flows upstream from the Atlantic coast toward the capital, insisting on a meeting with the presidents of all the Bolivarian nations in order to re-create Gran Colombia. Recalling Triana's and Montoya's experiences in the 1980s, people in the coastal towns rise joyously to welcome him as a savior. In the midst of his travels on the barge, a guerrilla group enters the scene; they identify themselves as the Coordinadora Guerrillera Simón Bolívar and intervene, or rather, join in the president's kidnapping and placing themselves under the orders of "El General Bolívar." In a clear allusion to the M-19, the guerrillas attempt to return to Miranda the sword of Bolívar they had earlier stolen from the Quinta de Bolívar, but Miranda eventually rejects them. (Gómez Pernia and Reyes discuss the M-19's appropriation of Bolívar's sword in their essays in this volume.) Confusion about who is in charge satirizes the authorial voice of the past that Miranda embodies. Miranda and the guerrillas, now joined by Alejandra as Manuela Sáenz, negotiate a meeting with the presidents of the Bolivarian nations at the Quinta de Bolívar in exchange for the Colombian president's release. Soon afterward it becomes apparent that the objectives of the guerrillas, Miranda, and the historical Bolívar do not line up.

Rather than the tragic ending in a botched operation (recalling the Colombian Palace of Justice tragedy in 1985) where all is lost in a fratricidal bloodbath, Triana blocks this finale. In an act of self-referentiality, the crew announces the film's directorial "Cut," thus leaving the end open for interpretation and imaginary reconstruction. The boundaries between the past and the present, reality and fiction are skillfully blurred by various strategies so that the continued relevance of Bolívar's ideals is highlighted. We now turn to the three strategies that foreground performativity.

Dressing the Part of Bolívar

The first strategy is costume. Bolívar's image, as frequently depicted in history books, paintings, and statues, is first and foremost a man in arms. Most costumes, when successful, are naturalized as part of the fiction world without alluding to the reality outside the story (Collins and Nisbet 2010). But a uniform worn by an actor can bring the supposedly real world to bear upon the fiction world by intertextually referencing a historical army and a contemporary one. Roland Barthes (1979) describes "two kinds of history: an intelligent history which rediscovers the profound tensions, the specific conflicts of the past; and a superficial history which mechanically reconstructs certain anecdotic details." He adds that costume has "long been a favorite realm for the exercise of the latter" (42). In *Bolívar soy yo* the character of Miranda is largely believable as Bolívar due to the authenticity of his costuming, which in turn serves to revive the whole historical era. The cut and shape of the uniform Miranda wears seem to summon up the codes of behavior of that historical period, codes that directly affect his posture and movements. When reciting the script for his role in the soap opera and dressed the part, Miranda becomes even more the virile hero. The epaulettes make his shoulders seem broader, the high collar extends his neck longer, and the gilded laurels ornamenting the uniform puff up his chest, all of which are crucial to the iconography of military masculinity and ritual.

It is this image that gives him the authority to pronounce some of Bolívar's most famous speeches.

Maurice Bloch (1975) finds that language in rituals is, by its very nature, constrained and thus constraining, since what can be said on such occasions is limited to a pre-existing repertoire. However, I argue that ritual is not mainly verbal but is also constituted by its ability to enable participation. Bloch fails to take this very important aspect into account. In other words, performance not only constructs a symbolic reality through verbal argumentation but also creates a situation for participants to experience symbolic meanings. *Bolívar soy yo* calls attention to the ritual invocation of Bolívar's words and the audience's participatory choices, for example, in the opening scene. Bolívar's body before the firing squad is a symbolic body, dressed in a uniform whose bright red, yellow, and blue are now so closely associated with the Colombian, Venezuelan, and Ecuadorian flags. About to be executed, Bolívar utters fragments from a 1830 speech that, according to historian John J. Johnson (1992), represent the heart of his thinking, namely a concern with the four priorities of unity, control, stability, and security. The famous speech from Bolívar's final year is quoted in the film:

> Colombian people: as I am about to leave you, I am guided by my love for you when considering my last will. The sole glory to which I aspire is the consolidation of Colombia. Everyone must work for the precious good that unity is. People: obey the present government to rid yourselves of anarchy. Ministers: raise your prayers to heaven. And soldiers: raise your swords to protect individual freedom. Colombian people: you have witnessed my efforts in trying to bring freedom where tyranny reigned before. . . .
>
> Colombian people: my last vows are for the motherland's happiness. If my death contributes to the end of Parties and the consolidation of the Union, I shall gladly descend to my grave. (Bolívar 1830/2007, 310)

The first performance of Bolívar (in the film) is thus only accomplished in a ritual that highly engages its audience, that is, the ritual invocation of Bolívar's famous call to unity reiterated by politicians in all sorts of ceremonial contexts. This Bolívar, made authentic through costuming, finally achieves a moment of unity when the soldiers assigned to kill him are moved to tears, as are the set staff and crew, and the execution is thwarted.

Later in the film, costume is also employed to blur the boundaries

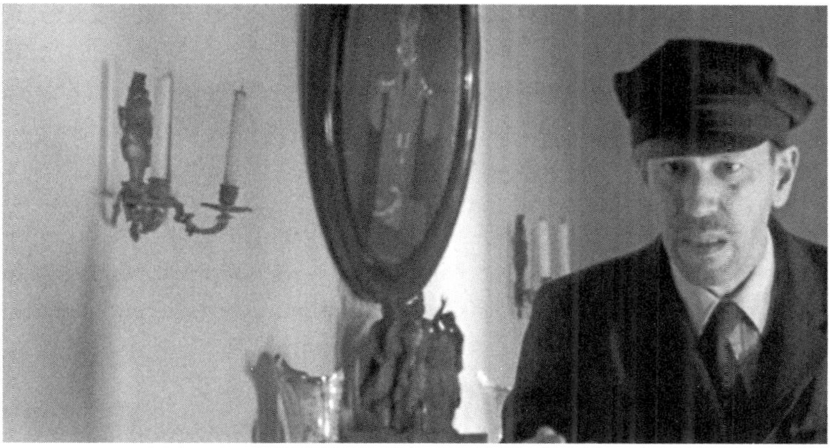

FIGURE 10.1. Quinta museum caretaker. Film still from *Bolívar soy yo* (Jorge Alí Triana, 2002).

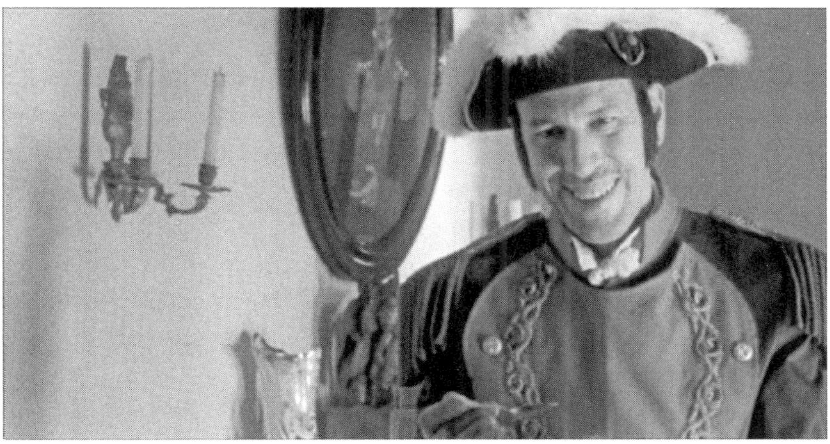

FIGURE 10.2. "Sucre, my only friend!" Film still from *Bolívar soy yo* (Jorge Alí Triana, 2002).

between the past and the present by establishing parallels with Bolívar's friends and enemies who are given contemporary roles as guerrilla leaders (General José Antonio Páez) or museum caretakers (General Antonio José de Sucre). Even the president of Colombia morphs into Francisco de Paula Santander. Arriving at the Quinta de Bolívar, the actor Miranda at first sees a museum and its caretaker, but as Bolívar, he recognizes Sucre, and their costumes revert to military uniforms (figures 10.1 and 10.2).

The film further blends reality and fiction by having Miranda utter speeches and quotations from letters and texts written by Bolívar within the fictional world of the soap opera and the reality of Miranda's daily life. Bolívar's words are juxtaposed into contemporary situations and so made to be completely appropriate. Thus, having been betrayed even by his partner Alejandra/Manuelita and disappointed at having his attempt to revive Bolívar hijacked by the guerrilla and the media, Miranda reads, "There is no good faith in America, neither amongst people, nor amongst nations. In America, treaties are paper, constitutions—books; elections are combats; freedom is anarchy, and life is a torment" (Bolívar 1853, 72).

Acting Methods: Identification with or Alienation from Bolívar

The film also benefits from drawing upon two opposite but complementary traditions of acting. On the one hand, Western traditions have long relied on naturalism to produce suspension of disbelief, with the actor mimetically representing a role and the drama largely unfolding through character development. Famously, Constantin Stanislavski (1926/2013) and later Lee Strasberg (1987) pioneered methods for acting that required the actor to identify with the character, such as creating a score of psychological actions in response to a script text so that the actor seems to merge with the character. Ironically, in *Bolívar,* the soap opera producer comments on the way Miranda had no interest in history and knows nothing about Bolívar before learning his part. Instead, performing Bolívar has the effect of a "reverse method." Miranda does merge with Bolívar but becomes Bolívar's "score"; that is, the spirit of Bolívar appropriates Miranda's body, life, and emotions. This is yet another important way in which Bolívar refuses to die.

This reverse method occurs when Miranda, running away from the producers, takes refuge with his mother, only to have neighbors and friends come to petition Bolívar for favors. When they ask his intervention in obtaining scholarships for their children and lighting on the streets, Miranda pitches his responses in the ways he assumes Bolívar would have reacted. Here, performing Bolívar means fulfilling the cultic role of saints and virgins in the Catholic tradition, hearing the needs and requests of the faithful and promising to comfort them. The actor's name, Santiago Miranda, is highly loaded with references, religious as well as historical. Santiago is the patron saint of Spain for his role as Matamoros in the reconquest of the

Iberian Peninsula and then as Mataíndios in the conquest of the Americas. He thus serves as a reference to the reconquest of a Catholic Colombia in the Conservative regime of Laureano Gómez (1950–53) during La Violencia. Moreover, Francisco Miranda was a Venezuelan revolutionary whose ideals of liberty and Spanish American unity are considered forerunners to Bolívar's. Thus, even the character's name serves here as a vehicle to invoke multiple pasts to bear upon the present, adding to the cult and contested dimensions of Bolívar.

On the other hand, traditions of acting that followed Bertolt Brecht's alienation effect (1978) required the opposite of identification with characters, that is, distancing the audience from emotional involvement in the play by drawing attention to its artificiality. This was in part achieved through the actors maintaining a distance from their characters by various means, such as speaking of themselves in the third person and directly addressing the audience. The aim was to break down the barrier between actors and audiences, to drive the audience into active engagement, questioning, and participation. The film clearly draws from this tradition as well, particularly in those scenes when Miranda, as he enters and leaves the Bolívar character, proposes new ways of interpreting what Bolívar means. These interventions strongly recall Brecht's *Three Penny Opera* (1928/2005) in the way they stress agency on the part of the audience, such as in changing the ending, and in the innovative use of music. Triana cleverly interrupts the film's finale and calls attention to its artificiality with a directorial "Cut" of the *Bolívar soy yo* film, thus intervening in the tragic end. This gesture recalls the opening scene when Miranda/Bolívar refuses to die by firing squad, a scene that signals the film's recurring invitation to the spectator to imagine an alternative ending.

While the credits are rolling, the 2002 song "Final feliz" (Happy ending) by the contemporary Colombian pop group Aterciopelados plays; and the credits to Bolívar and Manuelita and not to Miranda and Alejandra insist on the capacity of the audience to transform the ending. In this case, the song's lyrics play on rhyme and linguistic innovation to invoke new meanings and transform horror to beauty. The simple transformation of a single letter in a word completely changes its meaning, rendering, for instance, death (*muerte*) as luck (*suerte*) and bullets (*balas*) as wings (*alas*): "En vez de muerte yo quiero suerte, en vez de llanto, canto. En vez de balas yo quiero alas. En vez de trágico que sea mágico . . . un final feliz" (Instead of death I want luck, instead of tears, song. Instead of bullets, I want wings. Instead of tragedy, magic . . . a happy ending). Indeed, music is in the film a third and very important way of creating a situation for the performance of Bolívar to occur. It is to the use of music that we now turn.

Music and the Call to Action

Contrary to Bloch's contention, the effectiveness of ritual lies less in spoken language than in the kind of participation the ritual allows or constrains. In *Bolívar soy yo*, music, song, and dance are privileged ways to hold attention, create mood and pathos, and enable participation. Audiences all over Colombia are shown reacting with glee to Miranda's attempt at reviving Bolívar. They dance and improvise songs that interpellate him as "Santiago Miranda, who will soon come back as Simón Bolívar, [bringing] freedom." These depicted audiences do not interrupt official or state-sponsored rituals. Rather, they create their own ritual by means of music and dance. At the same time, the film audience watching *Bolívar soy yo* is placed in a position parallel to that of the audience in the film. The film's audience and the portrayed audiences are participants in a shared ritual through sound. Since hearing is three-dimensional, it creates an acoustic space shared by the imagined and actual audiences. The shared space is what Thomas Elsaesser and Malte Hagener have called the "imaginary topography" of cinema (2010, 130).

The song the audiences sing in greeting Miranda/Bolívar is "Canto a Bolívar," a Colombian vallenato composed and sung by Iván Ovalle, a star of the genre. Both the song and Pablo Neruda's poem of the same name are, like Bolívar's final speeches about unity, ritually invoked in many official ceremonial contexts. The vallenato is a genre that may have originated with Spanish minstrels, West African griots, or traveling singers as a means of telling stories and spreading news. In the film, it is the news of Bolívar's return that this vallenato celebrates. At the same time, it calls for dancing. In this context, what Halifu Osumare has said of hip-hop is also applicable to the audiences dancing in *Bolívar soy yo*, that dance is a way of mapping identity into the muscles, producing sociocultural bodies, and moving in often subversive ways. To Osumare, the movement of the hip-hop dancer, and I think the vallenato dancer of the film, "transcends nation-states and generates a global Intercultural Body that we are only beginning to fathom" (2002, 42).

This transnational body, the film suggests, may well be Latin America, as the popularity of vallenato is today high not only in Colombia but also Panama, Venezuela, Ecuador, and even Mexico. Indeed, when Plato forcefully condemned theater, he contrasted it with what in his view was a good form of art: dance. As Rancière interprets Plato, it is in the choreographic where the community "sings and dances its own proper unity" (2004, 14). The potential of singing and dancing to inscribe community through participation is thus a central part of the way Bolivarian ideals are performed in the twenty-first century.

Bolívar and Latin American Unity Today

Let us now conclude by taking a closer look at the issue of Latin American unity, since it ends up being the film's proposed meaning for Bolívar as an anchor for this yet-unresolved ideal. For while costume, script, and music are central to reviving the Liberator in *Bolívar soy yo*, it is Bolívar's insistence on the need for Latin American unity that stands out as practically synonymous with his name today. Unity is the recurring theme from the first speech in the opening scene to the climax of the film, when Miranda kidnaps the Colombian president, to the end, when Miranda demands that the Bolivarian presidents meet to reintegrate Gran Colombia. Unity is, as claimed by the psychiatrist in the film, "the key and ongoing, permanent obsession of the character." Miranda puts it thus:

> I have risen from the grave because the continent deserves another opportunity. I came to call you back to reintegrating Gran Colombia. The only possibility for our countries to overcome the underdevelopment in which they still find themselves is to unite into one great nation. Everything else is a lie, ready-made phrases for occasions such as this.

It is the relevance of this idea that I wish to explore here since, especially in light of recent history, it has become clear that the development of capitalism has continued to have profound effects on the size and nature of the polities that are regarded as legitimate and sustainable units for self-governance.

To theorists of the nation like Ernest Gellner (1983) and Benedict Anderson (2006), the misnamed nation-states we presently inhabit are the polities resulting from modernization, entailing the formation of vernacular languages, the downward spreading of so-called high culture and vice versa, and the engagement of various elites and intelligentsias in nation and state-building through a variety of institutions—not least of which is cinema. Ideology, imparted mainly by the educational system as well as other institutions such as the family, has played a large role in the formation of the soldier-citizens that the nation-state requires. Nationalism becomes, as it were, a religion suitable for secular times, a call for awareness of the "community of history and destiny" that is the nation (Smith 1991).

What gives life meaning no longer resides in the afterlife but in the connected fate of ancestors and descendants. It has also become commonplace to note, however, postmodern transformations in capitalism, such as what David Harvey (1991) characterizes as a metamorphosis of the multinational corporation into a transnational entity that engages in "flexible accumulation." Such transnational entities have rendered nation-states obsolete in their relentless drive toward ever-larger markets and more efficient means of production, and the soldier-citizen has been replaced with the consumer-customer of a globalized era. In accounts such as this, the Fordist model of the mass society of industrialization has given way to fragmented and dispersed forms of production. Importantly, production itself has been marginalized as the key means of accumulation and supplanted especially by financial and information services and plain speculation. With a focus on the social consequences of these developments, Zygmunt Bauman (2007) has called the period leading to globalization "liquid modernity," as institutions, including the state, cannot keep their form for long. Older forms of solidarity are giving way to extreme individualism.

Whatever one thinks of Bolívar and contemporary Latin American politics, it is impossible not to ponder the possibilities—and the limitations—that a Bolivarian civilization-state would afford. It may be that during our era of globalization, the relevance of Bolívar's dream of subcontinental unity has lost its luster and indeed seems more of a nightmare. In the final scene of the film, Miranda's eyes bleed as a montage of victims of the Colombian armed conflict flashes in and out of the frame. The Bolivarian vision of Spanish American unity seems delusional, Quixotesque as Miranda implies in the opening scene, amid the current bloody unraveling. As Santiago

Miranda agonizes, he utters his last breath: "Corten" (Cut). The director's clapboard—in a self-referential gesture not to the soap opera but to another film—reads "Bolivar yo soy," inverting the words of the film's title and thus emphasizing the *mise-en-abime*: the narrative's inconclusive, artificial, and performative character. It invites the viewer to respond as Miranda did at the beginning of the film, by refusing to accept the story's ending and rather embarking on a quest to rescript an alternative path. By foregrounding the performativity of "Bolívar," *Bolívar soy yo* raises questions that are not limited to the Colombian context. What story of "unity" or "nation" or "people" will bind the collective psyche and retrieve it from the madness of self-destruction and violence? What myths, cults, and rituals organize and inhibit our social imaginary? What metamorphoses in embodiment or identification with and alienation from an/other need to take place for the poetics of possibility to transform our social order? These remain open questions.

References

Anderson, Benedict. 2006. *Imagined Communities.* London: Verso.

Austin, John L. 1962. *How to Do Things with Words.* Oxford, England: Clarendon.

Bakhtin, Mikhail. 1984. *Rabelais and his World.* John Wiley and Sons.

Barthes, Roland. 1972. "The Diseases of Costume." In *Critical Essays,* 41–50. Translated by Richard Howard. Evanston, IL: Northwestern University Press.

Bauman, Zygmunt. 2007. *Liquid Times: Living in an Age of Uncertainty.* Cambridge, England: Polity.

Bloch, Maurice, ed. 1975. Introduction to *Political Language and Oratory in Traditional Society,* 1–28. New York: New York Academic Press.

Bolívar, Simón. 1830/2007. *Discursos y proclamas de Simón Bolívar,* edited by Rufino Blanco-Fombona. Caracas: Biblioteca Ayacucho.

———. 1853. *Proclamas de Simón Bolívar, Libertador de Colombia.* New York: D. Appleton.

Bourdieu, Pierre. 1977. *Outline of a Theory of Practice.* Cambridge: Cambridge University Press.

Brecht, Bertolt. 1928/2005. *The Three Penny Opera.* York, England: Methuen.

———. 1978. *On Theater.* Edited and translated by John Willett. New York: Methuen Drama.

Butler, Judith. 2006. *Gender Trouble: Feminism and the Subversion of Identity.* London: Routledge.

Collins, Jane, and Andrew Nisbet, eds. 2010. *Theatre and Performance Design*. London: Routledge.

Elsaesser, Thomas, and Malte Hagener. 2010. *Film Theory: An Introduction through the Senses*. London: Routledge.

Gellner, Ernest. 1983. *Nations and Nationalism*. Oxford, England: Blackwell.

Harvey, David. 1991. *The Condition of Postmodernity*. Oxford, England: Blackwell.

Jacques, Martin. 2011. "Civilization State versus Nation-State." *Süddeutsche Zeitung*, January 15. http://www.martinjacques.com/articles/civilization-state-versus-nation-state-2/.

Johnson, John J. 1992. *Simón Bolívar and Spanish American Independence 1783–1830*. Anvil Series. Malabar, FL: Krieger.

Kantaris, Geoffrey. 2007. "Soapsuds and Histrionics: Media, History and Nation in *Bolívar Soy Yo*." In *Contemporary Latin American Cinema*, edited by Deborah Shaw, 117–33. Lanham, MD: Rowman and Littlefield.

Melo, Jorge Orlando. 2010. "Bolívar en Colombia: Las transformaciones de su imagén." In *Entre el olvido y el recuerdo: Íconos, lugares de memoria y cánones de la historia y la literatura en Colombia*, 103–38. Bogotá: Universidad Javeriana.

Osumare, Halifu. 2002. "Global Breakdancing and the Intercultural Body." *Dance Research Journal* 34, no. 2 (Winter): 30–45.

Pollock, Della. 2008. "Moving Histories: Performance and Oral History." In *The Cambridge Companion to Performance Studies*, edited by Tracy C. Davis, 120–35. New York: Cambridge University Press.

Rancière, Jacques. 2004. *The Politics of Aesthetics: The Distribution of the Sensible*. Translated by Gabriel Rockhill. London: Continuum.

Reyes Posada, Carlos José. 2012. "Adaptación de la historia para la televisión en 'Bolívar, el hombre de las dificultades.'" Paper presented at Latin American Studies Association annual conference, May, San Francisco.

Smith, Anthony D. 1991. *National Identity*. London: Penguin Books.

Stanislavski, Constantin. 1926/2013. *An Actor Prepares*. New York: Bloomsbury.

Strasberg, Lee. 1987. *A Dream Of Passion*. New York: Little, Brown.

Tzvi, Tal. 2010. "Libertadores de celuloide: San Martín y Bolívar en películas de la globalización." *El Ojo Que Piensa*, June 29. Posted at http://www.researchgate.net/publication/44844453_Libertadores_de_celuloide_San_Martn_y_Bolvar_en_pelculas_de_la_globalizacin_%28Axe_VI_Symposium_26%29.

Part III

Re-Anchorings in the Late Twentieth and Early Twenty-First Centuries

11

The Liberator's Sword

The Most Precious Relic of the Bolivarian Revolution

ALEJANDRO E. GÓMEZ PERNIA

In the chaos of events, there are always examples
to support the most foolish theories.

ANDRÉS BELLO, 1848

On December 3, 2012, the Venezuelan president Hugo Chávez, in his last televised appearance, evoked once again the sword of Simón Bolívar. By doing this, he showed for the last time the great significance the sword had for him and for the revolutionary process he had been leading for more than a decade. A month later Chávez was dead, and his successor, Nicolás Maduro, placed a copy of that symbolic weapon over his coffin in a pompous burial attended by several heads of state and broadcast live throughout the world by Telesur. Although filled with contemporary references to the revolution that the deceased president led, the ceremony was very much positioned within a long-lasting national "religion" that began in the mid-nineteenth century. In Germán Carrera Damas's seminal work (1970), in the Bolivarian nations the figure of the Liberator played a central role in the formation of their national identities, but only in Venezuela did it become a true national religion. This has also fostered the development of a popular perception of Bolívar in which he is considered a champion of the poor, a bearer of their claims, and even a sort of deity (Salas 1987). Popular practices are evident by the tradition of displaying Bolívar's image in domestic shrines where he often shares a place of honor along with other Creole mythical figures.

To understand the present extreme-left version of the Bolivarian cult in Venezuela, it is necessary to focus on what is unequivocally its most symbolic element: the swords of the Liberator. I analyze the political and liturgical usages given to that bladed weapon since the outset of the so-called Bolivarian Revolution, the eschatological meaning Chávez and his followers gave to it as well as the wider significations attributed to the sword by other far-left movements in northern South America.

A Republican Fetish

Starting at the end of the eighteenth century with the revolutionary era, many new republics began the practice of burying their great men in classically inspired necropolises known as pantheons. In 1842, Simón Bolívar's remains were reburied at the Holy Trinity Church of Caracas. Some four decades later, President Antonio Guzmán Blanco launched an ideological project in which he appropriated the regenerative character of the Bolivarian cult, solidified his power, and claimed that he was putting an end to a period of disorder and chaos (Carrera Damas 1969, 126). That Catholic church was later appropriated and renamed the Panteón Nacional as part of a larger Parisian-inspired urban project undertaken by the Venezuelan president (discussed in the essays by López Maya and Straka in this volume).

The republican pantheon was modeled after the Catholic church in that it aimed to transmit a series of symbolic messages to the new generations of citizens, but instead of ensuring the continuation of the ancien régime with its partnership between the church and the monarch, the pantheon functioned to preserve the republican system. As in the case of churches, the images displayed in pantheons follow a strict hierarchical order conforming to the canon of the Western "art of memory" as inherited from ancient times (Yates 1966). In the case of the Caracas pantheon, for many decades Bolívar's sarcophagus was located in what had been the altar of the former church, and his statue stood on the place normally reserved for the crucified Christ, while the other "great men" of the republic were buried at the periphery of this central monument. Bolívar's position at the altar location thus connected his sacrifice and martyrdom with Christ's. More recently, Chávez's Bolivarian government invested in a multimillion dollar extension to the building—a huge mausoleum that in the words of the

Venezuelan minister of culture constitutes a dignifying temple more worthy of the "majesty" of the Liberator (López Bohórquez 2012).

Something similar occurs with objects of memory such as religious relics that are also valorized according to their mythical importance or even by their alleged thaumaturgic properties, which can have regional, national, or international importance. Thus the tongue of Saint Anthony is not known very far beyond the Italian town of Padua, while the bones of the Apostle Peter, buried under the altar of the Vatican, are known and revered by Catholics around the world. This phenomenon is reproduced with certain republican fetishes, as is the case of the swords of Bolívar; they have become true symbols of the struggles for the independence of Spanish America in which the Liberator played a leading role. These objects are even attributed with mystical qualities and mnemonic functions, as if they were true sacred relics. The combination of the two elements aims to remind Catholics of the immaterial and material duties they ought to have toward religion and the Church, respectively. Similarly, the Bolivarian cult has, since the late nineteenth century, served to remind Venezuelans of the historic debt they have toward the founding father of their nation and the political support they ought to give to those who claim to continue his original project.

At least three of these Bolivarian relics have been preserved. Due to their material and symbolic importance, they are jealously guarded in museums and national banks. There are two sabers, one at the National Museum of Peru, which was given to Bolívar by Haitian President Alexandre Pétion in 1816, and the other of unknown origin, now located at the Quinta de Bolívar museum in Bogotá. The third sword, the subject of discussion here, until recently was exhibited at the Central Bank of Venezuela in Caracas. The first two may have been brandished by the Liberator during the wars of independence, as sabers were more fashionable for senior officers and more efficient when riding horseback. However, it is the third piece, the sword stored in Caracas, that is considered the most valuable in the Venezuelan and Latin American Bolivarian imaginary.

This sword was presented to the Liberator in 1825 by the government of Peru, thus its name, the Sword of Peru, as a reward for Bolívar's victory at the Battle of Junín. This masterpiece of goldsmithing is richly elaborated in solid gold and inlaid with precious stones. It was publicly displayed for the first time in Venezuela in preparation for Guzmán Blanco's spectacular 1883 centennial celebration of Bolívar's birth. At that time, the sword's value already exceeded its material worth, and it became known as a "rich talisman." Since it was in private hands, Aristides Rojas, a renowned nineteenth-century historian, appealed to future leaders by stating that one day it should belong either to Venezuela or Peru (Rojas 1872/1924). In 1889 the Venezuelan government acquired the sword from the Bolívar family for 120,000 bolivares (approximately $600,000 in today's U.S. currency) (Andueza Palacio 1891, 299–300).

At the beginning of the twentieth century, Bolívar's sword underwent a major symbolic transformation when it was introduced into the Venezuelan army's ritual iconography as part of military professionalization under the dictatorship of Juan Vicente Gómez (1908–35). His successor, General José Eleazar López Contreras (1936–41), gave the Bolivarian icon an even more important role in military ceremonies. This process of symbolic appropriation was accentuated when another military president, General Marcos Pérez Jiménez (1952–58), decided that the Sword of Peru would become the emblem of the generals. In addition to attaching increasing honor and status to all of the swords, the Sword of Peru consequently became the main object of veneration of the Venezuelan armed forces.

Although the Venezuelan civilian presidents who followed Pérez Jiménez introduced new elements to the worship of the Liberator, apparently none personally brandished the sword and none dared question the particular significance conferred by the military on the Sword of Peru. Actually, before Chávez's assumption of power in 1999, the sword had only been displayed in public on a few occasions: during a civic celebration under the presidency of Isaías Medina Angarita (1941–45); in a commemoration in 1980 of the 150th anniversary of the death of Bolívar; and during the 1983 bicentennial of Bolívar's birth. As in the case of other religious figures, none of the fetishes or relics associated with him matches the power his body and physical image represent as a whole, not even his swords. Nevertheless, Bolívar's Sword of Peru has, like the Lobera Sword in Seville, become a symbol of worship. The Lobera Sword, which belonged to "The Saint" Ferdinand III, is a Catholic relic exhibited in the Cathedral of Seville paraded every year on the date of the reconquest of the city from the Moors.

A Relic at the National Bank

After the election of Chávez as president in 1998, the cult of Bolívar, including the symbolism of his swords, took a new turn. To explain this phenomenon, we now focus on that contemporary charismatic leader in order to understand him from a threefold perspective: as a military man, as a politician, and as a Christian.

Chávez was trained in the Venezuelan army and achieved the status of lieutenant colonel. He studied at the Military Academy of Venezuela, where the worship of the Liberator was omnipresent in the education of cadets. In this academy, as with similar institutions and armies in the Western world, officers and cadets proudly wear their swords as symbols of honor. The influence of this particular military environment on Chávez's thinking can be seen not only in the solemn respect he showed toward the Sword of Peru but also in the frequent references he made to it. He often evoked it as a symbolic threat against those who opposed his Bolivarian Revolution, both inside and outside Venezuela, but also to diminish the eschatological barriers between him and the Liberator and so increase his identification with Bolívar before his followers.

As a politician, Chávez led a movement whose historical aim was to complete the Bolivarian project allegedly interrupted by the Latin American oligarchies whose heirs held power before him. It is with this objective in mind that in 1983, he and other officers created the Bolivarian Revolutionary Army 200 (EBR-200). In February 1992 the group attempted a coup d'état, which, although unsuccessful, gave Chávez the political and media exposure that launched his successful campaign for the presidency six years later. The campaign win was largely accomplished thanks to the support of the Fifth Republic Movement (MVR), the political arm of the EBR-200. The MVR's name was intended to make a historical connection between the goals of the new Bolivarian revolutionaries and those attributed to the Liberator, who founded the Second Republic. In doing so, the MVR bypassed more than 150 years of republican history, from the collapse of Gran Colombia in 1830 to the present time, a period they considered a sort of dark age and disdainfully called the Fourth Republic (Langue 2002).

With respect to Chávez's religious convictions, besides his Christian beliefs, we know he was deeply mystic, an aspect of his personality that also affected his perception of the potency of Bolívar's swords. Chávez's mystical belief in the ongoing power of Bolívar's spirit is manifested in a number of anecdotes. One U.S. diplomat who met frequently with Chávez in 2000 reported that on one occasion, while holding a replica of the Sword of Peru, Chávez asked the diplomat and other visitors if they could feel the presence of the Liberator (Lifsher 2003). It was also said that Chávez often left an empty chair at cabinet meetings for the spirit of Bolívar. Chávez expressed his mystical communications with Bolívar in other forms, such as in a kind of prayer dedicated to the Liberator (doubtlessly inspired by Pablo Neruda's 1950 poem "Un canto para Bolívar"), whose regenerative character recalls Guzmán Blanco's aims more than a century earlier.

The very first public invocation of that prayer was probably when Chávez chanted it at a ceremony at the pantheon on July 24, 2000, commemorating the anniversary of the Liberator's birth and shortly after the approval of the new constitution, which changed the name of the country to the Bolivarian Republic of Venezuela. Chávez prayed,

> We humbly come to you, Father, to offer you with all our hearts this new Republic that carries your name. We offer you a nascent Republic and every year we shall come here, Father, to bring your sword to you and take it out from its sheath so it can shine under the sun of Caracas, and feel the breeze of the people stroking its invincible and liberating blade. Every year we shall come here, Father, and when we leave [earth] to join you where you are, then it will be our children who will come. (Chávez 2000)

As he concluded the prayer, Chávez dramatically unsheathed the sword and paraphrased the legendary (and probably apocryphal) oath that Bolívar made in 1805 at Monte Sacro, Rome, when he promised to liberate his people. In restaging that oath, Chávez with an expression of defiance made a vow before Bolívar's coffin: "never to let my soul rest nor give respite to my arm until I have eradicated the last vestige of the oligarchy that betrayed your dream and destroyed the work you began 200 years ago" (Chávez 2000).

Thus he aimed to remove the temporal, spatial, and even eschatological barriers that separated him from his "tutelary figure," to borrow Jung's term (1964); he addressed the prayer as though he were part of a Bolivarian trinity in which Chávez represents the role of the son to Bolívar as father. Furthermore, for many of the president's followers, his esoteric filiation with the Liberator goes far beyond a privileged metaphysical relationship, since some even consider Chávez to be Bolívar's reincarnation. Not coincidentally, Carrera Damas has indicated that one of the guidelines of the Chavista political project is to prepare for "the second incarnation of Simón Bolívar" (2005, 183).

A Bolivarian Act of Memory

To explain the ideological importance of the figure of the Liberator and his swords to contemporary Bolivarian revolutionaries, it is necessary to analyze their symbolism as mnemonic devices. As argued by Maurice Halbwachs (1952), who first posited the concept of "collective memory," and others who have nuanced his ideas, the evocations and interpretations of the past are made according to the present needs of human groups. People can thus remember and represent the same past in different and, at times, conflicting ways. Consequently, even though the Liberator is considered to be the founding father by all Venezuelans, the Chavista ideology highlights the popular image that Bolívar has in the collective memory as well as the avenging character he represents for certain sectors of the extreme left, not only in Venezuela but also in Colombia and other Latin American countries. Furthermore, this avenging image of Bolívar has even contributed to the survival of radical socialism in Latin America after the ideological crisis of the 1990s.

However, Bolivarianism is also a secular religion, hence the importance of analyzing it in the legacy of memorial traditions developed within Christendom since the early modern age. In this sense, icons function as a form of social memory, a claim asserted by Matteo Ricci, a sixteenth-century Florentine monk and Christian evangelist in the Ming Dynasty: "[E]verything we seek to remember must have an image, and each of these images should be assigned a place to rest peacefully until required for an act of memory" (in Spence 1985, 2). Following this definition, we can recognize *grosso modo* at least three types of such acts: acts of continuity, as in the processions in religious festivities when effigies are taken out of churches and paraded to remind the congregation—and the population in general—of the spiritual power of the church; acts of alteration, when those same effigies or other religious objects are attributed a different signification without breaking away from the original tradition, as in the case of the picture of the Virgin of Guadalupe in Mexico during the Mexican Revolution; and finally, acts of erasure or iconoclasm, as when people destroyed the Cluny Abbey and decapitated the statues of saints at Notre Dame de Paris during the French Revolution.

The new symbolism that Chávez and his followers attached to Bolívar's swords caused them to function within the second type of memory acts: those of alteration. To understand this phenomenon, we must start by considering a slogan often sung at pro-Chávez assemblies: "¡Alerta, alerta, alerta que camina, la espada de Bolívar por América Latina!" (Beware, beware, beware, the sword of Bolívar walks on in Latin America!). This slogan does not seem to have emerged in Venezuela but in Colombia as a protest motto used by the radical leftist groups of Bolivarian inspiration that first appeared in the late twentieth century.

The slogan first emerged in January 1974 in the context of a subversive action carried out by the urban guerrilla Movimiento 19 de Abril (M-19). On that occasion, members of M-19 broke into the Bolivarian Museum of Bogotá and seized one of the original swords of the Liberator. Shortly thereafter, M-19 leaders issued a declaration to explain the reasons that motivated them to carry out that action:

> Bolívar, your sword is fighting again. . . . [T]he struggle of Bolívar continues, Bolívar is not dead. His sword rips through the museum's cobwebs and faces the struggles of the present. It is now in our hands, in the hands of the people in arms. And now it points at the exploiters of the people. Against domestic and foreign masters. Against those who left it locked up to rust in museums. Those who distorted the ideas of the Liberator. Those who called us subversives, stateless, adventurers, bandits. For them this reunion of Bolívar with his people is an outrage, a crime. And for them the "Liberating" sword in our hands is a danger. . . . But Bolívar is not with them—the oppressors—but with the oppressed. This is why his sword has passed to our hands. To the hands of the people in arms. And by joining the struggles of our people it [the sword] will not rest until achieving the second independence, this time total and final. (In Anrup 1999, 45)

As is evident in their declaration, M-19 members claimed that their intention was to return the sword to its legitimate owner: the people. Therefore, removing the sword from the museum could not be considered robbery but a legitimate action. With the mythical sword of their hero in their power, they, "the people in arms," could now successfully undertake the "second struggle to free South America." For them, the political and economic elites had distorted the ideas of Bolívar and profited from his liberating legacy. This explains why the elite had "hidden" that important symbol of struggle for so long from the eyes of the common people.

Historian Roland Anrup (1999) has argued that this action had a very symbolic character since it was aimed, for the first time, to identify the cause of a left-wing radical movement with a populist version of Bolívar's independence project as well as the eschatological character of his swords. This ideological position was later explained by Vera Grabe, one of M-19's main leaders:

> With this action that only few understood, we broke into public life, breaking traditional schemes: because Bolívar was for many a figure not locatable within revolutionary theories. From that moment on, a Bolivarian consciousness was born and grew and its symbol of struggle [the sword] acquired its real value. No wonder that when we were arrested, they tortured us to ascertain its whereabouts or get clues to find it. (In Anrup 1999, 47)

Despite the revolutionary character of the M-19, the ideological evocation they made of the Liberator seems to be inspired by the official worship he had in Colombia. This is apparent in claims that were made much later by one of its leaders, Alvaro Fayard, who argued that their intention was to vindicate Bolívar, release him from the history books, and associate his iconography with the objectives of the movement. Thus, their aim was that the Liberator would not just be remembered on "the commemorations of each August 7 [the anniversary of the Battle of Boyacá] and of each December 17 [the anniversary of his death]" (in Behar 1985, 138). If we consider the importance of the Liberator for the traditional national imagery of the Bolivarian countries, the proposals of the M-19 and other extreme-left groups to socialize Bolívar's thoughts could be seen not as a rupture but rather as a schism. In Venezuela, this became the central issue of a true competition over history and memory, to paraphrase James Young (1993), between the Bolivarian revolutionaries supporting a new official history that Chávez imposed after his ascent to power in 1998 and the revolution's opposition.

In the years that followed the M-19's theft of Bolívar's sword, the movement continued to gain public attention. In 1980 a squadron took over the embassy of the Dominican Republic, and in 1985 another one assaulted the Palace of Justice in Bogotá. This latter action seriously affected the image of the M-19 movement since more than a hundred people died after the Colombian army tried to take over the building. Eventually, this smear upon their revolutionary ideals, along with the refusal of the leaders to fund the movement through drug trafficking and the ideological vacuum created after the downfall of the Soviet Union, led many of its members to transition to peaceful political life in Colombia. On January 31, 1991, as part of the installation of the Constituent Congress, in a symbolic gesture of reconciliation, they returned the sword of Bolívar the M-19 had stolen twenty-six years earlier.

The ideological aim of completing the work of Bolívar did not end when the M-19 laid down their arms. Other groups followed their ideological example to pursue similar political objectives. One was the Coordinadora Guerrillera Simón Bolívar (CGSB), which organized the Ejército de Liberación Popular (ELP), the Ejército de Liberación Nacional (ELN), the Fuerzas Armadas Revolucionarias de Colombia (FARC), and even the remaining combating elements of the M-19 between 1985 and 1987. Another was the Movimiento Bolivariano para la Nueva Colombia (MBNC), the FARC's political arm, and the Bolivarian Revolution in Venezuela. These movements give great importance to the symbols associated with the Liberator. The emblem of the MBNC is a tricolor flag with the face of the Liberator intentionally looking to the left; the new Venezuelan national coat of arms was changed in 2006 by the Chavista-dominated National Assembly and by express petition of Chávez so that Bolívar's white horse gallops to the left.

In the political imaginings of these movements, Bolívar's swords have the most important symbolic role. It is as if the struggle that began with the M-19's daring action in 1974, allegedly to pursue the unfinished liberating enterprise of Bolívar, would thereafter be permanently attached to those sharp objects. According to Chávez's oneiric interpretation of the Sword of Peru, the inherent revolutionary legacy is reflected by the materials embedded in it as well as by the motifs in the engravings that adorn it. With respect to the materials, Chávez argued that the metal with which it was manufactured ("gold from Peru") would have been extracted "by the men freed by Bolívar." Consequently, he asserts, it "is the sword of the people, the gold of the people, the hope of the people." Regarding the engravings, he underlines certain indigenous-related aspects such as the Native American who presumably manufactured it and the face of Atahualpa that decorates the handle (Chávez 2001).

As with the M-19, Chávez's deep admiration for Bolívar led him to harshly criticize the fact that the Sword of Peru, like the Colombian one, had been "hidden" for so long from the eyes of the people. In the words of the Venezuelan president, the mythical sword of Bolívar being "stored in a . . . cold vault at the Central Bank" was a true insult (Chávez 1999). In reality, the sword in question was exhibited in a secure area on the mezzanine of the bank's Caracas headquarters, which was open to the public from Mondays to Fridays between 8 a.m. and 4 p.m. Paradoxically enough, the Sword of Peru had been traditionally exhibited at the Liberator's birthplace in Caracas along with other Bolivarian items. It remained there until 1974, when the Ministry of the Interior had it deposited in the more heavily protected site of the Central Bank of Venezuela to prevent it from falling into the hands of any subversive movement, as had happened early that year with the sword in Bogotá. Due to Chávez's campaign, the Sword of Peru is exhibited in front of Bolívar's burial place inside the monumental extension of the Panteón Nacional.

An Iconic Struggle

For the Bolivarian revolutionaries, Chávez was entitled to wield the Liberator's sword at will. To them, this was perfectly logical and even necessary, considering the magnitude of the historic responsibility they believed he had on his shoulders. However, as the political crisis progressed in Venezuela in 2000 and 2001, more and more individuals began to condemn Chávez's symbolic monopolization of the sword and other objects of patriotic veneration. The opposition increasingly criticized what for them was clearly a lack of respect for the Father of the Nation. Many criticized Chávez's frequent brandishing of the sword as a sort of sacrilege, and some historians defended these criticisms with articles about the collective memory of Venezuelans (Gómez 2005). The reactions were even more emphatic among Chávez's military opponents, who in one way or another shared the president's military mentality and therefore were more sensitive to his frequent use of the Sword of Peru as an "insult" to the patriotic symbol, not to mention its arbitrary handling by a former mid-range officer. This state of mind is evidenced in a text published by a member of the Institutional Military Front (FIM), consisting of anti-Chávez retired military officers:

> He has again brandished the Sword of Peru, which will probably lose—as it already has—another jewel from its aged embeddings. Just so that little Hugo can play with the gift that the Viceroyalty [of Peru] gave the Liberator in thanks for its emancipation, while he continues his project of falsifying and manipulating the history of our country according to his own whims and for his personal profit. (Coronil Hartmann n.d.)

Nowadays, no one in the opposition really cares how Chávez and his regime used the Sword of Peru. This is undoubtedly due to the aggravated political climate and the violent situations that have taken place in Venezuela since late 2001. On July 24, 2002, three months after the massacre at Llaguno Bridge and a failed coup d'état, Chávez once again visited the Panteón Nacional. This time Chávez went not only to pay tribute to Bolívar on another anniversary of his birth but also to thank Bolívar for having protected him and his revolution. During the ceremony he once again drew the sword and condemned what he cast as a new attempt to assassinate the Father of the Nation (Pérez 2002), thus describing the challenge to his government as an attack upon Bolívar's body. The assassination theory acquired an even more extraordinary eschatological dimension when the Liberator's remains were publicly exhumed on July 17, 2010, with great pomp and ceremony for purposes of an autopsy.

The theory that Bolívar was assassinated is shared by other extreme-left figures of the region the secretary of the FARC-EP (People's Army) Luciano Marín Arango, alias Iván Márquez, who made a statement to that end in a video that was made public in February 2010 (in Anncol 2010). However, sharing his views about the death of the Liberator was not the main reason for the message. Rather, Márquez wanted to make known to the public that his movement was in possession of the original "battle sword of Bolívar, the one that accompanied him in his final days." It was actually a saber and would be the fourth weapon of the sort said to have belonged to Bolívar. The previously unknown saber that Márquez showed in the video allegedly fell into the group's hands as if by fate in an anniversary year of national independence after having been extracted from a catacomb at Santa Marta where Bolívar passed away in 1830. In the FARC-EP secretary's speech which references José Martí's "Nuestra América" essay, we once again find the desire to use a sword to perform an act of memory:

> On behalf of the Secretariat of the FARC-EP, the commanders and Bolivarian combatants of Manuel [Marulanda Vélez] deliver today this holy sword as a symbol of triumph, unity, and freedom to the peoples of Nuestra América, to the Bolivarian Continental Movement, to the volcanic energy of our youth, to the men and women of this hemisphere, all fighting for independence, for humanity, against the Empire. (Anncol 2010)

The Sword against Globalization

The revolutionary symbolism of the swords of Bolívar has also inspired other individuals and movements beyond the borders of Colombia and Venezuela. The "Alerta!" slogan alluding to that weapon was often heard when the Venezuelan president visited other Latin American countries. On one occasion, Chávez even brought the Sword of Peru with him to perform a commemorative act outside his own country. This happened during the 10th Ibero-American Presidential Summit held in Panama City in 2000. On the first day of the event, the Venezuelan president ignored protocol in order to escort what he defined as "the sword of peace and [Latin American] integration." The procession continued for more than a mile through the streets of the historic center of the city until it reached the building of the Instituto Bolívar, an old convent, where in 1826 a pan-American congress was summoned by Bolívar with almost all the new nations of the Americas. Once at the entrance, Chávez proudly raised the sword before an enthusiastic multitude (Agencia EFE 2000).

The iconography of the swords has managed to migrate to other Latin American left-wing symbolic systems. The Argentine example is particularly interesting because the Guayaquil Conference of 1822, in which the Argentinean liberator José de San Martín granted Bolívar total command of the patriotic armies, continues to create tension between the national mythologies of Venezuela and Argentina. In an official trip to Buenos Aires in August 2003, Chávez had to share the glory of his tutelary figure with the southern liberator by acknowledging that "the sword of Bolívar and the curved saber of San Martín go forth [together] in Latin America" (Chávez 2003). This adaptation inspired the formation of Bolivarian–San Martinist Circles, Venezuelan civic groups of Bolivarian inspiration.

But the Sword of Peru has also served more diplomatic purposes. The Chávez regime often offered replicas of the original relic to individuals the president wanted to support, reward, or strengthen ties with as well as to important international personalities of very different backgrounds: Pope John Paul II, the Russian gunsmith Mikhail Kalashnikov, the chiefs of state of the other OPEC countries, the leftist presidents of Latin America, and world leaders not aligned with the United States. Some of these gifts were very controversial because of the questionable moral stature of some of the individuals who received them, among them Mahmud Ahjmadinejad, Muammar Gadafi, Robert Mugabe, Aleksandr Lukashenko, and Bachar al-Assad.

Conclusion

For Venezuelans, Bolívar's swords have been an important element of their national identity at least since the Peruvian item was acquired by the Venezuelan government in 1889. The current ideology of Bolivarian revolutionaries has been nourished by the traditional significance given to those weapons, to the cult of Bolívar, and to four other, more contemporary factors: the military symbolism developed since the beginning of the twentieth century; the popular image of the Liberator; the particular esoteric beliefs of Hugo Chávez; and the avenging doctrines of extreme-left movements especially in Colombia, Venezuela, and Peru. On this last point, the ideological importance that the M-19 attached to the Liberator's swords and the example it set by stealing one of them for political purposes in 1974 established a crucial precedent for other leftist movements. This connection was recognized by Chávez himself in one of his televised shows entitled *Aló Presidente*, transmitted in 2004:

> When we were thinking here about founding the MBR, which later became the MBR-200, a group of middle-class youngsters in Colombia . . . stole the sword of S. Bolívar from the Bolivarian Museum in Bogotá and left a slogan painted on the wall reading: "Bolívar your

sword has returned to the fight," and then they hid in the mountains of Colombia. That was an example for us. (Chávez 2004)

In spite of this example, in Venezuela, as we have been able to see, the current extreme-left perceptions of the Liberator and his swords are intrinsically associated with the more complex eschatologico-militarist view of Chávez and his former military companions. Hence Carrera Damas (2001) has called this new stage of the cult "Bolivarianism-militarism." The demise of Chávez and the arrival of a civilian to the presidency, Nicolás Maduro, does not seem to have undermined that mythical perception. Quite the contrary. Chávez having handled the sword so often has enhanced its liturgical value; in Maduro's own words (2013), by doing that his predecessor, whom he has defined as "the vindicator of Bolívar," had "cleansed it for history."

References

Agencia EFE. 2000. "Hugo Chávez anuncia que visitará Honduras el jueves." Published in *Diario Tiempo* (San Pedro Sula, Honduras), November 13.

Agencia de Noticias Nueva Colombia (Anncol). 2010. "Márquez asevera que la muerte de Bolívar 'fue fruto de una traición.'" *Aporrea*, February 25. http://www.aporrea.org/tiburon/n151795.html.

Andueza Palacio, Raimundo. 1891. *Recopilación de leyes y decretos de Venezuela*. Vol. 14. Caracas: Impresora del Gobierno Nacional.

Anrup, Roland. 1999. "La palabra y la espada: Lucha armada y discurso de poder en Colombia." *Anales Nueva Época*, no. 2:45–70.

Behar, Olga. 1985. *Las guerras de la paz*. Autores Colombianos. Bogotá: Planeta.

Bello, Andrés. 1848. "Modo de escribir la Historia." *El Araucano* (Santiago, Chile), January 28.

Carrera Damas, Germán. 1970. *El culto a Bolívar: Esbozo para un estudio de la historia de las ideas en Venezuela*. Caracas: Instituto de Antropología e Historia, Universidad Central de Venezuela.

———. 2001. *Alternativas ideológicas en América Latina contemporánea. El caso de Venezuela: El bolivarianismo-militarismo*. Caracas: Universidad Central de Venezuela.

———. 2005. *El bolivarianismo-militarismo: Una ideología de reemplazo*. Colección Ensayo. Caracas: Ala de Cuervo.

Chávez, Hugo. 2000. "Discurso del presidente de la república." Centro de Medios Independente–Sucre, July 24. http://sucre.indymedia.org/es/2004/01/5603.shtml.

———. 2001. "Cadena Nacional de radio y televisión." Bitblioteca. http://www.analitica.com/bitblioteca/.

———. 2003. "Seamos libres! Lo más no importa nada!" Speech, Facultad de Derecho, Universidad de Buenos Aires, August 19. http://www.catedranacional.4t.com/Autores/Venezuela/discarg.htm.

———. 2004. *Aló Presidente*. No. 203. Video. Gobierno Bolivariano de Venezuela. http://www.gobiernoenlinea.ve/.

Coronil Hartmann, Alberto. N.d. "El Comandante no juega limpio." Organo Divulgativo del Frente Institucional Militar. http://www.fimvenezuela.org/articulo.asp?ID=292. Accessed in 2004; no longer available.

Gómez, Alejandro E. 2005. "El papel de los intelectuales en la Venezuela de Hugo Chávez: Los historiadores a la palestra pública." *L'Ordinaire Latino Américain*, no. 202: 83–94.

Halbwachs, Maurice. 1952. *Les cadres sociaux de la mémoire*. Paris: Presses universitaires de France.

Jung, Carl G. 1964. *Man and His Symbols*. Garden City, NY: Doubleday.

Langue, Frédérique. 2002. *Hugo Chávez et le Venezuela: Une action politique au pays de Bolívar*. Collection "Horizons amériques latines." Paris: Harmattan.

Lifsher, Marc. 2003. "Venezuela's Chavez Is Ratcheting Up Anti-U.S. Rhetoric." *Wall Street Journal*, June 12. http://www.wsj.com/articles/SB105536607198636800.

López Bohórquez, Carmen. 2012. "Un mausoleo digno para el Libertador." *Ciudad CCS: Revolución a diario*. Alcaldía de Caracas. http://www.ciudadccs.info/.

Maduro, Nicolás. 2013. "Discurso—conmemoración de los 200 años de la entrada triunfal de Bolívar a Caracas al finalizar la Campaña Admirable." *Revolución o Muerte*, August 6. http://revolucionomuerte.org/index.php/discursos/discursos-de-nicolas-maduro/1288-lea-el-discurso-integro-del-presidente-nicolas-maduro-en-la-conmemoracion-de-los-200-anos-de-la-entrada-triunfal-de-bolivar-a-caracas-al-finalizar-la-campana-admirable.

Pérez, Nadia. 2002. "Chávez llamó a la unión nacional." *El Nacional* (Caracas), July 25.

Rojas, Arístides. 1872/1924. "La espada de Bolívar." In *El estandarte de Pizarro, y la espada de Bolívar*, by José E. Machado and Aristides Rojas. Caracas: Tipografia Americana.

Salas, Yolanda. 1987. *Bolívar y la historia en la conciencia popular*. Caracas: Instituto de Altos Estudios de América Latina, Universidad Simón Bolívar.

Spence, Jonathan D. 1985. *The Memory Palace of Matteo Ricci*. New York: Penguin Books.

Yates, Frances Amelia. 1966. *The Art of Memory*. London: Routledge and K. Paul.

Young, James Edward. 1993. *The Texture of Memory: Holocaust Memorials and Meaning*. New Haven, CT: Yale University Press.

12

When the Boat Comes In

Myth, Reification, and the Changing Face of Simón Bolívar in Venezuelan Politics and Culture

NICHOLAS ROBERTS

Throughout his work, the Venezuelan poet and essayist Eugenio Montejo was concerned with locating and poeticizing the central symbols of Venezuelan identity and being (Roberts 2009). It should therefore be no surprise that Simón Bolívar appears as the subject matter of one of Montejo's longest poems, "Nostalgia for/of Bolívar" (Montejo 2005, 105–9). The poem, dating from 1976, does what many good poems do: it resonates far beyond its literary borders. Using this poem as a starting point, I examine to what extent the Bolívar who is traced and metaphorized within its lines serves as a basis for understanding how the figure has been used and appropriated by politicians throughout Venezuela's history. I then explore how Hugo Chávez's appeal to the Liberator has, however, altered the way in which the figure operates as a political, social, and cultural icon, analyzing how the solemnity of "Nostalgia for/of Bolívar" has, as a result, given way to the satiric comedy of more recent cultural engagements. Finally, I ask whether these changes signal the end of the Bolívar depicted in Montejo's poem.

The Poetic Bolívar

In "Nostalgia for/of Bolívar," Montejo is not concerned with the flesh-and-blood Bolívar so much as with the mythic figure who grounds Venezuelan identity and being. This is clear from the poem's opening lines, which describe the Liberator as the essence of the Venezuelan land and people, coursing through both as their pulsing lifeblood:

On the birth map that we tattoo in our dreams
on the skin, the arms, the voices of this land,
Bolívar is the first of the rivers
that cross our fields. (Montejo 2005, 107)

As the poem advances, this fluvial metaphor continues, the river Bolívar picking up different elements and associations as it flows through the verses: the river has its wellspring "close to Manoa" (107) and offers the Venezuelan people "the keys to El Dorado" (108), as the identification of Bolívar as the mythic essence of the country is underlined. This is a river and a figure that at once is written into the being of the very stones of this land, as "it leaves its light written on the stones' veins" (108), and yet it is also bound up with a heady, ungraspable promised land, "until it [Bolívar] appears again, on horseback, / at the end of the rainbow, wrapped up in its colors" (108). Unsurprisingly, then, Montejo's poem carries within it a clear religiosity, evident not just in its reverential, almost incantatory tone but in its biblical references to how "on his bank the men congregate in line / they hear him speak alone with the earth / with the sun and the high astral spaces" (108), lines that allude to the figure of Christ and the pantheistic presence of the divine.

Moving toward the poem's dénouement, the historical and mythical identities of Bolívar converge. Already signposted in the reference to the "river" Bolívar as "on horseback," lines 38–43 of this 67-line poem bring in the historical personage more strongly, relating the Liberator's exile in sparse, terse lines:

Afterwards he starts to lose his clothes,
his horse,
his shadow,
everything . . .
When he heads out toward the ocean he is already very poor
he arrives almost in rags. (108)

The presentation of the mythic Bolívar as the central ontological river into which run all Venezuelan rivers, real and figurative (lines 5–9), ties in neatly with this movement into exile, as the flowing of the Magdalena River leads inexorably to the sea. Thus the historical exile in which Bolívar died in Santa Marta, Colombia, before setting sail is fused with the poem's metaphorical and mythic portrayal as the latter completes that exilic journey, in effect understanding Bolívar's death as the fulfillment of that movement out into the open sea:

> Faced with the final blueness he disappears,
> beyond, his wake dissolves into the sea,
> there are no steps which follow him,
> there are no boats. (109)

The mythic, fluvial Bolívar and the historical Bolívar (to be) carried on a boat thus combine in this final image, and the message of the poem is clear: the importance and role of the historical figure can only be fully grasped through an understanding of the mythical figure, and the relationship of Venezuela, as land and people, to the Liberator can thus only be understood through this final, mythified image.

So what is the nature and what are the implications of this image of Bolívar, as man and myth, exiled and separated from the land and people of which he is the essence and the lifeblood? Well, the poem ends by deepening its religious elements, as Bolívar becomes a Christlike figure to be remembered and invoked in rite and ritual when,

> at each table, bread is broken in his name,
> in each voice resound his words. (109)

As I have argued elsewhere (Roberts 2009, 170), ritual implies and confirms the absence of what is remembered while also pointing to the centrality of that absence. Bolívar thus appears here as the essential point around which society operates but, where this essence is unattainable, caught in a constant slipping away.

Reading this idea back into the body of the poem, we come to see it anew. Every image contained in it is bound up with unlocatability, ungraspability, slipping-awayness: the association of Bolívar with the mythic locations of Manoa and El Dorado, with the evanescent end of the rainbow; his depiction as a river inexorably flowing through and out of the land; the flitting between different allusions to Bolívar as Christ, as the divine, as the historical figure. The poem was written, we must remember, from the condition described in its final lines, and its portrayal of Bolívar is, then, a portrayal of Bolívar as already absent, as that elusive, ungraspable essence of Venezuela.

Yet "Nostalgia for/of Bolívar" does more than just speak of the absent, religious nature of the Liberator. Rather, Bolívar's role within the Venezuelan sociopolitical imaginary is found in a more literal appreciation of his imagined watery exile, in that, with the implied image of the historical Bolívar carried on a boat, he appears—quite literally—as a floating signifier. The implication is that Bolívar functions as a signifier without a fixed meaning, open to different referents being attached to it. With this reading in mind, we see that the poem's varied depictions of Bolívar show not just the inexorable always-already slipping away of the essence that the figure is but, more specifically, this sense of its/his lack of fixed valency.

Bolívar in Venezuelan Political History

Moving outside of the poem to a consideration of the sociopolitical reality of Venezuela since the death of Simón Bolívar, we can now examine how the main elements to emerge from our reading of Montejo's poem map onto and elucidate the ways in which Bolívar has functioned in the country. First, there is general scholarly consensus that Bolívar has, as "Nostalgia from/of Bolívar" describes, come to be synonymous with national identity and being. José Pascual Mora-García describes how "it is impossible to understand Venezuelan-ness without Bolívar; because Bolívar is the foundational myth" (2005, 8), with Luis Castro Leiva stating simply that "being Bolivarian is the same as being Venezuelan" (1991, 10). Emphasizing this inclusiveness, Nikita Harwich describes how Bolívar foments a sense of "national cohesion" (2003, 11).

Second, there is the identification of Bolívar as a divine figure. Again, this understanding of Bolívar is widely commented on by scholars (in particular in Elías Pino Iturrieta 2004): he is the central being of a "civic religion" (Harwich 2003, 11). The implications of this divine characteristic, as set out by Montejo's poem, are also evident in Venezuelan historical reality. When Germán Carrera Damas speaks of the idea of "the return of he who was the soul of the nation, overcoming thus the effects of an irreparable loss" (1983, 114–15), he is conjuring the same image as "Nostalgia for/of Bolívar," of the Liberator as the nation('s essence), distanced and absent from it. Moreover, Carrera Damas proceeds to underscore the condition in which this leaves the country, determined by a "paradigm, always present but unattainable in its perfection" (131), at once putting under erasure the adjective "present":

Bolívar operates as the presence of an absence, invoked by rite but essentially elusive.

The third significant element of Montejo's poem is the identification of the Liberator as a floating signifier. The history of the cult of Bolívar confirms that this is not merely an amusing coming together of literal and semiological descriptions but an apt way of understanding how Bolívar has functioned over the past two centuries. Even a brief survey of the prominent political figures who have invoked Bolívar discloses to what extent he has become a vessel into which different meanings, contexts, and discourses are poured. The nineteenth-century president Antonio Guzmán Blanco, the first properly to develop the cult, worked to "project the image of himself as the continuer of Bolívar's work" (Harwich 2003, 12), and many subsequent leaders followed his model (discussed in the essays by López Maya and Straka in this volume). Juan Vicente Gómez, the de facto dictator of Venezuela from 1908 to 1935, took advantage of "the foundations that the Guzmán regime had laid, [and] was able to maintain and widen the official heroic image of the Liberator" (Harwich 2003, 13).

Perhaps most notable, however, is that this use of the figure is found among leaders and movements of different natures, many of which were attempting to distinguish themselves from previous or current administrations. Thus, in the difficult transition period after Gómez's death, the new president Eleazar López Contreras called upon and claimed Bolívar as being at the heart of his own thought and ideology, focusing on "unity and solidarity" (Carrera Damas 1983, 140). Similarly, just as the dictator Marcos Pérez Jiménez (1952–58) declared himself to be Bolivarian, so too did governments of the *puntofijista* democratic system, which ran from 1958 to 1999. Named after the Punto Fijo Pact of 1958, the *puntofijista* democratic system was an accord among the main political parties aimed at preserving the nascent democratic system. The *puntofijista* parties appealed to the Liberator in the promotion of their different political ideologies and projects. Pino Iturrieta (2004, 163–64) has discussed examples from Luis Herrera Campins's government (1979–83). In short, what marks the appeal to Bolívar down the years in Venezuela is the remarkable polyvalence of the figure as successive political leaders and movements have invested him with a context, ideology, and politics designed to fit their own requirements and to confer legitimacy on themselves.

Yet, while this polyvalence underpins an understanding of Bolívar as a floating signifier, Montejo's poem is important in signaling the particular way in which this operates within Venezuela. Specifically, in its implied depiction of Bolívar floating out at sea, its wake having long since vanished, the poem allows us to understand the political appeals to Bolívar not as presentings or reifications of the figure but rather as the laying down of paths by which Bolívar might be found and returned. That is, in foregrounding his resistance to being brought back and moored at land, the poem underscores Bolívar's resistance to political hegemonization through the application of a fixed valence.

At once, then, the poem carries with it the sense that Bolívar's status as a common, unifying denominator depends, somewhat paradoxically, on its being a figure in which competing visions and understandings clash, thus fulfilling the role that such a signifier must fulfill if it is to carry with it the possibility of a democratic turn. Chantal Mouffe observes,

> Democratic politics does not consist in the moment when a fully constituted people exercises its rule. The moment of rule is indissociable from the very struggle about the definition of the people, about the constitution of its identity. Such an identity, however, can never be fully constituted, and it can exist only through multiple and competing forms of *identifications*. . . . Hence the importance of leaving this space of contestation forever open, instead of trying to fill it with the establishment of a supposedly "rational" consensus. (2013, 178)

Bolívar, then, is the space of contestation, the polyvalent floating signifier that acts as a potential locus for the (continued?) construction of liberal democracy within Venezuela.

Chávez and the Bolivarian Revolution

In 1999, with the arrival of Hugo Chávez as Venezuelan president, the story of the political use of the figure of Bolívar began a markedly different chapter, with Chávez going much further than any predecessor. Irma Chumaceiro Arreaza notes that in the case of Chávez, the extent to which Bolívar was linked with every aspect of the Bolivarian Revolution is remarkable, with "the profuse, reiterated, and systematic appeal to the figure of the

Liberator, his ideas and his feats" (2003, 25). But, with Montejo's poem in mind, I would argue that what sets Chávez's use of Bolívar apart from previous appropriations is a striking move away from Bolívar as being, above all, a guiding (absent) spirit, a goal to work toward, in favor of something decidedly more corporeal.

At the swearing in of the Revolutionary Commando in 2002, for example, Chávez declared that

> the eternal commander of this revolution is none other than Simón Bolívar. . . . Viva Bolívar! Bolívar has returned and is made [into the] nation [pueblo]. (In Chumaceiro Arreaza 2003, 31)

The religious language is there, but Bolívar is not a divine figure to be remembered and honored; rather, he is reincarnate in the pueblo, in the nation of and under Chávez. This present-ing or reifying of Bolívar is further evident in Chávez's renaming the country the Bolivarian Republic of Venezuela in 2005, asserting the (essential) nation/fatherland/republic as having been realized, as well as in his practice of leaving a seat for Bolívar at cabinet meetings. This shift from absent to realized essence and the ways it has been internalized and taken on by those who support the *chavista* revolution are nowhere made more stark than in the usage by Nicolás Maduro's government and its supporters of the slogan "We have fatherland" ("Tenemos patria").

Most significantly, though, this present-ing of Bolívar as the realized essence of the nation is accompanied by an alignment of Chávez with and as Bolívar. This is evident in the interchangeability of the recurrent epithets *boliviariano* and *chavista* in the description of the Venezuelan political project post-1999, but there were also numerous specific examples of this fusion in Chávez's discourse. In Caracas on February 6, 2010, at an event marking the birth of the Frente de Juventudes Bicentenaria 200, Chávez brandished Bolívar's sword and pronounced an oath that reenacted and recontextualized Bolívar's 1805 "Oath of Monte Sacro":

> I swear by the God of my parents, I swear by them, I swear by my honor, I swear by the country, I swear by my people, I swear by the youth I carry within, that we will not rest body or soul until we have freed the nation, until we have crowned our independence by building socialism. (Chávez 2010)

These were Bolívar's words:

> I swear by the God of my parents, I swear by them, I swear by my honor, and I swear by the country that I will not rest body or soul until I have broken the chains with which Spanish power oppresses us! (Bolívar 2013, "Documento 28")

Likewise, Chávez's exhumation of Bolívar's remains in 2010 was widely seen as designed to enable Chávez to entrench yet further the idea that he was the heir, even reincarnation, of Bolívar. He did so in his speeches surrounding the event and in implicitly suggesting that he was in danger of being assassinated by his enemies, just as, Chávez claimed, Bolívar met his end by foul means rather than the official cause of tuberculosis, a thesis not proven by the exhumation. Frédérique Langue has commented that the exhumation episode came down to bringing together "the present hero and the past hero: Chávez is the new Bolívar" (2011, 40). A more withering response appeared on the satirical Venezuelan online publication *El Chigüire Bipolar* (2011b) in the article "Study Reveals Chávez and Bolívar Had Bones, Therefore They Are the Same Person."

Put simply, the extent of Chávez's appropriation of Bolívar has led to a significant shift in the nature of the Liberator as signifier. He is no longer absent, floating, the bobbing boat implied in Montejo's poem, onto which leaders and sociopolitical groupings project different meanings and contexts, tracing different paths by which he might be brought back. The empty, floating vessel that was Bolívar has been moored to the land, to the present, and to the figure and revolution of Hugo Chávez. He is, quite simply, no longer a floating signifier.

Cultural Response, from Solemnity to Satire

The questions thus pose themselves: If Montejo's pre-Chávez poem acted as a reflection of a multivocal, divine Bolívar, how has recent Venezuelan culture changed its appeals to the Liberator in the face of his new political role and identification? And how does this cultural engagement enable us better to understand the nature of the port at which Bolívar has come to be moored? Perhaps the most significant material for answering these questions is found in Venezuelan humor, in particular in the routines of arguably the two most popular Venezuelan comedians of the past two decades, Emilio Lovera and Er Conde del Guácharo, and in articles published in *El Chigüire Bipolar*.

Lovera, in a 2010 routine, recounts a comic version of Bolívar's independence campaigns in which the Liberator drags an increasingly tired and hungry group of Venezuelan peasants around Latin America. Central to this narrative joke is that Lovera uses his well-known impression of Chávez in imitating Bolívar. The fusion of present/Chávez and past/Bolívar underscores how much the two have become one within the contemporary Venezuelan imaginary, but it has the additional effect here of showing how this fusion leads to both figures being satirized. Put simply, the target of this narrative is, to be sure, Hugo Chávez, but the satire and comedic critique of Chávez unavoidably tips over into a satirizing of Bolívar and his actions. Thus, the early part of this story has Lovera, playing Bolívar in Chávez's voice, telling the peasants he is trying to take any horse that is not being used and any land they want, including land that belongs to the Bolívar family, in a clear allusion to Chávez's policies of property appropriation. Yet this comes at Bolívar's expense, as it undercuts the grander nature of his motives as well as his intelligence in telling them, unwittingly, to take his own family's land. Perhaps the most significant part of the narrative, however, occurs when, surveying the vast emptiness of the part of Bolivia that they have reached, one of the peasants asks Bolívar-Chávez why they have come here. Bolívar-Chávez replies, "To liberate this beautiful nation [pueblo]," to which the peasant retorts, "But there's no one here. . . . What are we going to liberate it from? . . . Bolívar, the fact is we're hungry." A satire on Chávez's priorities and anti-imperial (anti-U.S.) discourse is—ineluctably even if unwittingly—at once a satire on the priorities and actions of Bolívar himself in liberating much of Latin America.

Turning to Er Conde del Guácharo, whose humor is somewhat more risqué than Lovera's, we find that the treatment of Bolívar is, if anything, even more subversively satirical. In one of the staple jokes in his routine (2009), Er Conde sends up the extent to which Chávez sought to do everything as Bolívar had done it. He ends the joke by satirizing this near-amorous obsession on Chávez's part, as he refers to (one assumes apocryphal) graffiti he apparently saw in Caracas that read, "'Chávez, take it out of my ass ["Chávez, sácamelo"],' signed Simón Bolívar." While the target here is Chávez, the implied image of the graffiti shows the extent to which the alignment of the two figures has led to a peeling away of the layers of sacrosanct reverence that have traditionally surrounded public discourse regarding the Liberator. In a traditionally *machista* society in which attitudes toward homosexuality often remain mired in insult and denigration, the placing of Bolívar, the "man of the nation," in a homosexual act—and in the passive role—represents a significant shift in the ways it is deemed acceptable to engage with Bolívar in cultural output. Despite a move to reassess the cult, deeds, and reputation of Bolívar by historians such as Carrera Damas, subjecting the iconic Bolívar to denigrating satire is novel in the public sphere in Venezuela.

In both of these examples, the solemnity of the cultural presentation of Bolívar in Montejo's "Nostalgia for/of Bolívar" has been replaced by a satire operating at the level of his ideas, actions, and virility, an ineluctable correlate of the primary satirical target being Chávez. Moreover, a brief examination of the articles found in *El Chigüire Bipolar* discloses to what extent this satire has pervaded all aspects of the Bolívar cult as a result of Chávez's own all-pervading employment of it. Since emerging during the 2000s, *El Chigüire Bipolar* has published many articles that make reference to Bolívar in relation to Chávez and his appropriation of the figure. The two most recurrent themes are Bolívar's sword and bodily remains. In the case of the former, the satire takes aim at the large number of replicas given out by Chávez to different world leaders, most notably in a mock infomercial for the "Bolívar Sword 3000" (2010a) and an article describing how dictators around the world have returned their swords, fearing they are cursed after seeing the fate of recipients such as Gaddafi (2011a).

The humor here, while aimed at Chávez, nonetheless has the effect of grounding what was the most sacred relic of Bolívar, the symbolic sword with which Venezuela was liberated, and tying it into a consumerist, kitsch paradigm, signaling the defeat rather than the triumph of those who (metaphorically) wield it. It seems, here at least, as if there is no space left for a representation of Bolívar's sword that is not bound up with a satirical swipe at Chávez's appropriation of it. Arguably the most significant examples, however, are the references to the Liberator's bodily remains, in particular *El Chigüire Bipolar*'s article "Bolívár's Bones Catch Dengue" (2010b). Alluding heavily to Chávez's exhumation of Bolívar, the article has the latter's bones catching dengue fever, upon which the Liberator declares his determination to rid Venezuela of the disease:

> If my death contributes to the end of the mosquitos and the death of dengue fever, I shall be lowered in peace into my grave.

The satirists' words recast the last line of the historical Bolívar's final declaration:

> If my death contributes to the end of partisanship and the consolidation of the union, I shall be lowered in peace into my grave. (Bolívar 2013, "Documento 191")

Clearly, the presentation of Bolívar's bones as both talking and catching dengue is a far cry from the reverent, quasireligious respect granted to his remains in sociopolitical discourse and in cultural representations of the type found in "Nostalgia for/of Bolívar," where, implying immanence, we are told that "his bones are scattered throughout the world" (Montejo 2005, 108). But the *Chigüire Bipolar* article also underscores what is at stake in its satirical move in other ways. Key here is the image that accompanies the piece, which is an altered version of Antonio Herrera Toro's famous painting *Los últimos momentos del Libertador* (1883), a work that symbolizes the cultural sanctity and reverence in which Bolívar has traditionally been held. In this new version, the face of Bolívar on his deathbed appears as a skull, and the painting on the wall behind the dying Bolívar, which in the original is of the Holy Trinity crowning the Virgin, has been replaced by one of Hugo Chávez.

This is significant in several ways. First, it reverses the usual media image of Chávez during his presidency appearing in front of a painting of Bolívar, suggesting the now profound interchangeability of the two. Beyond that, however, placing the image of Chávez in such an anachronistic setting carries with it the idea that Bolívar can no longer be imagined or portrayed without reference to Chávez; the Bolívar of history (the scene depicted in the painting) and Bolívar in culture (the painting as perhaps the most iconic cultural depiction of Bolívar) can now only be seen through the lens of the present, of the Bolívar-Chávez conflation. And third, in replacing a painting of divine iconography with a portrait of Chávez, the image underscores to what extent the sacred (and, as Montejo's poem shows, attendantly polyvalent) associations of the Liberator have been, to return to our metaphor, moored at the shores of contemporary historical reality. Humorous the article may be, but it is a highly revealing piece of popular culture.

Hegemonization and Democracy

Given these comedic engagements, it might be tempting to conceive of the port at which Bolívar now finds himself as having a carnivalesque quarter alongside the official Bolívar-Chávez reverence. Certainly, the characteristics of the Bakhtinian carnivalesque, most importantly at the expense of higher authorities and "the profanation of everything sacred" (Bakhtin 1984, 130), including the debasement or carnivalization of high culture, are explicitly present in the examples analyzed above. But rather than acting in an emancipatory manner, as Bakhtin describes (122–24), these popular culture engagements both depend upon and entrench the official, hegemonic Bolívar-Chávez conflation. This entrenchment then contributes to the contemporary inability of other political figures and groups to successfully avail themselves of Bolívar as the signifier of the nation, as was evident when the Venezuelan opposition Democratic Unity Roundtable (Mesa de la Unidad Democrática) named its 2013 presidential and municipal elections headquarters the Simón Bolívar Command Center. The response, even among opposition-supporting media, was muted, to say the least, with Clodovaldo Hernández writing in March 2013 in *El Universal* that

> Bolívar . . . is a complex concept that President Chávez interpreted and loaded—in his own way—with contemporary associations. . . . Nowadays, whether you like it or not, the concept of the Bolivarian is linked to Chávez's system of ideas and twenty-first-century socialism.

In short, the attempted reappropriation of Simón Bolívar is unsustainable and unsuccessful post-Chávez because Bolívar has been hegemonized and is no longer a site of contestation. That this has been accompanied by dismantling the separation of powers in Venezuela (Human Rights Watch 2008, 36–63), together with a catalogue of other significant blows to the democratic and pluralistic claims of the Chávez and Maduro governments (Kornblith 2013), sends us back to Mouffe's warnings about the detrimental impact on democracy that results from the loss of such a site (2013, 178).

Conclusion

So where does this leave Bolívar for future generations in Venezuela? What must become of this figure if there is to be a move outside of the current social and democratic crisis in the country?

First it is necessary to underscore that although my discussion has leaned upon the notion of an empty signifier to be filled as well as that of a floating signifier, as Montejo's poem shows, with its implied image of Bolívar floating away in exile, it is, finally, the concept of the floating signifier that offers the most accurate and useful way of understanding the nature and role of Bolívar in post-independence Venezuela. For Bolívar the signifier is never and has never been truly empty; it bears traces of the different contexts, meanings, interpretations assigned to it: the caudillo figure, military strongman, fighter against imperialist forces. The traces have remained attached to the figure of the Liberator and been variously incorporated into the more complex, contingent uses to which he has been put by leaders such as Guzmán Blanco, Gómez, and Herrera Campins, all of whom have themselves added to the accrued meanings associated with the signifier. The final result of such an accrual of traces is, then, either the sinking of the floating signifier, weighed down by its semiological baggage, or its mooring back at shore, as one meaning and context inscribes its mark on Bolívar with particular vigor and purchase, reifying and hegemonizing it, as has occurred with the *chavista* appropriation of the figure.

The implication thus is clear: what is needed is not so much the opening up of a specific floating signifier as a space of contestation; rather, it is at the level of the signifier itself, as well as the significations assigned to it, that contestation needs to be kept open. That is, the floating signifier of the nation itself needs to be open to change, to reassessment, to renaming. Only thus can Venezuela truly open itself up to democratic possibility, and only thus can Bolívar's load be lightened and his name allowed to dissolve into the Caribbean Sea that delimits and defines the Venezuelan nation.

References

Bakhtin, Mikhail. 1984. *Problems of Dostoevsky's Poetics*. Edited and translated by Caryl Emerson, introduction by Wayne C. Booth. Minneapolis: University of Minnesota Press.

Bolívar, Simón. 2013. Archivo del Libertador. Gobierno Bolivariano de Venezuela, Ministerio del Poder Popular para la Cultura. http://www.archivodellibertador.gob.ve/escritos/inicio.php.

Carrera Damas, Germán. 1983. "Simón Bolívar, el culto heroico y la nación." *Hispanic American Historical Review* 63, no. 1:107–45.

Castro Leiva, Luis. 1991. *De la patria boba a la teología bolivariana*. Caracas: Monte Ávila.

Chávez, Hugo. 2010. *Chávez desenvaina espada de Bolívar y jura construir el socialismo*. Video. Posted to YouTube by NoticieroDigitalcom, February 6. http://www.youtube.com/watch?v=ZKmmdLNqYkg.

El Chigüire Bipolar. 2010a. "El infomercial de la 'Espada de Bolívar 3000.'" April 4. http://www.elchiguirebipolar.net/13-04-2010/el-infomercial-de-la-"espada-de-bolivar-3000"-2/.

———. 2010b. "Huesos de Bolívar contraen dengue." July 24. http://www.elchiguirebipolar.net/24-07-2010/huesos-de-bolivar-contraen-dengue/.

———. 2011a. "Dictadores del mundo comienzan a devolver espadas de Bolívar." February 21. http://www.elchiguirebipolar.net/21-02-2011/dictadores-del-mundo-comienzan-a-devolver-espadas-de-bolivar/.

———. 2011b. "Estudio revela que Chávez y Bolívar tenían huesos por lo tanto son la misma persona." July 25. http://www.elchiguirebipolar.net/25-07-2011/estudio-revela-que-chavez-y-bolivar-tenian-huesos-por-lo-tanto-son-la-misma-persona/.

Chumaceiro Arreaza, Irma. 2003. "El discurso de Hugo Chávez: Bolívar como estrategia para dividir a los venezolanos." *Boletín de Lingüística* 20: 22–24.

Er Conde del Guácharo. 2009. "El Conde del Guácharo y Hugo Rafael Chávez Frias." Video. Posted to YouTube by Ramón Perazza, December 11. http://www.youtube.com/watch?v=VgkZrM1oYnM.

Harwich, Nikita. 2003. "Un héroe para todas las causas: Bolívar en la historiografía." *Iberoamericana* 3, no. 10:7–22.

Hernández, Clodovaldo. "Todo lleva tu nombre, Bolívar." *El Universal*, March 15, 2013. http://www.eluniversal.com/opinion/130315/todo-lleva-tu-nombre-bolivar.

Human Rights Watch. 2008. *A Decade under Chávez: Political Intolerance and Lost Opportunities for Advancing Human Rights in Venezuela*. New York: Human Rights Watch.

Kornblith, Miriam. 2013. "Chavismo after Chávez?" *Journal of Democracy* 24, no. 3:47–61.

Langue, Frédéric. 2011. "Reinvención del Libertador e historia oficial en Venezuela." *Araucaria: Revista Iberoamericana de Filosofía, Política y Humanidades* 13, no. 25:26–45.

Lovera, Emilio. 2010. "Emilio Lovera—Simón Bolívar.flv." Video. Posted to YouTube by suarezfco, August 19. http://www.youtube.com/watch?v=BgYzF3A1XvA.

Montejo, Eugenio. 2005. *Alfabeto del mundo*. Mexico City: Fondo de Cultura Económica.

Mora-García, José Pascual. 2005. "Bolívar en el imaginario venezolano." *Mañongo* 24:7–21.

Mouffe, Chantal. 2013. *Hegemony, Radical Democracy, and the Political*. Edited by James Martin. London: Routledge.

Pino Iturrieta, Elías. 2004. *El divino Bolívar: Ensayo sobre una religión republicana*. Madrid: Catarata.

Roberts, Nicholas. 2009. *Poetry and Loss: The Work of Eugenio Montejo*. Woodbridge, England: Tamesis.

13

Embodiments and Disembodiments of the Nation, the People, and the State

Disputing Bolívar's Body, and the Uses of Bolivarianism in Contemporary Venezuelan Politics

LUIS DUNO-GOTTBERG

> Once while some Israelites were burying a man, suddenly they saw a band of raiders; so they threw the man's body into Elisha's tomb. When the body touched Elisha's bones, the man came to life and stood up on his feet.
>
> 2 KINGS 13:21, NIV

> Hello my friends. What an impressive moment we lived last night! We've seen Bolívar's remains! I must confess that I've cried. I must tell you this: such a glorious skeleton has to be Bolívar, because one can feel the flames.
>
> HUGO CHÁVEZ FRÍAS, TWITTER, JUNE 16, 2010, 12:46 A.M.

> We have attended the funeral! We have fulfilled our promise to a dead Bolívar. Now I invite you to salute a restored Bolívar, to all his great deeds, in the memory of his immortal services.
>
> FERMÍN TORO, 1843

Picking Bones with/for the Nation

Human remains may constitute the ultimate and most contentious "site of memory," defined by Pierre Nora as "where memory crystallizes and secretes itself" (1989, 7). Following this logic, a corpse can function as the most powerful mnemonic device when processed through rituals of burial, reburial, mummification, or embalming. The bone fragments of Columbus or Cuauhtémoc, the leg of Santa Ana, the embalmed body of Evita, and even the mutilated bodies of Juan Perón and Ché Guevara are all well-known examples of the important role that dead bodies or body parts have played in the staging of the past. I am concerned here with an eschatological dimension of Bolivarianism—or a set of doctrines and cultural practices that celebrate the legacy of the nineteenth-century hero of the nation's independence—in contemporary Venezuela. I approach this topic through a recent controversy regarding the remains of Simón Bolívar. I contend that beyond the populist instrumentalization of those "heroic bones," the source of conflict might relate more closely to the ways in which the body of Simón Bolívar condenses a particular conception of the state and a certain notion of sovereignty—a contemporary polemic anchored in a tradition that dates back to the second half of the nineteenth century.

In the early hours of June 16, 2010, Venezuelan President Hugo Chávez Frías announced on Twitter to his then half-million followers that Simón Bolívar's body had been exhumed in response to his own request to find out if the national hero had died of poisoning. Another stated purpose was to ascertain whether the bones in Bolívar's grave were in fact his. Although Chávez had spoken earlier of the need to find "the truth" about the remains of Venezuela's founding father, it would take three years for the exhumation to take place. When it did, as with many other aspects of the Bolivarian Revolution, it was televised. National media—including television, radio, and newspapers—played a large role in orchestrating this ritual as Venezuelans bore witness to an uncanny image: a team of forensic experts, dressed in white aseptic suits (figure 13.1), working ceremoniously on the remains of El Libertador. Except for the national hymn that played on a continuous loop, the group performed its task in absolute silence, combining the solemn operation with scientific rigor and religious fervor. In many ways, this was an inquiry about both identity and treason.

The exhumation generated numerous reflections about ulterior motives for the process and about the meanings of the sacred corpse. Responses to the act were deeply emotional, ranging from patriotic enthusiasm to outrage and indignation. Nevertheless, the range of reactions articulated a pugnacious political landscape where the figure of Simón Bolívar embodied, for good or for bad, the legitimacy or illegitimacy of the Chávez era. The debate over the meanings of Bolivarianism dates back to the mid-nineteenth century, but its current significance must be read against the background of the mid-1980s, when institutions like COPRE (Comisión para la Reforma

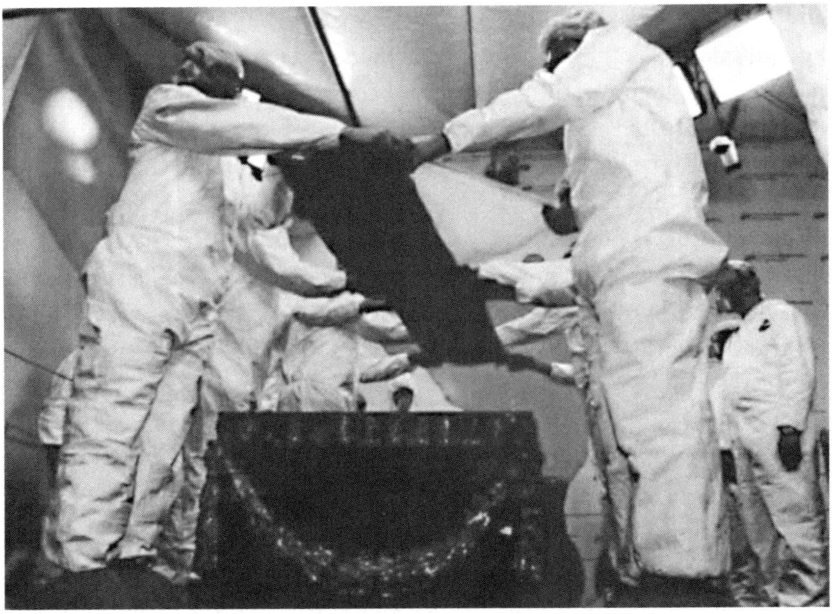

FIGURE 13.1. The opening of Simón Bolívar's coffin, June 16, 2010. Venezuelan National Television. The event, broadcast nationally, captured the imaginations of Venezuelans.

del Estado) enthusiastically championed neoliberal state reform. The two prevailing readings of the incident concerning the remains of Simón Bolívar can be briefly characterized as follows.

On the side of the government, opening the coffin was an act of embodiment and disembodiment. In one sense, those bones were not only the genesis of *venezolanidad* but, more poignantly, the material trace of the original nation, the tangible remains of the first state. At the same time, an act of disembodiment took place as the corpse was sublimated into a spiritual presence. Indeed, the celebratory discourse of the president pointed to the transcendence of Bolívar beyond the grave and the continuation of his struggle through the people and the Bolivarian state. Those fragile bones were instrumentally positioned to rearticulate the "nation" through the revolutionary spirit of the people. Such a double movement—of embodiment and disembodiment—transformed the exhumation of Bolívar's body into a genealogical gesture for the Bolivarian government, or a claim of sovereignty. That is to say, those bones were part of a foundational ritual for a new revolutionary republic and also embodied the struggle of the people that legitimized this rule. Further, the bones entailed not one body but two, one deceased and another resurrected in the flesh of the popular masses. In *NotiTarde* of July 22, 2010, Chávez wrote, "My Christ, our Christ; while I was praying in silence, looking at those bones, I thought of you! And I wanted you to come back and demand, like you did with Lazarus: 'Raise Simón, it's no time to die.' But I immediately remembered that *Bolívar is alive. Bolívar is alive, damn it! We are his flame*!"

Chavez's opposition was quick to respond to the apotheosis. The renowned historian Elias Pino Iturrieta, director of the Venezuelan National Academy of History and fierce critic of the government, declared in *El Universal* of July 28, 2010, that the president wanted to "appropriate the memory of the nation" and that his ultimate end was to establish an analogy between himself and Bolívar. Other criticisms included expressions of race and class hatred, as another historian, Manuel Caballero, declared: "The cult of Bolívar is an old one, with popular and official expressions. The difference today is that this adoration has even descended into Santería" (Caballero 2010). Quite often Chávez's detractors like the pioneering broadcast journalist Oscar Armando Yanes González viewed the exhumation and its years of public planning as, in Yanes's words, either a theatrical manipulation meant to distract "the ignorant masses who submit themselves to the designs of an ignoramous" or an obscure profanation connected with rituals of Santería—"Bolívar's remains will be used clandestinely by this lowlife from Miraflores [national palace] to comply with 'sacro-magical' rites . . . that will ensure his permanent presidency" (2008).

From various perspectives the body of Bolívar became the site of a struggle for the nation and the state. More specifically, it became the place from which contending national designs were projected. Some visions of the country relied on a utopian revolutionary impetus tied to nationalist discourse and the intertwining of popular participation and vertical representation. Others were explicitly postnational and rejected what was perceived as recycling a nineteenth-century imaginary as well as a threatening expansion of an authoritarian state. Along with these contending views, popular appropriations of Bolívar articulated syncretic forms of religiosity that included a plurality of revolutionary aspirations.

My inquiry into the exhumation is informed by three ideas. First, the remains of Bolívar function as a site of sovereignty, and the appropriations of those so-called monumental bones entail a contradictory transfer of this sovereignty, sometimes to Chávez and at other times to the people. This contradiction relates directly to the logic of populist representation that oscillates between cooptation and empowerment. To explore a different angle of this idea, I find Ernst Kantorowicz's landmark *The King's Two Bodies* (1957/1997) particularly useful. He describes a profound transformation in the concept of political authority since the Middle Ages in which sovereignty became a signature feature of modern politics. Kantorowicz finds that the change began when the understanding of the body of Christ evolved into a notion of two bodies. The *corpus naturale* became the consecrated host on the altar, while the *corpus mysticum* stood for the social body of the church with its attendant administrative structure. This notion of these two bodies would come to be transferred to other political entities. The king would be said to have both a natural, mortal body and an enduring, supernatural one representing the mystical dignity and justice of the body politic. Sovereignty thus migrates.

Eric Santner (2011), in his discussion of "the people's two bodies," draws on Kantorowicz to argue that the traumatic investiture of sovereign power in the people at the moment of the French Revolution entailed a similar dichotomy as that of the king's body politic. After the French Revolution, the previously split corporeality of the monarch—at once the divine and transcendent body politic and a natural body both mortal and corruptible—was deposited onto the people. Such a power transfer was full of conflict and contradictions. The people never quite fit the new symbolic authority, and this political theology of sovereignty produced a kind of excess that Santner calls a "surplus of immanence" and describes in terms of a "strange materiality," or "the flesh." That flesh, he writes, organizes the symbolic networks of authority (4). This process of continuous displacement or transfer of sovereignty has emerged during the Chávez era as citizens—their bodies, *su carne*—take over the streets. Here I argue that the corpse of a national hero has once again become the privileged site of memory embodying the substance of the nation and the authority to rule.

Second, I contend that the dispute over the remains of Simón Bolívar condensed and displaced a struggle over the form of the Venezuelan nation and the role of the state within it. The heated discussions over the race of El Libertador or the role of the *oligarquía* in his death offer two clear examples.

Third, I propose that the accusations of populist manipulation of historical remains tend to dismiss agency in popular politics and overlook the productive appropriations of Bolívar's body. Popular groups aptly appropriate images of the body of El Libertador, reading into the bones of the nation beyond the narrow dichotomy of opposition versus *chavismo*. It is worth remembering here that Germán Carrera Damas (1987) made a distinction between the Simón Bolívar "for the people" and the Simón Bolívar "of the people." Along these lines, the works of the anthropologists Yolanda Salas (1987) and Michael Taussig (1980) are also useful in understanding the active reconfiguration of national symbols among groups aligned with Chávez. In exploring this last point, I want to revisit the role of performance in the construction of collective memory to allow a more fluid understanding of how Bolívar's bones are a site of negotiation between the state and the *chavista* constituency.

The Roads to/from the Venezuelan State and the People

My overarching argument is that the polemic surrounding Bolívar's bones is yet another articulation of Bolivarianism connected to a tradition that dates back to the mid-nineteenth century and responds to a very precise circumstance that arose in the mid-1980s. The important movement of historical revisionism in the field of Bolivarian studies cannot be decoupled from the reflections on the role of the state and the contours of the nation under the auspices of neoliberalism and the Washington Consensus. The role of the state in national affairs and the legitimacy of that state to represent the people are precisely what becomes displaced and condensed in the bones of Bolívar.

The historical revisionism of the Bolivarian legacy is connected to the construction—and neoliberal reform, or destruction—of the Venezuelan state and the constitution of political legitimacy, or the problem of sovereignty. Asking "Whose bones?" opens a space to understand popular agency in engaging with historical remains; tracing the fate of Bolívar's bones addresses rituals of the state's claim to authority.

Whose Bones?

The configuration of Simón Bolívar as the cornerstone of Venezuela's nation-state takes place a few decades after independence, but the argument between Bolivarians and anti-Bolivarians precedes the construction of the myth and informs, to a degree, the contemporary debates surrounding the legacy of El Libertador. Whether those evaluations are correct is beyond my scope here. I would like to point out the origins of a specific reading beginning in the 1980s that connects with a desire to reform or dismantle (or modernize according to a neoliberal model) the Venezuelan state and, toward the end of the 1990s, with the consolidation of the Bolivarian state and its popular/populist program. In this sense, the historical revisionism of the Bolivarian legacy is closely connected with concerns about state formation and sovereignty.

I am most interested in the ideas that Simón Bolívar may for some represent a model of authoritarianism and centralized power and that this legacy permeates the Bolivarian Revolution of Hugo Chávez in the form of an atavistic political ideology. The first assertion relates to a specific reading of a particular moment in the career of Bolívar, who opted for a vertical and rather conservative power structure to rule former colonies in the context of a brutal war. This decision was motivated initially by the military and political setbacks that led to the fall of the First and Second Republics as well as by the existence of very real threats against the unity of Gran Colombia.

After successfully liberating an extensive territory from Spain, Simón Bolívar presented the Congress of the newly formed Republic of Bolivia a constitution that called for a lifelong presidency and a hereditary vice presidency. His adversaries immediately expressed outrage with what they perceived as an excessive concentration of power and a challenge to their regional interests. They claimed that El Libertador had in fact become an enemy of liberty. In 1828, as more divisions and tensions further threatened the unity of Gran Colombia, Bolívar declared a dictatorship that lasted two years. Although those actions beg to be read in context, their authoritarian nature has informed and continues to inform criticism. Nevertheless, as we shall see, the most recent revision of the myth of Bolivarianism might have motivations that go beyond a strict concern for the centralizing push of Simón Bolívar almost two centuries ago, amid the construction of a new republic. I will address this point as I trace the process of monumentalization that informs the idea of Bolívar as nation-state, to which the writings of Germán Carrera Damas (1970), Luis Castro Leiva (1991), Elias Pino Iturrieta (2003), Inés Quintero Montiel (2011), and Alicia Ríos (2013) are fundamental. More recently, the excellent contributions of Christopher Conway (2003), Javier Guerrero (2012), and Juan Antonio Hernández (2010) help trace the different parts of what I would call a body politics puzzle that transformed the remains of a nineteenth-century hero into the body of the nation.

As Conway explains, the origin of this myth is paradoxical, considering that post-independence Venezuela was born "out of a conspicuous rejection of Bolívar" (2003, 19). Indeed, the separation of the province of Venezuela from Gran Colombia in 1830 presupposed a break with a fundamental project of El Libertador. It is only with the repatriation of his body twelve years later that his figure becomes intertwined with ideas of national identity. "From 1842 onward, Bolívar was no longer to be considered a former president or *caudillo,* but rather the guiding spirit of the nation," explains Conway (19). This marks the beginning of a process of sacralization as well as a paradoxical gesture of disembodiment—in the Chávez government's handling of the same remains more than a century later. In both instances, the bones transcend their materiality into something else that exceeds the mere human remains. Such excess serves the nation-state in that it becomes invested with those forces that accompany religious fervor, as Luis Castro Leiva has explained in *De la patria boba a la teología bolivariana* (1991). The excess also allows for a complex mechanism of legitimization and transfer of symbolic power beyond the co-optative appetite of the state. Sujatha Fernandes's work on rap and popular culture (2010) is crucial in this regard, as it shows the ways in which historical figures including Bolívar are used to channel popular demands in contemporary Venezuela.

What does this all mean? It is clear that legitimacy is transferred from the founding father to the nation-state, as it preserves and honors his remains while arrogating power to represent his heirs. Many critics have pointed out that the process was centered in the now deceased president Chávez, who captured the surplus of political capital generated by the Bolívar monument after his death (Guerrero 2012; Lynch 2006; Pino Iturrieta 2003; Ríos 2013; Taussig 1980). I am more interested in the contradictory and multidirectional flow of power generated by the "magic excess" of those bones.

What some authors like Luis Castro Leiva have left out of their discussion is that the masses also have a claim to authority through the cult of Bolívar ("they are Bolivar's children"). As Carrera Damas (1970) first noticed and especially as Yolanda Salas (1987) and Michael Taussig (1980) have explained in more detail, popular sectors have long invoked a kind of ownership of El Libertador through aesthetic practices and religious rituals.

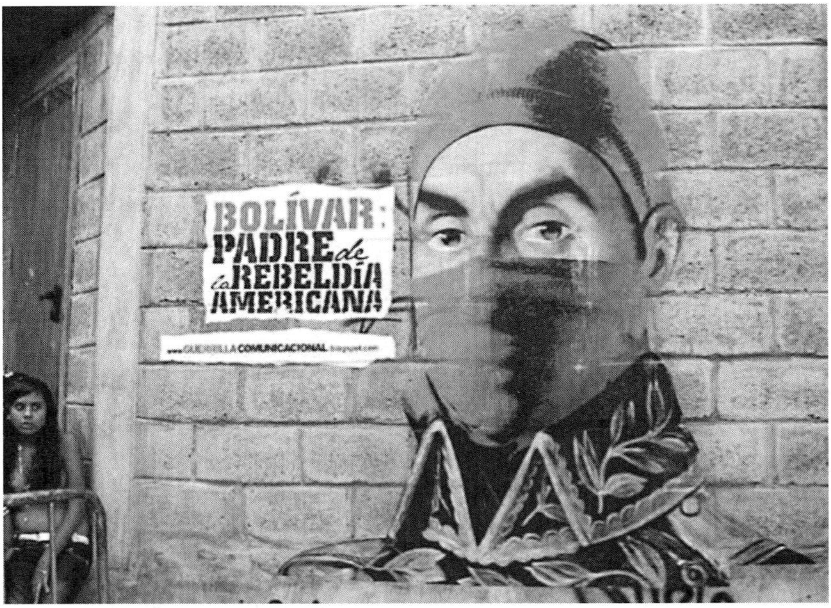

FIGURE 13.2. An *encapuchado* Simón Bolívar. Colectivo La Piedrita, ca. 2000. Mural, 23 de Enero neighborhood, Caracas. The nineteenth-century hero accompanies "the people" in their revolutionary struggle.

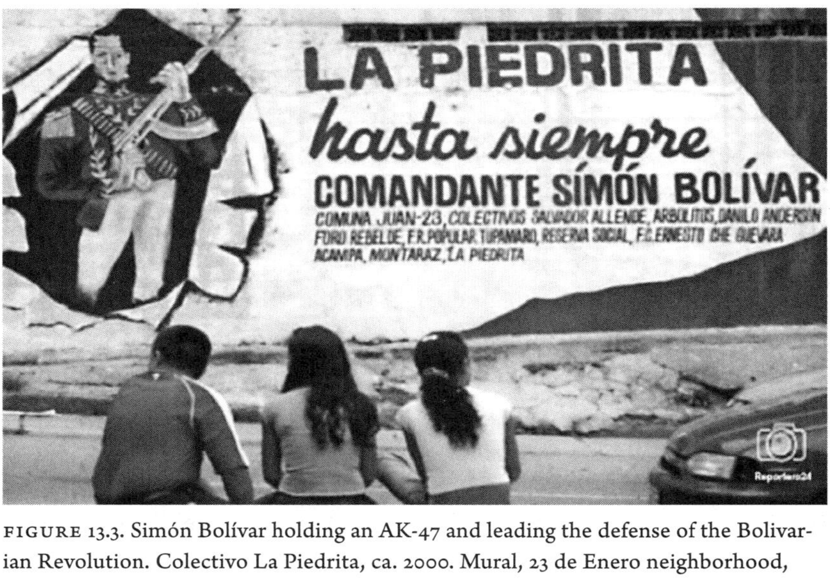

FIGURE 13.3. Simón Bolívar holding an AK-47 and leading the defense of the Bolivarian Revolution. Colectivo La Piedrita, ca. 2000. Mural, 23 de Enero neighborhood, Caracas.

As such, they find venues to relate to the symbols of the state by appropriating them. In fact, as Taussig explains, El Libertador talks to and/or through them in a process distinct from the monumentalization that we have seen thus far in state-orchestrated rituals (1980, 91–92). This other communication is intimate and entails an empowering effect (95). As such, it might be worth exploring further the ways in which this monumentalization of heroic remains contributed to the symbolic consolidation of the Venezuelan state while serving as a mechanism to transfer sovereignty from the body of the founding hero to the state, to the people, and/or to Chávez.

As an example, the Colectivo La Piedrita, a grassroots, now government-sponsored political organization from a Caracas neighborhood called 23 de Enero, has repeatedly represented Bolívar as a hooded man, as *un encapuchado* (figures 13.2 and 13.3). Nelson Santana, a member of the group, has asserted that "if he lived today, Bolívar would have worn and reclaimed the hood. For our generation the hood was, and continues to be, a symbol of popular resistance. It is the same rebellious and contestatory Bolívar that history brings us but I wanted to present him actualized, modern, the face of the future" (in Fernandes 2010, 148).

Through this imaginary, is the state machine just sucking the life out of social movements? Popular leaders have invoked the tradition of Bolivarianism to denounce contradictions in the current revolutionary process without necessarily aligning themselves with the opposition. Sujatha Fernandes provides a telling testimony when recalling that one of those activists, Freddy Mendoza, "compared Chávez's Fifth Republic to the Third Republic of 1819, when Bolívar presided over a post-Independence order. According to [him], the Third Republic was lost because Bolívar and the *mantuanos* could not conceive of governing along with the indigenous and black populations. Today, [he says,] the Fifth Republic will also be lost if bureaucrats in Chávez's administration resist the inclusion of the people" (2010, 157).

Picking Bones with the State

The repatriation of Simón Bolívar's remains in 1842 was a seminal gesture. Fermín Toro's 1843 *Descripción de los honores fúnebres consagrados a los restos del Libertador Simón Bolívar* played an important role in the early narrativization of the "cult of Bolívar" (Carrera Damas 1987). Toro's text was written upon the request of President Antonio José Páez and, in that sense, may be considered the writing of the state. It is worth remembering that Paéz is the second president to consolidate the Venezuelan state (if Bolívar is the first).

In Fermín Toro's account, the honors due to the remains of Bolívar play a fundamental role in the consolidation of the republic: those bones unified and pacified it. Contained in their coffin, they offered an emotional experience among the masses who, by witnessing the funeral ceremony, became one. Indeed, Toro explains, the sight of Bolívar's casket exerted a powerful effect over the multitudes who became normalized as a corpus of citizens: "It would have seemed impossible if it hadn't happened: to see such a diverse multitude, in terms of age and condition experiencing such intense and uniform sentiment, and behaving with the gravitas that the occasion demanded" (1843, 25). This ideal is accentuated in a biography written twelve years later by Felipe Larrazábal, who suggested that "social harmony results from the internalization, in each citizen, of the Bolivarian canon. . . . Bolívar is thus abstracted into an order of signs capable of shaping the inner and outer life of the nation" (in Conway 2003, 20).

This is a clear instance of disembodiment, furthering the process that would constitute the cult of Bolívar as a transcendental practice and a malleable discourse. But what I would like to emphasize here is that in regard to Fermín Toro, the instrumentalization of the hero employs the body itself to consolidate the state. Toward the end of his chronicle, Toro connects the solemn experience of collective unity among "el pueblo"—the people—with the need to reinforce the formal structures of the state. He expresses such ideas through the notion of patriotic duty, "se lo debemos al padre" (we owe it to the father): "We have just one more duty: to consecrate to the Liberator a monument deserving of his glory. The consolidation of Venezuelan institutions is due to the wisdom of its legislators, the integrity of its magistrates, the enlightenment of its People, and the unification of all Venezuelans" (1843, 49). In short, the sons of the nation pay their tribute to the father, Bolívar, by embracing the institutions that constitute the sovereign state.

Toro's chronicle bears resemblance to several elements found in the ceremony organized 160 years later by President Hugo Chávez. Both talk about restitution and aim at connecting Bolívar—or his remains—to the substance of the nation, just as both point to the transcendence of his labor and sacrifice. Toro declares that "honors to Bolívar are honors to the fatherland"

(8). Later he says, "At the foot of the altar and the grave's edge lies man's immortality and the hero's eternity" (10). Again, though similarities may be found in this and the ceremony organized by Chávez, one crucial difference is that the nineteenth-century writer calls on Bolívar as a pacifying figure, bringing reconciliation to those factions divided by the Federal War (1859–63) and laying the foundations for constitutional order. In his turn, Chávez invokes Bolívar as a revolutionary spirit that would guide the "people-government as one" into the continuation of a long struggle against oppression.

The use of Bolívar's legacy to consolidate the legitimacy of the state and the unity of the nation predates Chávez's rhetoric. Indeed, it continued after Páez's ceremony through a long process of commemorations and construction of public monuments. In 1883 President Antonio Guzmán Blanco celebrated the centennial of Bolívar's birth and staged the first actual monumentalization through the opening of the Panteón Nacional and the construction of Plaza Bolívar. In the 1930s writer Laureano Vallenilla Lanz (1934/1991) articulated a notion of authoritarian rule, "cesarismo democrático," to suggest that dictator Juan Vicente Gómez was called, like Bolívar, to unify and pacify the nation. Further, President Eleazar López Contreras, who led from 1935 to 1941, promoted the so-called Crusadas Cívicas Bolivarianas. The promenade Los Próceres was built under the dictatorship of Marcos Pérez Jiménez (1952–58) to commemorate the heroism of 1810.

When Carlos Andrés Pérez took office in 1979, he conceived his international agenda throughout Latin America as an integrationist gesture akin to Bolívar's. As he transitioned into his second mandate (1989–93), the populist caudillo shifted into the neoliberal camp. In this second period, the former popular-populist consensus that built legitimacy through the symbolism of the nation and its founding heroes was displaced by technocratic arguments and transnational agendas; the symbol of Bolívar as people and warrior had become irrelevant and even uncomfortable. The fact is that the figure of Bolívar faded out or, rather, was transformed. At Pérez's second inauguration, the poet Luis Gottberg (this author's cousin) read an unpublished text in which Bolívar literally lays down his sword.

It is not a coincidence that such important challenges to the civic religion of Bolivarianism emerged in the writings of philosophers like Luis Castro Leiva (1991) precisely when the governmental reform commission COPRE was created. The association between the need to modernize the state and the elimination of the cult of Bolívar is explicit in Castro Leiva's often-cited book on the Bolivarian theology. It is therefore surprising that, with the notable exception of literary critic Juan Antonio Hernández (2010), the connections with neoliberal state reform have been missed by the critics. It also happens to be quite clear that the deconstruction of the cult is followed by the inflation of a new cult of individualism and free enterprise. Castro Leiva notes,

> Indeed . . . a democratic Venezuela debates between the cult of the State and a regime of political parties (both asphyxiating freedom), and the emerging but "morally" pure and enslaved civil society. The latter, when not experiencing pressure from the State, suffers the weight of the iron law of the party oligarchies. In this form . . . freedom is doubly curtailed: by the absence of individual initiative and entrepreneurial spirit, and the control of social spontaneity under the civil police of the state or the government. (1991, 229)

If the uses of Bolivarianism have been transparent, the questioning of Bolivarianism might be less so. Nevertheless, looking at the demise of the Bolivarian myth in the context of a profound transformation of the Venezuelan state in the late 1980s, one can speculate that the demystification also responds to a redefinition the sites of sovereignty in a postnational, neoliberal order.

In Closing (the Coffin)

John Lynch, one of the best-known scholars on Bolívar, has claimed that "Chávez's heresy" derives from his falsification and appropriation of Bolívar:

> But the new heresy, far from maintaining continuity with the constitutional ideas of Bolívar, as was claimed, invented a new attribute, the populist Bolívar, and in the case of Cuba gave him a new identity, the socialist Bolívar. By exploiting the authoritarian tendency, which certainly existed in the thought and action of Bolívar, regimes in Cuba and Venezuela claim the Liberator as a patron for their policies, distorting his ideas in the process. (2006, 304)

I wonder if this is the most productive approach to the uses of Bolivarianism in contemporary Venezuela. Is such criticism not trapped in the same cult logic while pretending to be above it? Regardless, it petrifies a fluid cultural practice appropriated by the state and the people. Chávez's uses of Bolivarianism are but one dimension of a complex negotiation of symbols within the contentious power dynamic that exists not between *chavismo* and the opposition but within *chavismo* itself.

An obsession with Simón Bolívar and the ritualistic celebration of his body is clearly connected to the formation of the Venezuelan state. As stated previously, his body transfers legitimacy from the founding father to the people and/or the state that presidents have actively tried to channel. All attempts to consolidate, reform, or dismantle the power structure of the state have dealt in one way or another with Bolívar's bones. Perhaps one of the most telling indicators of the weight of Bolivarianism in matters of state formation was the anxious gesture of those who took power after the 2002 coup against Chávez. Their first act was the removal of Bolívar's portrait from the Salón Ayacucho of the Presidential Palace, while the second came with the decree of the newly inaugurated government—"We reestablish the name of the Venezuelan Republic"—thus erasing the Bolivarian qualifier.

Like the process of forming new bone tissue following every fracture, sovereignty in Venezuela has functioned through a kind of heroic osteogenesis, laying down new material in the deceased body of El Libertador—new bone for every new social tissue and every new monument needing to be assimilated and contained in the body politic, the body of the nation. The strategy captures and deploys that excess (of sovereignty) released in the transition of power to/from the people, illuminating why the embodiments and disembodiments of the nation, the people, and the state have been channeled through a dispute of Bolívar's body.

Acknowledgments

This essay owes a great deal to two friends with contending views on Venezuelan politics: Javier Guerrero and Juan Antonio Hernández. Over the past few years, our conversations have helped me shape my understanding of what I call here "the uses of Bolívar's body" but also about the political and cultural debates of the past decade.

References

Caballero, Manuel. 2010. "Chávez estaría bajando un peldaño del culto official y popular hasta el nivel de la brujería." Interview by Manuel Flores García. *Petroleumworld Venezuela,* July 25. http://www.petroleumworldve.com/edito 10072601.htm.

Carrera Damas, Germán. 1987. *El culto a Bolívar.* Bogotá: Universidad Nacional de Colombia, Centro Editorial.

Chavez, Hugo. 2010. *NotiTarde,* July 22. http://www.notitarde.com.

Castro Leiva, Luis. 1991. *De la patria boba a la teología bolivariana: Ensayos de historia intelectual.* Caracas: Monte Avila Editores.

Conway, Christopher B. 2003. *The Cult of Bolívar in Latin American Literature.* Gainesville: University Press of Florida.

Fernandes, Sujatha. 2010. *Who Can Stop the Drums? Urban Social Movements in Chávez's Venezuela.* Durham, NC: Duke University Press.

Guerrero, Javier. 2012. "Culturas del cuerpo. La sagrada familia venezolana." *452°F. Revista Electrónica de Teoría de la Literatura y Literatura Comparada* 6:17–38. http://www.452f.com/pdf/numero06/guerrero/06_452f_guerrero_indiv.pdf.

Hernández, Juan Antonio. 2010. "Los dos cuerpos del Libertador: Una introducción a la teología política bolivariana." *El Eje del Mal,* October 8. http://nomostierra.blogspot.com/2010/10/teologia-politica-bolivariana.html.

Kantorowicz, Ernst. 1957/1997. *The King's Two Bodies: A Study in Mediaeval Political Theology.* Princeton, NJ: Princeton University Press.

Lynch, John. 2006. *Simón Bolívar: A Life.* New Haven, CT: Yale University Press.

Mouffe, Chantal. 1993. *The Return of the Political.* London: Verso.

Nora, Pierre. 1989. "Between Memory and History: Les Lieux de Mémoire." *Representations* 26:7–25.

Pino Iturrieta, Elías. 2003. *El divino Bolívar: Ensayo sobre una religión republicana.* Madrid: Catarata.

———. 2010. "La guerra con Colombia." Opinion. *El Universal,* July 31. http://www.eluniversal.com/opinion/100731/la-guerra-con-colombia.

Quintero Montiel, Inés. 2011. *El relato invariable: Indepdendencia, mito y nación.* Caracas: Editorial Alfa.

Ríos, Alicia. 2013. *Nacionalismos banales, el culto a Bolívar: Literatura, cine, arte y política en América Latina.* Pittsburgh, PA: Instituto Internacional de Literatura Iberoamericana, University of Pittsburgh.

Salas de Lecuna, Yolanda, Norma González Viloria, and Ronny Velásquez. 1987. *Bolívar y la historia en la conciencia popular.* Caracas: Instituto de Altos Estudios de América Latina, Universidad Simón Bolívar.

Santner, Eric L. 2011. *The Royal Remains: The People's Two Bodies and the Endgames of Sovereignty*. Chicago: University of Chicago Press.

Taussig, Michael T. 1980. *The Devil and Commodity Fetishism in South America*. Chapel Hill: University of North Carolina Press.

Toro, Fermín. 1843. *Descripcion de los honores fúnebres consagrados a los restos del libertador Simon Bolívar: En cumplimiento del decreto legislativo de 30 de abril de 1842: Hecha de órden del gobierno*. Caracas: En la impr. de Valentin Espinal.

Vallenilla Lanz, Laureano. 1934/1991. *Cesarismo democrático y otros textos*, edited by Nikita Harwich Vallenilla. Caracas: Biblioteca Ayacucho.

Yanes, Oscar. 2008. "Ritos mágicos con los huesos del Libertador." February 17. https://towelto.wordpress.com/2008/02/17/oscar-yanes-ritos-magicos-con-los-huesos-del-libertador/ (site discontinued).

Contributors

Armida de la Garza is senior lecturer in screen media and digital humanities at University College Cork, Ireland. She is a member of the Lingnan Centre for Film Studies Advisory Board, editor of the book series entitled *Topics and Issues in National Cinemas,* and co-editor of the *Transnational Cinema Journal.* Before joining UCC, Armida founded Communication and Media Studies at Xian Jiaotong-Liverpool University, and prior to that she was a founding member and for four years deputy head of the Division of International Communication at the University of Nottingham Ningbo. She has also lectured in Latin American cinema at the University of Nottingham UK, and in global media at the London School of Economics. Her interests include screen media and their relation to culture, industry, and education and collaborative, interdisciplinary research that bridges the gap between science and the arts.

Luis Duno-Gottberg is associate professor and college master at Rice University. He previously taught at Universidad Simón Bolívar in Caracas, and Florida Atlantic University (FAU), where he was director of Caribbean and Latin American studies, and director of comparative literature. He specializes in nineteenth and twentieth century Caribbean culture, with an emphasis on race and ethnicity, politics and violence. His current research project, *Dangerous People: Hegemony, Representation and Culture in Contemporary Venezuela,* explores the relationship between popular mobilization, radical politics, and culture. He is the author or editor of numerous books including: *La Politica Encarnada. Biopolítica y Cultura en la Venezuela Bolivarniana; Submerged. Sumergido. Alternative Cuban Cinema* (co-editor); *Miradas al margen. Cine y Subalternidad en América Latina; Solventando las diferencias: La ideología del mestizaje en Cuba; Imagen y Subalternidad. El Cine de Víctor Gaviria;* and *Cultura e identidad racial en América Latina.*

Emily A. Engel is an independent scholar specializing in the art and history of early modern Latin America. Previously, Engel was assistant professor of art history and chair of the Fine Arts Department at the College of Mount Saint Vincent in New York City and assistant professor of art history in the Herron School of Art and Design, Indiana University. Engel has received fellowships from the Interdisciplinary Humanities Center at the University of California, Santa Barbara and the Getty Research Institute. She has published on eighteenth-century art in South America, and co-edited with Thomas B.F. Cummins *Manuscript Cultures in Colonial Mexico and Peru: New Questions and Approaches*. Engel is currently working on a book project exploring civic art sponsorship in urban South America at the end of the viceregal period and editing a volume on sixteenth-century Lima.

Alejandro E. Gómez Pernia holds a doctorate from the École des Hautes Études en Sciences Sociales. His dissertation, completed in 2010 on the Haitian revolution, received multiple awards, including the annual prize from the Comité pour la mémoire de l'Esclavage for advancing the history of slavery and the award for best doctoral dissertation from the Institut des Amériques. His principal areas of research include socio-racial issues, revolutionary conflicts, and the study of sensitivities in the Atlantic World. He is currently *Maître de conférences* of Latin American history at the Université de Lille 3. He has published two books: *Le Spectre de la Révolution noire: L'impact de la révolution haïtienne dans le monde atlantique, 1790–1886* and *Fidelidad bajo el viento. Revolución y contrarevolución en las Antillas francesas*.

Juan de Dios López Maya is a Venezuelan composer and musicologist. He is an aggregate professor of musical analysis at the Universidad Central de Venezuela where he is also coordinator of the master's program in musicology. López is currently a doctoral candidate at the Universidad Central de Venezuela and his research deals with Masonic music written by Venezuelan composers of the nineteenth century. He has also edited and produced concerts featuring works from the nineteenth century Venezuelan repertoire.

Paul Niell is assistant professor in the Department of Art History at Florida State University. He holds a PhD from the University of New Mexico and studied under Ray Hernández-Durán. Niell's research focuses on architecture and imagery in the early modern Spanish Caribbean and the material culture of the African Diaspora. He co-edited with Stace G. Widdifield *Buen Gusto and Classicism in the Visual Cultures of Latin America, 1780–1910*. He has published in *Cultural Landscapes: A Journal of Cultural Studies*, the *Bulletin for Latin American Research*, *The Latin Americanist*, and the *Colonial Latin American Review*. He is also the author of *Urban Space as*

Heritage in Late Colonial Cuba: Classicism and Dissonance on the Plaza de Armas of Havana, 1754–1828.

Tina Potočnik is a Slovenian art and architectural historian. She holds a PhD in architecture and a master's degree in art history from University of Ljubljana. Until 2013 she was employed as a researcher at the France Stele Institute of Art History, Scientific Research Centre of the Slovenian Academy of Sciences and Arts in Ljubljana. In 2013 she co-founded RI19+, the Research Institute for Visual Culture from the 19th Century to the Present Time, in Ljubljana, where she is carrying on with her work as an independent researcher. Her research and scientific work focuses on the built heritage and architecture of the nineteenth and twentieth century in Yugoslavia with special regard to politics, ideology, and identity. She has published her research in numerous scientific and professional journals and presented them at several international conferences.

Ana María Reyes is assistant professor in Latin American art history at Boston University and Santander Visiting Scholar at Harvard's David Rockefeller Center for Latin American Studies. She holds a PhD from the University of Chicago. She has published articles on cultural *desarrollismo* and the São Paulo Bienal, commemoration and the aestheticization of violence in contemporary Colombian art, metaphoric burial as political intervention, as well as the art criticism of Marta Traba. She is a founding member of the Symbolic Reparations Research Project (SRRP) that currently studies the role of commemorative arts in transitional justice. She is also preparing her book manuscript *Dis-Cursis: Beatriz González and the Limits of Modernization in 1960s Colombia.*

Alicia Ríos is associate professor of Spanish at the Department of Languages, Literatures, and Linguistics at Syracuse University. She is the author of *Nacionalismos banales: el culto a Bolívar (literatura, cine, arte y política en América latina)* and co-editor of *The Latin American Cultural Studies Reader*, among numerous articles and chapters. Her research has concentrated on nineteenth-century Latin America, in particular on the relationships of the press, war, and race in Venezuela's Independence Era, as well as cultural and literary theory. She is currently working on representations of Simón Bolívar in twenty-first century film.

Nicholas Roberts is a senior lecturer in Hispanic studies at Durham University, in North-East England. He completed his BA and MPhil at King's College, Cambridge University, before going on to obtain his PhD at King's College, London University. He held the position of Mellon Career Development Fellow at St Catherine's

College, Oxford University, before taking up his current post at Durham. Roberts spent approximately two years living and working in Venezuela. Roberts specializes in Latin American literature, and has published articles on Roberto Arlt, Julio Cortázar, and Eugenio Montejo, on whom he has also written a monograph entitled *Poetry and Loss: The Work of Eugenio Montejo*.

Maureen G. Shanahan is professor of art history at James Madison University. She holds a PhD in art history from University of Michiagn and a JD from Loyola University in Los Angeles. She has published on early film and French modernism in *Cinema Journal, Konsthistorisk Tidskrift, Michigan Feminist Studies,* and the *Journal of Colonialism and Colonial History*. She has also published articles on Fernand Léger and other modernists in numerous edited collections, encyclopedias, and exhibition catalogs, and a forthcoming book, *The Colorist Doctor: Fernand Léger and the Aesthetics of Trauma*. She has been awarded the inaugural Florence Gould Foundation fellowship in French art and visual studies at the Sterling and Francine Clark Art Institute and a Fulbright award. These awards support her research on the psychiatric and photographic works of Gaëtan Gatian de Clérambault and the French colonial subject.

Juan Francisco Sans is a Venezuelan composer, pianist, conductor, and musicologist and currently the director of the School of Arts, Universidad Central de Venezuela. He is the general editor of the complete symphonic works of Juan Bautista Plaza and of the collection *Classics of the Venezuelan Pianistic Literature*. He has published more than thirty articles in specialized journals and edited collections. As a pianist and composer he has recorded more than ten compact discs.

Tomás Straka holds a doctorate in history from the Universidad Católica Andrés Bello (UCAB) and a masters in history from the Universidad Central de Venezuela. He is the director of the masters program in history at UCAB and a researcher at the Instituto de Investigaciones Históricas "Hermann González Oropeza, SJ" of UCAB. His publications include: *La voz de los vencidos: Ideas del partido realista de Caracas, 1810–1821, Hechos y gente: Historia contemporánea de Venezuela,* and *La épica del desencanto: Boliviarianismo, historiografía y política en Venezuela*. He is also the editor of *La tradición de lo moderno: Venezuela en diez ensayos* and *Las independencias de Iberoamérica* (with Michael Zeuske and Agustín Sánchez Andrés). He was recently awarded a Fulbright Scholar Award to conduct research on the American Technical Missions in Venezuela.

Index

Note: Italicized page locators indicate illustrations; plates are designated as Pl.